Praise Page

"By viewing the events in Derry through the prism of those in Selma, Forest Jones draws attention to the striking commonality in cause and consequence of both the American and Northern Irish Civil Rights movements, and the awful violence which attempted to silence those twin cries for equality. In doing so, he creates an insightful and compelling examination of a terrible period in our shared histories and highlights the need for society to learn from the past for a more equitable future."

—*Brian McGilloway,* Sunday Times and NY Times *bestselling author*

"Jones is a detailed researcher, and *Good Trouble* is based on a wide array of material, old and new—Jones offers affecting accounts of both the Selma to Montgomery march and the Belfast to Derry march. His book reads like a historical thriller at times. A must read."

—*Richard Moriarty, North West District Editor of* The Sun

"The first comprehensive look at the connection between the two Civil Rights movements in the USA and Northern Ireland. Jones has written a book that is worthy of its subject."

—*Chris Riches, Correspondent for North-West England and Wales on the* Daily Express

"An important book that traces the parallels between two different fights for civil rights."

—*Sharon Dempsey, Author, Queens University in Belfast*

"*Good Trouble* is a fascinating read that connects America's Civil Rights movement with Northern Ireland's movement to end discrimination against Catholics in the 1960s. Woven through with firsthand accounts from Jones's family, this personal telling of the two countries' common struggles is moving and enlightening."

—*Kristen Green,* NY Times *bestselling author*

GOOD TROUBLE

GOOD TROUBLE

THE SELMA, ALABAMA, AND DERRY, NORTHERN IRELAND, CONNECTION 1963–1972

BY
FOREST ISSAC JONES

INTRODUCTION BY
JULIEANN CAMPBELL

FIRST HILL BOOKS
An imprint of Wimbledon Publishing Company Limited (WPC)

This edition first published in UK and USA 2025
by **FIRST HILL BOOKS**
75–76 Blackfriars Road, London SE1 8HA, UK
or PO Box 9779, London SW19 7ZG, UK
and
244 Madison Ave #116, New York, NY 10016, USA

Copyright © Forest Issac Jones 2025

The author asserts the moral right to be identified as the author of this work.

All rights reserved. Without limiting the rights under copyright reserved above, no part of this publication may be reproduced, stored or introduced into a retrieval system, or transmitted, in any form or by any means (electronic, mechanical, photocopying, recording or otherwise), without the prior written permission of both the copyright owner and the above publisher of this book.

Library of Congress Control Number: 2024951840
A catalog record for this book has been requested.

ISBN-13: 978-1-83999-461-6 (Hbk)
ISBN-10: 1-83999-461-4(Hbk)

ISBN-13: 978-1-83999-462-3(Pbk)
ISBN-10: 1-83999-462-2(Pbk)

Cover Credit: Marco Culbreath

This title is also available as an e-book.

CONTENTS

Acknowledgments	ix
Introduction	xiii
Prologue	xvii

CHAPTER 1	Coming to Derry, Summer 2022	1
CHAPTER 2	The Roots of the Conflict: Michael Collins and Easter Rising	7
CHAPTER 3	The Rise of the IRA	17
CHAPTER 4	Student Nonviolent Coordinating Committee	23
CHAPTER 5	1963 March on Washington	31
CHAPTER 6	The Courageous Eight	37
CHAPTER 7	Selma to Montgomery March	45
CHAPTER 8	The People's Democracy in Northern Ireland	53
CHAPTER 9	John Lewis	57
CHAPTER 10	Bernadette Devlin	61
CHAPTER 11	John Hume	67
CHAPTER 12	Eamonn McCann	73
CHAPTER 13	Selma to Montgomery March—Bloody Sunday	77
CHAPTER 14	Bloody Sunday—the Impact	89

viii   *Contents*

CHAPTER 15 The Aftermath—The Selma to
Montgomery March   95

CHAPTER 16 The Beginning of the Catholic Civil Rights
Movement   107

CHAPTER 17 Belfast to Derry March—the Beginning   121

CHAPTER 18 Day one—January 1, 1969, Belfast to
Derry Long March   127

CHAPTER 19 Day Two: Belfast to Derry—Toome   133

CHAPTER 20 Day Three of the Belfast to Derry March 137

CHAPTER 21 Last Day of the Belfast to Derry March 141

CHAPTER 22 Battle of the Bogside   153

CHAPTER 23 Conflict with the Police, Paramilitaries,
and the Marchers   169

CHAPTER 24 Conclusion   183

Brexit, Irish Unity, and the Troubles in Northern
Ireland Today   187

Epilogue   193

Notes   201

Bibliography   215

Index   219

ACKNOWLEDGMENTS

Good Trouble is based on over two years of research, three trips to Northern Ireland and close to 20 interviews. In addition to interviews, the book is based on extensive archival research, including newspaper accounts, declassified government papers, published memoirs and archival footage.

There are so many people to thank for their support and assistance in bringing this book to life. A big thank you to my family, friends and loved ones for their incredible support over the years. Thanks to everyone I spoke with concerning the topics of this book and the vast quantities of material that did not or could not make it into this book. I appreciate their bravery in their honest comments.

This book will always have a special place in my heart, not because it is my first book but because it has been part of such a long and fun journey. It has been a passion piece of mine since I was at Hollins University as a graduate student.

For one of my independent studies, I did a research project on the Troubles in Northern Ireland under one of my all-time favorite professors, Dr. Peter Coogan. With that project, I was intrigued by this small country that had so much in common with the African American population in the United States. They were fighting for voting rights, housing rights, and unjust policing. What was stunning was that they used the blueprint of the US Civil Rights movement in the early 1960s.

However, as I got into teaching and administration, the years flew by until the invention of Twitter.

That social media piece has its negatives, but it was through that I met my friend, Julieann Campbell. We finally met, and after visiting the city of Derry, the idea came to me about a book that would link the two civil rights movements. She is "Jules" to me. There is no doubt she is one of the smartest people that I know and one of the funniest. We had so many good times in Sandino's

Bar over the last couple of years. She helped me with numerous books, articles and pictures. You were an invaluable resource in writing this book. I am lucky and proud to call you my friend.

But before that, I had met another good friend on social media, Rachel Scilley. Rachel and I became friends during the first months of COVID-19. We would talk quite a bit about civil rights because her background was studying the Troubles as well. Rachel was the person who introduced me to one of the people I interviewed, Delia McDermott.

Rachel and I finally met in spring 2024, and she was the one who took me to Magilligan Beach. She is truly one of the sweetest people I've ever met, and her friendship has meant a lot to me. We also had some fun times in Bushmills and Belfast this past year.

The face-to-face interviews were something I will never forget. A big thank you to Eamonn McCann. I truly appreciate your humor, your laughter and your honesty with me.

Billy McVeigh, I will never forget taking a selfie with you when we first met. You make me laugh constantly, and you don't know how much I appreciate your text messages on a weekly basis. I am grateful and honored that we've become friends.

Gerry Duddy, a huge thank you for drinking some pints of Guinness with me and telling me your stories about those difficult times in the late '60s and early '70s. You were a pleasure to talk to!

Reverend E. T. Burton, thank you for inviting me into your home in Roanoke and taking the time to sit down with me and tell me your story. You are an amazing man, and your outlook on life inspires me.

Delia McDermott, a big thanks to you for spending time with me on the phone over Christmas holiday. I so enjoyed you telling me your story, and I'm glad I was able to incorporate it in the book. I also appreciate the picture you shared with me. You are still a beautiful woman inside and out.

However, not only was a book born from it; several friendships came from my visit to Derry.

Many thanks to the wonderful people of Derry. I will always cherish your kindness and hospitality. My deep gratitude goes to Kaysi at the Bishops Gate Hotel in Derry. The hotel was my home away from home for many days doing the research for this book. Kaysi and the rest of the staff at the hotel always made me feel at home, and I will never forget the hospitality.

A big thank you to the people that I talked to on the phone for interviews. They provided so much insight on the Bloody Sunday march in Selma and the march from Selma to Montgomery—Carolyn Doyle King, Dr. Shannah

Acknowledgments

Tharp-Gilliam, Linda Gildersleeve-Blackwell, Richard Smiley, Alan Reese Sr., Marvin Reese Jr. and Dr. Sheyann Webb-Christburg.

A special thank you to Saleen Martin for helping me reach many of the folks who talked to me about Selma, and Anastasia Barnes Holmes, who helped me set up the interview with Reverend Reese's grandsons. Dr. Wornie Reed, you were a huge help getting me in contact with Dr. Christburg.

Also, thank you to William Calloway. I appreciate your help in acquiring an interview with a marcher from Selma. Sadly, he had already passed away, but I thank you for your efforts.

Many other dear friends and colleagues read the manuscript and offered help along the way. Dr. James Soltis, Dr. Wayne Tripp, Dr. Sharon Dempsey, Dr. Deborah Flynn, Brian McGilloway, Rebecca Jones, Mike Stevens and the staff at the Linen Hall Library in Belfast (Sean and Judith), the wonderful staff at the Free Derry Museum in Derry—thank you for helping me with my research. Jill Beecher, thank you for our crazy and fun journey up North, which gave me the idea about the book in the first place. Thank you for taking good care of me on that trip. I appreciate your friendship and banter.

A big thank you to Alan Lewis. Your picture was great, even though we ended up not using it for the cover. I appreciate your patience with the trouble we had with our initial emails! Your permission to use the iconic picture meant a lot to me.

Tracy Martin, thank you for your kindness and your help in choosing pictures for the book. Your father's pictures spoke to me, and I believe the readers will enjoy seeing them. I also love that we share the name, Issac.

Thank you to the numerous newspapers from which I have quoted a wealth of important relevant archive material, including the *Derry Journal*, the *Guardian, Irish Times, New York Times, Washington Post, BBC News, RTE, Cain (Conflict Archive on the Internet)* and *Daily Mirror*, and also to the team that made the incredible documentary, *Once Upon a Time in Northern Ireland*. Bernadette Devlin's autobiography, *The Price of My Soul*, was also integral to completing this book, as well as John Hume's biographies. Tim Pat Coogan's fantastic books on both the *Troubles* and the *IRA* were an invaluable wealth of information. Thank you to Livingstone College for their help with the pictures from the 1960s. I appreciate you all—Laura Johnson and Tracy Johnson.

A big thank you to the book team that helped put this project into completion—the team at Anthem Press: Tej Sood (I knew after our first call that you were the perfect person to team with on this project), Golda Merline, Srini, Jebaslin and everybody at Anthem. Thank you for believing in me and in this project. I cannot thank you enough for giving me the space and grace to complete this project.

Huge thanks to Kristin Clifford and her team at Finn Partners (Adrienne and Nick Fontaine)—you all were great to work with and I appreciate your support and push every step in the process. Jon Kirk, thank you for your fantastic help across the pond—I appreciate all that you did.

Thank you to Marco Culbreath, my cousin. Your drawing for the cover was incredible, and I truly appreciate you working me into your busy schedule. You are one talented dude!

I also want to thank my brother and my sister-in-law, Anton Forest Grant Jones and Katherine "Kat" Larson Jones, who have read a lot of my work over the years and served as a welcome dose of reality in terms of what needed to improve with the writing. Their friendship, humor and unconditional love have influenced me in so many ways. I appreciate and love both of you.

The best parts of this book were being able to meet and spend time with the various people that I interviewed, including two special interviews—with my parents, Betty Coates Jones and Forest Grant Jones. My mother and father read multiple versions of the manuscript, provided insightful feedback, and encouraged me to finish the book and do whatever it took to complete the project. Thank you both for always being there for me and supporting me. I couldn't have asked for better parents.

I love my family, and they are and always have been my guiding light.

Finally, thank you to everyone who purchased and read the book. I appreciate your support.

INTRODUCTION

The humble television set is mentioned among the many catalysts for Northern Ireland's civil rights movement. Like people everywhere throughout the late 1950s and 1960s, people in Derry and across the north welcomed their first-ever television sets in the family home—replacing the radio as the main source of entertainment.

With this new global view, Irish Catholics/nationalists witnessed for the first time how America's Black communities were treated by their country. They watched on as these same communities challenged their oppressors—rising to demand change and an end to discrimination and racial segregation. Seeing the US movement unfold reinforced the north's fledgling movement as more and more realized the potential of collective action.

Centuries of British-led hardship and discrimination had long since polarized the north. After the Partition of Ireland in 1921, unionists loyal to the British state ruled the new Northern Ireland with little regard for their fellow Catholic countrymen. By establishing his 'Protestant parliament and a Protestant State' (1934), Northern Ireland's unionist prime minister, Sir James Craig, isolated this community even more.

By the late 1960s, the situation in Northern Ireland had reached a boiling point. Pockets of activism sprang up across the north—spurred on by inhumane housing conditions, a historic lack of jobs and opportunity and no voting rights. The Northern Ireland Civil Rights Association (NICRA) was born, and its first and loudest demand became One Man, One Vote. NICRA organized marches across the region, each swelling in numbers until basic reforms were granted.

It's no exaggeration to say that our own early civil rights activists gleaned ideas and inspiration from their US counterparts. They borrowed their hard-hitting slogans and adopted protest anthems like "We Shall Overcome." More importantly, they observed how civil disobedience and peaceful demonstrations

xiv *Introduction*

could bring attention to their cause—and so they took to the streets in pursuit of change.

The struggle for civil rights and equality impacted my own family, too. Several of my aunts tell stories of going for their first job interviews—only to be rejected once the employer realized they were Catholic based on the name of their school (schools with a Saint-prefix were a dead giveaway).

My mother had 15 brothers and sisters, all crammed into a tiny maisonette together. Other families were much worse off, with often three or four whole families crammed into one house, a single dilapidated room per family. The housing conditions became so bad for many that a group of frustrated parents chose to occupy an abandoned US army base and its 302 corrugated-iron Nissen huts to escape such dire conditions.

My grandad Willie Duddy was among the first people to squat in Springtown Camp. Families needed something physical to put down inside, and my grandad carried the base of an old spring bed for miles to stake his claim to a camp hut. They lived there until the Creggan estate was built, squeezing yet more Catholics into one area of the city.

Alongside peaceful protests and rallies came the fear of police brutality. Marches were often attacked by members of the Royal Ulster Constabulary (RUC) and their unionist supporters. As fate would have it, Derry's Duke Street march on October 5, 1968, would change everything. A lone cameraman from Irish broadcaster RTE broadcast scenes of batoned police beating marchers mercilessly—images that went around the world and illuminated just how badly Irish nationalists and their supporters were treated. The reality of our 'Protestant parliament and a Protestant State' was visible at last—and international condemnation swiftly followed.

The city of Derry was—and remains—a majority Catholic/nationalist city, and yet this section of the population was corralled into the sprawling electoral area of South Ward to gerrymander votes and ensure unionist supremacy.

In August 1969, residents' anger at seeing Orange Order parades march through Derry's Catholic Bogside spilled over. This led to three days of rioting against police and their unionist supporters. On the third day, the RUC and their allies retreated in defeat. Thus, known as the Battle of the Bogside, this incident exhausted local security forces and led to British troops being deployed to Northern Ireland for the first time on August 14, 1969. Despite only being deployed for a few months, the army stayed for decades, eventually siding with the RUC and its British masters to quell any perceived uprising.

In August 1971, during the introduction of internment without trial, hundreds of Catholic nationalists were rounded up and put in prison indefinitely.

Introduction   xv

Throughout all this, Northern Ireland's civil rights movement continued to swell in both stature and numbers—much to the chagrin of the British government. This all changed when British troops opened fire on an unarmed crowd during an anti-internment march on January 30, 1972. Bloody Sunday, as it is now known, extinguished the peaceful civil rights movement and led to a generation of young people joining armed groups to fight back—extending the conflict for decades. Over half a century later, however, the achievements and courage of the early civil rights era and its street radicals are widely recognized as the turning point in our recent history.

While much has been achieved on both sides of the Atlantic, there is more work to do. Ireland's colonial legacy continues to cause suffering throughout the north, and justice evades the majority of those affected by the Troubles. We still march and protest, but about different things nowadays like austerity, racism and global awareness.

In the United States, Black Lives Matter reignited the embers of defiance within the Black populace—incensed at police brutality and too many needless deaths. To an onlooker, it seems that history repeats itself across the United States, the achievements of the past no longer enough. It seems that, once again, the need for action is too great to ignore if we are to live peacefully and in parity with our neighbors.

We have come so far, but there is a long road ahead for all of us who continue to challenge oppression, regardless of place, race or religion. American activism dared to let us dream. Now the actions of our collective ancestors can inspire others around the world to dream, to persevere and to overcome.

Julieann Campbell
Derry, 2024.

Julieann Campbell is an award-winning author, poet and oral historian from Derry who has worked extensively to document the civil rights movement 1968–72 and Bloody Sunday in 1972. Her 17-year-old uncle, Jackie Duddy, was the first fatality of Bloody Sunday 1972—shot in the back as he fled advancing British soldiers. Julieann is currently a PhD researcher at Ulster University exploring the impact of storytelling on post-conflict Northern Ireland.

PROLOGUE

Why, when we talk about the Black Civil Rights Movement in the United States and the Catholic Civil Rights Movement in Northern Ireland, have we forgotten about the close connection between the two? It is hard for many people to understand the experiences of Catholics living in the North during the Troubles and Blacks living during segregation unless you, yourself, lived it. I talk from experience—as my great-grandfather, Issac Coats Sr., disappeared off a Black sharecropping farm in Georgia in the late 1930s. My friend, Nichola Mallon, former Lord Mayor of Belfast, who I've had the privilege of working with, lost part of her hearing because of an IRA (Irish Republican Army) bomb that went off in her backyard when she was a young girl. In the 1960s, a new generation of politically and socially aware Catholics in Northern Ireland looked at the civil rights movement in America as a model for ending what they saw as blatant anti-Catholic discrimination in their country. Young civil rights leaders like John Hume, Eamonn McCann and Bernadette Devlin refused to accept this way of life. They saw what was occurring in the United States and how peaceful mass protests had shined the spotlight on Blacks who were living under Jim Crow's segregation laws.

When many people think about Northern Ireland, they think of a war between the IRA and the British government. Not many people remember the very short civil rights movement there in the late 1960s and early 1970s. I believe it has been forgotten by many because of the shame associated with the widespread discrimination that was ignored by the British government, both the Labour and Conservative leaders. Even today, some people believe that the marchers who peacefully demonstrated in Belfast, Derry or Londonderry (as named by Protestants) and other places were to blame for 'The Troubles' that started in Northern Ireland in the late '60s and lasted until 1998.

Northern Ireland was a dysfunctional and broken society, the same as the United States during those turbulent times.

xviii   *Prologue*

Decades later, it breaks my heart that so many people suffered the way they did during those times in both countries. Nobody—Black, White, Catholic, Protestants, policemen and soldiers were immune to suffering during those dark times. Starting in the mid to late 1960s, Northern Ireland and the United States were torn apart by violence that would trickle into the present.

I was in graduate school when I became interested in the connection between the two movements and headed to Northern Ireland for the first time to do research for my independent study for my Master's degree in History. The year was 2001, just three years after the Good Friday Agreement had been signed to allow a power-sharing government between Catholics and Protestants in Northern Ireland. Belfast and the country were changing at a breakneck pace.

Having experienced racial bias in the United States, I was fascinated by the lack of overt racism in Northern Ireland. As one young man told me on a side street near the Crown Bar in 2001, "More people are worried about having a bomb stuck up their arse than they are about your color."

Experiencing less racial bias in Northern Ireland than in the United States deepened my curiosity about how the Nationalists used the Black Civil Rights movement in America as a playbook. Upon returning to Virginia, I immersed myself in research, looking at interviews of various Catholic leaders and talking to both of my parents, who found themselves in the middle of the Civil Rights Movement in North Carolina as college students. In the summer of 2022, I went to Derry for the first time and learned more about the march that had ignited the Civil Rights movement in Northern Ireland. People on both sides of the Northern Irish divide were left speechless by the beatings that occurred during the march from Belfast to Derry, the British response and the confrontation on Burntollet Bridge on January 4, 1969.

As an African American student back in the 1990s, the country intrigued me because of the connections to our own fight for rights here in the United States. Just like the Civil Rights movement in the United States, the Catholic movement in Northern Ireland was led and put together mostly by young people and students.

In the 1960s, Catholics were inspired by the Civil Rights Movement in the United States, and protests in Northern Ireland began with Catholics demanding equality. Their demands included better access to jobs and housing, and a fair voting system where all votes counted. Their slogan was "One Man, One Vote." In local government elections, Britain had changed to universal suffrage for all citizens over the age of 21 in 1945. Northern Ireland maintained a system in which young adults living in their parents' households were not

Prologue xix

allowed to vote. This policy disproportionately limited Catholic votes because many Catholics resided in multi-family households. Significantly, social housing at this time was mainly allocated by the local councils, meaning that there was discrimination in housing allocation against members of the Catholic community. With fewer Catholics allowed to vote, the Protestant community and their Unionist politicians were able to pass legislation that further marginalized Catholics.

On January 1, 1969, a People's Democracy march, made up of mainly students from Queens University in Belfast, left Belfast City Hall on a four-day march to Derry. This march lacked the backing of the Northern Ireland Civil Rights Association, a group that supported the suspension of demonstrations because of their differing views with the students.

Governor George Wallace said this when Civil Rights was mentioned in America, "Segregation today. Segregation tomorrow. Segregation forever."[1] The Loyal Citizens of Ulster (an extremist group of Protestants), led by Major Ronald Bunting, issued a statement about the march from Belfast to Derry calling on "all those who value their heritage" to take every possible action within the law to hinder and harass the "so-called civil rights marchers."[2]

Reverend Ian Paisley, leader of the Free Presbyterian Church, was one of the most fervent anti-Catholic protestors in Northern Ireland. He said at one of the demonstrations in 1969, "All our life and heritage are at stake."[3] At another of his sermons, he said, "Romanism has controlled this land for many centuries. And Romanism has bred poverty, ignorance, witchcraft, and superstition."[4] Another one of Paisley's soundbites was, "No Surrender."[5] These samples of his public speeches demonstrate Paisley's suspicion, hate and prejudice toward Catholics.

The parallels of the quotes are stunning to read. The connections between both groups of people fighting for their rights are indelible. Both groups were being beaten off the streets by counter-protestors and the police. One has to remember the police in the United States were predominantly white and in Northern Ireland, predominantly Protestant.

This book is the story of the march, the major leaders and the events that led up to it and the events that followed it. It also chronicles the Selma to Montgomery march, which heavily influenced the Belfast to Derry one, and the events surrounding it as well.

The Civil Rights movement was a landmark for both countries. Passionate fighters for Catholics and Blacks in Northern Ireland and the United States paid the ultimate price, which were their lives, for what they believed in. So many families on all sides were impacted by the loss of precious life.

xx *Prologue*

This is a personal story because my mother took part in the 1963 March on Washington. She saw firsthand the impact that marching for democracy can have on a nation's society. My mother was born in Hickory, North Carolina and my father in Walkertown, North Carolina, both in 1943. Their parents were born and raised in the early twentieth century. Both of their parents took their first steps in the shadows of cotton and tobacco plantations in Georgia and North Carolina respectively. My grandparents came of age in the shadows of post-Reconstruction in the United States, when opportunities were promised for all people, regardless of color. However, this never came to fruition. My grandparents, like many other Black Americans at that time, were only provided the opportunity to work in the fields and other menial jobs. Because of their circumstances, only one of my grandparents graduated from high school.

Both of my parents grew up with legal segregation and voter disenfranchisement being the norm during their teenage and college years. My mother met my father while at the historically Black college, Livingstone College. Livingstone was located in Salisbury, North Carolina. This region was home to the Grand Dragon of the Ku Klux Klan. My parents were dedicated to the non-violent social movement and campaign from 1954 to 1968, the year of the death of Dr. Martin Luther King, Jr. I will talk about their marches in downtown Salisbury to integrate the lunch counters and movie theaters there later in the book. My parents understood Dr. King's famous words, "Freedom only comes through persistent revolt, through persistent agitation, through persistently rising up through the system of evil."[6] They knew that direct action and protest, not negotiation, was the only way to make true progress for equal rights.

I've been fortunate enough to visit Belfast numerous times since 2001. I was able to visit Derry for the first time during the summer of 2022 and again during the spring of 2024. Both cities are two of my favorite places to visit. The backdrop of my Twitter page is a photograph of Civil Rights icon John Lewis walking across the Peace Bridge with Northern Ireland Civil Rights icon John Hume. That image still makes my heart proud because of the connection between the two Civil Rights movements.

However, to understand the connection, we need to look at the beginning of the movement on both sides and how the Catholics were influenced by what the African Americans did in the United States.

I tell everyone I can about the murals in both Belfast and Derry, where I saw gorgeous images of both Dr. King and Malcolm X. One of the former IRA men who gave me a black taxi tour of Belfast in the summer of 2022 told me, "We took a lot from your movement for Black Civil Rights in the States."

Prologue xxi

The connection between my people and the Catholic population was strong and remains that way today. My goal was to weave together personal stories in an intimate, kaleidoscopic portrait of two Civil Rights movements and how the United States one influenced the one in Northern Ireland. The result, I believe, is a spellbinding account of the Belfast to Derry march, a propulsive piece of forgotten civil rights history in Northern Ireland, and a poignant reminder of the emotional toll on those who stood on the front lines of social change in both countries.

You may have never heard of Salisbury, North Carolina and Burntollet Bridge, but what happened in both locations will forever change how I viewed the Black Civil Rights movement in the United States and the Catholic Civil Rights movement in Northern Ireland. This is a tremendously personal book. I chose to write about people that I knew, people I've met and people who taught me about the connection between the two movements, such as Bernadette Devlin, member of the Courageous Eight and Eamonn McCann.

I chose to focus on the attack on Burntollet Bridge, which was eerily similar to the attack on the Edmund Pettus Bridge in the Selma to Montgomery, Alabama march in 1965. The ambush of the Catholic civil rights group that day in 1969 became a defining moment of the Troubles in Northern Ireland. Most books about the Catholic Civil Rights movement begin with Bloody Sunday when thirteen unarmed Catholics who were marching against internment without cause were murdered by British paratroopers in January 1972. My friend and fellow author, Julieann Campbell, is the niece of Jackie Duddy, one of the youngest killed on Bloody Sunday. He was 17 years old. I am touched by the stories of Blacks and Catholics who were killed unjustly due to a lack of understanding and empathy among different groups in the United States and Northern Ireland.

The history between our two countries goes back to Frederick Douglass, the famous escaped slave and human rights campaigner. Douglass visited Ireland in the years 1845 and 1846, just before some of the most horrific years of the Great Famine. Douglass gave over 50 speeches there. He developed an affection for the country and recognized the connection between the treatment of Blacks in the States and the nineteenth-century rule by the British over the Irish citizens. The anti-slavery movement in Ireland was active during his visit. In his own words, Douglass said, "Ireland was transformational."[7] He also witnessed the dreadful conditions that the Irish peasants lived in.

Deep-rooted connections between the United States and Northern Ireland continue today. In August 2023, a crowd of over hundreds turned out for the unveiling of a statue of Frederick Douglass on Lombard Street in the city of

xxii   *Prologue*

Belfast. Northern Ireland continues to respect the work Douglass did and the work that remains to be done in terms of racism and poverty in both the United States and Northern Ireland, respectively.

We've come so far, but there's still a lot to do in both countries.

This is the story that binds us.

CHAPTER 1

COMING TO DERRY, SUMMER 2022

The city of Derry is nestled poetically on the gorgeous River Foyle where you can see the gentle, rolling lands up on the hill that foster a community of some 83,000 people. The city is now known for the Peace Bridge that ties both banks together, the Cityside on the west side and Waterside on the east. For this book, we will call it Derry, but you'll hear and see people in here call it Londonderry, depending on the community they come from. Derry's original name was Daire Calgaich (Oak Grove of Calgaich). In the tenth century it was renamed Doire Colmcille (Oak Grove of St Colmcille), in remembrance of the sixth-century saint. However, in 1609, when the English government decided to develop Derry, it signed an agreement with the Corporation of London to provide the necessary land settlers. To commemorate this fact, the city's name was lengthened to Londonderry (a name many Protestants still use today).

It is truly a beautiful city, almost a valley-like place where you look up and see the clouds right behind the houses, gathering the morning fog from the rain that will no doubt hit during the time people visit. Erosion and time have worn the mountaintops of the city's distinctively hilly topography.

There had been a settlement on the site where Derry is today since the sixth century when St. Colmcille (also known as St. Columba) founded a monastic community on the hillside. Most people think it is where the Church of Ireland Chapel of St. Augustine is today. In the late sixteenth century, Elizabeth I became determined to conquer the pain in the side that Ulster had become, and an English group arrived in Derry in 1566. In 1600, another, better attempt to take over the city was made during the Nine Years' War between 1594 and 1603 against the O'Neills and O'Donnells. In 1609, James I was determined to finish the matter for good; he gave land to English and Scottish settlers and the wealthy London trade guilds were put in charge of planning the expansion of Derry and were responsible for the present layout of the walled city and for the actual walls you see today.

In 1688, eighty years after James I, the gates of Derry were slammed shut by 13 apprentice boys. Months later, the great siege of Derry had begun behind the Catholic forces of James II. For 105 days, the Protestant citizens of Derry withstood heavy attacks, disease and starvation. They rejected the proposed peace terms and proclaimed that they would eat the Catholics first before ever surrendering to them. A relief ship broke through the boom on the River Foyle and ended the siege. However, by that time, an estimated quarter of the 30,000 people there had perished. It wasn't a final winning blow for the Protestant forces, but the timely distraction gave King William the time he needed to increase his army's numbers. This helped King William in his historic victory at the Battle of the Boyne on July 12, 1690. This turned things around for the negative in James's failed attempt to regain the British crown and aided in ensuring the Protestant rule in Ireland.

During the nineteenth century, Derry was one of the main ports from which many Irish citizens emigrated to the United States. It also played an important role in the transatlantic trade in shirts and other items. Local factories also provided uniforms for both sides in the American Civil War.

Northern Ireland's second-largest city is a walled city. Its walls are thought to have been influenced by the French Renaissance town of Vitry-le-Francois, designed in 1545 by Italian engineer Hieronimo Marino. The city was based on a grid plan with two main streets and four gates, one at either end of each street. The walls were completed in 1619, and they are 8 m high and 9 m thick. Interestingly enough, they are the only city walls in all of Ireland to have survived almost completely intact. When I was there in 2022, you could walk to the highest part of the walls of the city and look directly down on the area where Bloody Sunday occurred.

The Bogside area, to the west of the walled city, was developed in the nineteenth and early twentieth centuries. It was settled as a working class, mostly Catholic housing area. By the 1960s, its rows and rows of terrace houses had become overcrowded and hindered by poverty and rampant unemployment. Because of these issues, the area became a prime focus for the emerging Civil Rights movement. Even today, there are murals throughout the Bogside that either showcase past events in the area or continue the rhetoric of 'Free Derry' corner, one of the most famous murals in Derry.

There are still rumblings in the area, especially during the marching season in July when Protestants celebrate the Battle of the Boyne and Catholics burn certain people in effigy with huge bonfires in the middle of the Bogside. The city center was given a beautiful makeover for its year as the UK City of Culture in 2013 with the construction of the Peace Bridge and the redevelopment of the waterfront, which has taken advantage of the city's gorgeous riverside setting.

***

I first went to Derry in the summer of 2022 with a good friend of mine from Dublin. I'd been to Belfast numerous times, but this was the first time in the city that I'd read about and was excited to visit. I would be there for three days to learn more about the city and its history and to meet author Julieann Campbell for the first time in person, someone that I now consider a good friend. We'd become friendly through Twitter, and I had enjoyed her book, *On Bloody Sunday*. A stunning fact-based book if you haven't read it. Though I had learned about the 1972 event of Bloody Sunday at Hollins University while I studied the Troubles, I really didn't know much about Derry beyond that. That didn't surprise many of the people I met during my visit. One of the workers at the Bishop's Gate Hotel said, "Bloody Sunday is what we're known for," he told me. "But we've tried to move past it, and show people that there is more to our city. We're a resilient lot."

The warmth of the people in Derry, I'd never seen anything like it. The Peace Bridge, the iconic picture that I had on my Twitter page with John Lewis and John Hume was stunning to see in person. Next, I checked into the Bishops Gate Hotel. This is definitely the city's grandest hotel, established in the 1880s by veterans of the Crimean War. Everyone was friendly, from the doorman to the young lady (Kaysi) at the front desk. I highly recommend this hotel if you're ever in Derry. However, it is a hilly city, so be prepared to walk and get a workout. The Bishops Gate was in the middle of the city center, a former Northern Counties gentleman's club that was transformed into the now 30-room boutique hotel, with people such as Winston Churchill staying there in the past. I spent the day with Julieann Campbell and later that evening, enjoying the best live Irish music I've ever heard in the raucous pub, Peadar O'Donnell's, named after the Irish radical. Too much fun and too much Guinness that night!

The next afternoon, another friend of mine and I did a tour of the Bogside (which is still 99 percent Catholic), with its amazing murals and down-to-earth atmosphere. In my humble opinion, some of the best people I've ever met and spent time with are from there. In the 1960s and 1970s, it was the site of many marches and battles for civil rights for the Catholics. Catholics living in

4   GOOD TROUBLE

the Bogside could see across the river where the Protestants lived in the best houses. Catholics living in the Bogside had houses with multiple bedrooms, with a family in each one and at the same time no bathrooms, outside toilets and no jobs. Two-thirds of the population in the '60s in Derry were Catholic, and they were ruled by the Protestant minority. The entire electoral system was unbalanced because, to be able to vote, you had to be a homeowner. For instance, a homeowner who had eight people in their family, even if they were all over 18, had only two votes—the owners of the house. The other issue was that very few Catholics owned their own houses because most of them were barely surviving and paid rent only to live where they could. Many Protestants did own their houses, and therein lay the problem. The country of Northern Ireland was designed so there would be a solid Protestant majority. It was similar in the United States, where African American voting was suppressed so the White majority rule would always win out. In Northern Ireland, it was the Unionist Party, and they were loyal to the British Crown (Unionists are sometimes called Loyalists as well).

The most famous march that I've mentioned was Bloody Sunday in January 1972. The day was tragically similar to Dublin's Bloody Sunday in November of 1920, when British security forces shot dead 14 spectators at a Gaelic football match in Croke Park stadium. On January 30, 1972, the Northern Ireland Civil Rights Association organized a peaceful march through Derry in protest against internment without trial, which had been introduced by the British government the previous year. Some 15,000 people marched from Creggan through the Bogside, but they were stopped by British Army barricades. The main march was diverted along another street to the Free Derry corner, but a small number of youths began hurling stones and insults at the British soldiers.

Soldiers of the first battalion, Parachute Regiment, opened fire on unarmed civilians. Thirteen people were shot dead, some of them shot in the back; six were aged just 17. One of those aged 17 was Jackie Duddy, the first fatality of the afternoon and the uncle of Julieann Campbell. A photograph of his limp body being carried by local men, while Father Edward Daly, who would later become Bishop of Derry, nervously walks ahead of them waving a white handkerchief, has since become the single most memorable image of that day's horror.

As the tour continued for us, I saw one of the streets where a marcher was shot, though now the building beside it is the Museum of Free Derry. There were still bullet holes in one of the neighboring buildings where the soldiers shot at the marchers. I couldn't help but imagine the scenes on these same streets, people running, hiding behind walls and praying for the shooting to stop.

Going down into the Bogside, our tour guide took us past Rossville Street where the marchers had been diverted to before the shooting began. I saw the area where the flats stood as shots rang out after British troops advanced on Rossville, opening fire with live rounds. Marchers were being hit by vehicles, paratroopers chasing men and women with batons and high velocity shots, as one man said, "I thought they were wasps flying around but they were actually bullets." I passed the Free Derry Corner, where everyone had panicked and started to lie down and looked for any type of cover that they could find from the shots coming from all directions. There were kids out there who had just wanted to see what all the commotion was about in the streets and to hear the speeches. I walked by the side alleys and saw the walls that many had hidden around to keep safe from the snipers.

Above me loomed the great city walls of Derry, where our tour guide had told us that British snipers had killed several 'suspicious' people over the years who had turned out to be Irish citizens minding their own business. The walls were amazing to see from inside the Bogside. The Free Derry Museum was right in the middle of the Bogside, on a side street where citizens had hidden from bullets during Bloody Sunday; now it is an educational area. As Julieann Campbell said, "Now, we're all about peace tourism. People are coming here for an education."[1]

Deciding about the narrative, or more accurately, whose narrative to feature in the exhibits at the Free Derry Museum was very challenging. The battle over the story of Derry's part in the Civil Rights Movement was part of, and still is, an ongoing struggle over the politics of memory for both sides of the argument. History, like everything in politics today, is seen as the truth that's in the eye of the one telling the story. But, memories are something that people believe are one hundred percent accurate even though they can fade with age. They do reveal truths that people are happy to talk about since their version of events has sometimes been ignored by certain entities. However, there is no doubt that we choose to remember certain things with our own personal perspective.

I was able to reconstruct these previously unknown stories because of research and interviews with people who were generous with their memories. As I've learned about the struggle with the Belfast to Derry march, I've been surprised at how the march is not as well known as it should be. The events of the march show the challenges that both the Catholic marchers and the Black marchers in the Selma to Montgomery march faced. Many of the best-known events such as Bloody Sunday and the 1963 March on Washington have been told in ways such as television highlights and movies that make us forget about other turning points for both countries. What happened with the Belfast to Derry march was the start of something big for the Civil Rights Movement and British responses to the country.

On the Belfast to Derry march and the Selma to Montgomery one, none of the participants could have ever guessed what was about to happen to them. They were doing something that would have been seen as a major turning point for both of their Civil Rights movements. Had they not done what they did— or had they been shut down and given up—where would Northern Ireland or the USA be today? Instead, everyone in both marches were knocked down, literally, but they got back up and it made them more powerful. Today, both countries continue to be split by religion and race respectively—the same ones that splintered the countries in the 1960s. Their experiences changed them, scarred them, and the trauma remains with many of them even today, evident by the comments in my interviews with them. Some were able to rebuild their lives, while others were not. Even my parents still talk today about those marches that they took part in and are amazed that nobody was killed.

The first lesson of this book is this: history is the story of human beings— individuals responding to events already in motion and rarely under their control. Along the way, many of them showed courage that they never knew they had. Their brave acts in the face of intense violence changed their countries for good.

There was a lot of bravery in both the Catholic and Black Civil Rights movements during those years.

CHAPTER 2

THE ROOTS OF THE CONFLICT: MICHAEL COLLINS AND EASTER RISING

What we now know as Ireland started hundreds of years before Michael Collins and Easter Rising. Pope Adrian IV gave Ireland as an inheritance to Henry II, the Norman king of England. At that point, there was no united Ireland, but a number of independent areas. These independent areas banded together against Henry II's armies and held them off. For hundreds of years after this, the English attempted to take over Ireland but to no avail, interestingly enough both of these were Catholic entities going against each other. This all changed with the Tudors coming into power when Henry VIII broke away from the Catholic Church. At the same time, the heads of Ireland stuck with Rome.

With this recognition of Protestantism, the best land was given to farmers from England and Scotland as the British troops pushed the Irish off their own land. The majority of the remaining Irish population was condemned to jobs working the land of the English and the Scots, very similar to the Black slaves in the United States. There was a bloody revolt in 1641 against the Protestant landowners by the Irish. Oliver Cromwell came over and crushed the insurrection and continued to bring in Protestants to take over more land. Now, almost all of the land was under British rule in Ireland.

This led to the defeat of James II, who had been kicked out by Protestant William of Orange, at the Battle of the Boyne by King William, which, as you will read later, is still celebrated today by many Protestants. James wanted power back, and the Catholics were excited about him returning to Ireland, but the revolt failed.

There is still an old toast that is made by some Protestants on the anniversary of the Battle of the Boyne: "To the glorious, pious and immortal memory of King Williams III, who saves us from Rogues and Roguery. Slaves and slavery, Popes and Popery; and whoever denies this toast may he be slammed, crammed an jammed into the muzzle of the great gun of Athlone, and the gun fired into the Pope's belly, and the Pope into the Devil's belly, and the Devil into Hell, and the door locked and the key kept in an Orangeman's pocket."

On January 1, 1801, Ireland officially became a part of the United Kingdom. The British did their best to keep the Irish down and not give them any hope for freedom or justice. It was very similar to what was happening around the same time with Blacks in the American Southern states. It was a desperate situation for the Irish, with the living conditions, lack of land and the potato famine, which killed so many and forced many to leave their country. This all led to a limited home rule in September 1914, because of the efforts of the Irish Nationalist Party The Ultra-Nationalists, including members of Sinn Fein, opposed home rule as they wanted complete independence.

However, many people didn't want home rule, limited or not. They wanted a completely independent Ireland.

This opened the door for Michael Collins and Easter Rising.

***

The birth of Michael Collins in a small location in West Cork provided what is now known as the Republic of Ireland with an intelligent and headstrong man who forced his country to take a big step from British property to a free land under Irish rule. Over many years, Protestants coming to Ireland had been given land, legal and political privileges.

From his boyhood, Collins remembered landlordism and pride in Irishness, both of which would form his character throughout his older years as he remembered how his family had come to blows a few times with the Protestant landlord classes.[1] Collins was taught at a young age to be proud of his Irish roots and heritage. Collins was a young boy who seemingly was destined to become a leader. Stories pop up of the young boy always wanting to be in charge of things. This is evident with his father telling his family while on his deathbed, "One day he'll be a great man. He'll do great work for Ireland."[2] Even as early as Collins's pre-teen years, there were already leadership qualities and determination in the mind of the good-looking, wavy, dark-haired young man. Very noticeable was the focused perception that the Irish boy would do everything and anything in his ability to survive and flourish in a world that was reserved exclusively for the Protestants and the British. Collins had grown into his stoic, handsome self that made him appear more like a prince than a dangerous revolutionary.

The Roots of the Conflict

Around the year 1916, the question of Irish independence from Britain became the most important issue for the Catholic population other than World War I. Many Irish wanted self-government and became more and more frustrated as two home rule bills had been defeated in parliament in 1886 and 1893. The third home rule bill was introduced in 1912 and encated in September 1914, but it was never enacted because of the start of World War I. However, not all Irish people wanted home rule. Most people in the nine counties of the North at that time, wanted to remain part of Britain; in the South, most wanted to become an independent republic. This bitter division dated back to the sixteenth century when English monarchs had put Protestant Englishmen and Scotsmen on lands taken from Irish Catholics as a way of increasing loyalty to the crown.

The Easter Rising of 1916 by the Irish volunteers against the British thrust the patriots into a social and political war and was the turning point for the argument of Irish nationalism. People who wanted Ireland to become a republic belonged to various organizations, including the political party Sinn Fein, the Irish Republican Brotherhood, the Irish Volunteers and the Irish Citizen Army. Two of the leaders of the revolt were James Connelly and Patrick Pearse. Connelly was a slightly balding man with a thick mustache and a trade union leader with a socialist mindset. Pearse was both a schoolteacher and a writer, who firmly believed that a stand in the city center of Dublin would attract the world's attention instead of a guerilla war campaign in the countryside. The clean-cut, dark-haired Pearse was known as a deep thinker and hardline revolutionary.

Word of the 1916 rising was spreading and Michael Collins also wanted to be there in the middle of it all. Wanting to organize and be in the middle of it all would be something that Collins would use quite a bit in his years of fighting for Irish nationalism, something that always made him the center of attention, as both a leader and a revolutionary.

A man who had traveled from Dublin to London said that word had started to spread about the insurgency even before it started. He said, "The invasion of the rebel army did not take the population by storm [...] For a long time there have been frequent dress rehearsals [...] and it was generally expected that sooner or later Dublin must be the theatre of serious disturbances. Only last week a private warning was issued in certain outlying districts of the city urging people to look out for help on Easter Monday. The police, too had received anonymous correspondence to the effect that the Sinn Feiners contemplated a big coup."[3]

10   GOOD TROUBLE

The first step of the insurrection was storming Dublin Castle. This attempt was foiled as the guards defeated the mob.

Out of all the places for a rebel headquarters, the place they picked was the General Post Office (I saw this in Summer 2022, and there are still bullet marks on the building from the uprising). The rebels took some British guards as prisoners and hoisted a green flag with the words 'Irish Republic' on it. Pearse came out, addressed the stunned crowd and announced the proclamation of the Republic. The post office was a strong and well-defended building, one that the British made little attempt at assaulting. This was a good choice by the rebels; people would see what they were doing and why they were doing it. Very few clerks were on duty because of Easter Monday, and when the rebels made their appearance in the building, there was little resistance. Now, there was no retreating from the beginnings of the Republic of Ireland.

While in the fiery Post Office during the 1916 Easter Rising, Michael Collins told a friend about his feelings inside there, "Machine gun fire made escape more or less impossible. Not that we wished to escape. No man wished to budge. In that building, the defiance of our men, and the gallantry, reached unimaginable proportions."[4] Truth be told, Collins played a very minor role in the Rising.

In the St. Stephen's Green neighborhood, the rebels took possession of several houses. They closed the gates of the Green and began digging trenches. Shots were fired at the Shelbourne Hotel and any soldier or policeman in the streets was shot down, which contributed to a number of deaths.

The rebels were dressed in uniforms and the majority of them carried old-fashioned rifles. Shots were heard in all parts of the city all day on Monday and that evening.

Once the armed gained possession of the Post Office, they were prepared for the siege. A group of rebels went with carts to the Metropole Hotel and persuaded the staff there to supply them with food. They barricaded the windows with sandbags and began to shoot at the police and soldiers indiscriminately. Perched high up, the rebels had a clear vantage point to pick off the soldiers one by one. They shot at unarmed soldiers who just happened to be out on the street at the time. One officer explained what he saw, "A soldier was shot down who was walking with his sweetheart."[5] Along with the seizure of the Post Office, the rebels took over other public buildings such as the College of Surgeons, the College of Science and numerous railroad stations. Easter Monday was the best day for the siege as the city was on holiday and many of the military and police were away at a meeting at Fairyhouse. One of the newspapers said, "Monday an ideal day for the raiders."[6]

The Roots of the Conflict   11

One soldier from Dublin reported what he'd seen at the Post Office seizure, "After they seized the building men at the windows fired at any man in uniform in sight. [...] They had a lot of explosives."[7]

During the day on Monday, a large part of the city was controlled by the rebels. Early on Tuesday morning, troops began to arrive as the air became colder. *The Manchester Guardian* said that the attack was "a crime against Ireland's honour and welfare."[8]

The unfortunate thing for the rebels was that General John Maxwell had arrived to lead England against the upstart rebels. This was a man who was not given an army to fight in France and he wanted desperately to show the young Republicans that insurrection would not be tolerated. Ironically, it sounded very much like what Bunting said in Derry in 1969. Maxwell was a large man with a dark mustache. He was born in Liverpool in 1859 and educated at the Royal Military College. He took part in the Boer War. He'd had a long and distinguished career in the British Army with commended postings in the Middle East and Africa. However, after the Easter Rising, Maxwell would be known as 'Bloody' Maxwell. The six months that he spent in Ireland during the Easter Rising days would be a turning point in the country's history moving forward.

The plan was to surround the rebels. The situation turned in favor of the military by early Wednesday. Nobody was allowed to be in the streets. Bullets sprayed many of the buildings in the city, and very little of the structures remained afterwards. Most of the rebels had to escape the buildings through exits in the back. More and more soldiers began to show up and prisoners were taken. The military was fighting back with force against the rebels.

By the end of the week, two things became evident to Pearse and the rebels fighting against the British. Number one was that they were wrong about the British being reluctant to damage the city of Dublin. Number two was that the people of Dublin did not rally to the defense of their fighting Republicans. The number of armed Dubliners barely represented one percent of men of military age.[9] The British were not the ones who were being blamed for the destruction of Dublin, but the Irish volunteers. The bombardment of the city was devastating as Dublin was filled with battle-weary men and starving women.

The British continued their fiery siege on the city. Also on Friday, the post office was set on fire once again as the rebels decided to move their headquarters to a factory back up the block since they could not control this fire. Pearse and Connelly knew they would not reach the factory. From the house, Pearse saw a family of three shot dead on the street as they attempted to leave their burning home. Pearse could not take any more of the killing, and this was the beginning of the end for the Irish rebels.

12   GOOD TROUBLE

Pearse sent a message to the British that he wanted to ask for terms of peace under a flag of truce.[10] Pearse heard the message return for an unconditional surrender by him and his men, and he wrote a letter of surrender, in his mind to prevent the further killing of Dublin citizens. By Sunday, it was all over, leaving many to question what went wrong. Another Irish legend who took part in the insurrection, Eamon de Valera gave his view: "If the people had risen en masse, if they had gone out with nothing but knives and forks in their hands, they could have won the country.[11]

The Dublin citizens did not care as many commented as the prisoners were marched through the city, "Shoot every bloody one of them!"[12] The irony here is that the cause that these Irish rebels fought for only began to gain support by the Dubliners when fifteen of the rebels were executed. The most famous one of them all, Pearse, gave an impassioned speech about Irish freedom. Afterwards, he was executed with fifteen others. Pearse was still seen as the embodiment of the rebellion. De Valera was one of the lucky ones, spared because of his American birth and British sensitivity to American support during World War I. Connelly did not survive the defeat. Following the loss of Easter Rising, and the arrest of the majority of its leaders, he was taken to Kilmainham Gaol (jail) and executed by firing squad for his participation in the insurrection. One of the last things Connelly said was a poignant quote, "If you remove the English army tomorrow and hoist the green flag over Dublin Castle, unless you set about the organization of the Socialist Republic, your efforts would be in vain. England would still rule you. She would rule you through her capitalists, through her landlords, through her financiers, through the whole array of commercial and individualist institutions she had planted in this country and watered with the tears of our mothers and the blood of our martyrs."[13]

The response to the rebellion prisoners was swift and devastating. One example of how they were treated was the case of Mr. Gerald Crofts, one of the rebellion prisoners. He was sentenced by Court Martial to ten years' penal servitude in connection with the Easter Week 1916 Rising, later commuted to five years. The executions galvanized an Irish population who at first were leery about the rebellion.

Dublin was in ruins. Hundreds of people had been killed and many more were wounded. In one month's time, close to 4,000 people had been arrested. British soldiers executed many in the courtyard of the famous Kilmainham Gaol. Despite the results of the failed rebellion, the Irish freedom fighters had landed a body blow to the powerful British Empire.

In May of 1917, one of the British MPs, Mr. T. P. O'Connor, brought up the chance of an early release for a number of Irish political prisoners. He said,

The Roots of the Conflict

"I'm perfectly sure the Prime Minister would approach the subject in a broad, generous and statesmanlike manner. He would know that after the close of one of those tragic outbursts which occurred in all counties under certain conditions that if the Government wanted to bring conciliation and peace nearer the final thing they had got to do was to clean the slate and release those who had been involved in it [...] and if they were released the result would be, he hoped, a new and brighter chapter in the history of Ireland."[14]

Both sides suffered casualties, with 485 total including 82 rebels, 143 from the British Crown and 260 civilians. Many public buildings in Dublin were destroyed or badly damaged in the conflict. The entire episode was seen has haphazard, plans for the rising had been lost and there was a lack of communication about how the attack would begin. There was even an announcement in the newspaper the day before the rising started, stating that everything had been called off. Not the finest way to start a revolution, in many people's eyes. Nonetheless, the feeling in Dublin was changing, with those who had been booed and spat upon now being seen as heroes by the citizens. However, there were many Irish citizens who called on the Government to release many of the Irish prisoners. Westmeath City Council said that the release would be essential to the creation of Ireland, which would convince all parties to take part in drafting an Irish constitution. At the same time, Irish prisoners were already planning the next step in their fight for the Republic.

The leaders who were killed and executed in the Easter Rising rebellion would haunt the British for many years to come. The Irish population would never forget those events.

***

Following his release, Michael Collins played an active part in the reorganization of the Irish Republican Brotherhood, the Volunteers and Sinn Fein. He remained vigilant despite the setbacks he'd endured. The IRB was determined to use the Volunteers for offensive action while Britain was tied up in the First World War. Their plan was to instigate a rising. Collins also began to take trips to London and Manchester to build up his smuggling network that would work so well in the future. In 1917, Collins was elected to the Sinn Fein executive, and with that, he became involved with the setting up of two underground newspapers, the building of an intelligence network, the organization of a national loan to fund a rebellion and a bomb-making factory.

Prime Minister Lloyd George was feeling the pressure of the situation. The Irish Independent had a letter from Dean McGlinchey that said the following,

14 GOOD TROUBLE

"There are two points in connection with the Lloyd George trap to which I would respectfully call public attention [...] the government has said that coercion of Ulster is unthinkable. It has been quite evident all along that these same advocates of liberty never hesitated for a moment to coerce Tyrone, Fermanagh and Derry City, and that they were prepared to establish a new division of Ireland which they called 'Ulster', into which they would force against their will the predominating Catholic population of two counties and a city."[15] This citizen could clearly see that the seeds were being sown from across the sea in London.

Going into 1918, Collins believed the following about Great Britain: "...to subvert the tyranny of our execrable government, to break the connection of England- the unfailing source of all our ills- and to assert the independence of my native country [...] these were my objects."[16] Interestingly enough, during these next few years, the viewpoint of Collins changed. It changed as the Irish issue fell into the hands of the Irish revolutionaries, and the main one was unexpectedly, Michael Collins himself.

In 1918, Collins was arrested and held in jail in Sligo, Ireland. He wrote a letter about what was happening at the time:

Arrested in Dublin just at 11:30 [...] detectives seized me were- O'Brien and Bruton. Refused to proceed until they produced warrant. Of course this was the purpose of annoying them. Crowd quickly gathered and like every other right minded crowd in Ireland were hostile to the police. [...] Of course the moral support of the mob was an acquisition. The miserable hound (Bruton) knew that a word from me meant a mauling for him [...] Both police uniformed and police detectives were very rough towards young boys and girls. Saw one member of the "B" division particularly brutally fling a slender girl of about 15 on the pavements at a point about 10 yards past the Red Bank restaurant. [...] The charge was read to me- and is as far as I remember somewhat as follows: Having incited reading for arms in a speech delivered at Legga, Co, Longford, on Sunday, March 3, 1918. It struck me that the charge was so framed as to deny me the rights of political treatment in case of conviction [...]Detained in Brunswick St. for a few hours in a filthy, ill-ventilated cell [...] (Collins was then sent to Bridwell jail) [...]Awful place the Bridwell- big, cold, filthy cells [...] Spent almost sleepless night and elf positively petrified in the morning.[17]

In early 1920, Michael Collins created an assassin squad called the Twelve Apostles, a group specifically formed to terrorize both British intelligence and the Royal Irish Constabulary (RIC).[18] The RIC was the police force in the land at the time. That made the year 1920 come to be known as the Year of Terror in Ireland, as the Black and Tans (in Irish—Duchronaigh) came into the land to devastate the Irish population with brutal violence. The Black and Tans were constables recruited into the RIC as reinforcements during the Irish War of Independence, with about 10,000 men enlisting. The majority of them were unemployed former British soldiers who had fought in the World War I. These forces put a curfew and martial law on the Irish. A full-throttle Anglo-Irish War was in gear now, with Sinn Fein terrorizing RIC officersand Collins thinking that much would be gained by pulling England into the war. As the violence continued to spiral out of control, many people around the world began to see the British as the oppressors of the Irish.

The public started to doubt the direction of the Irish conflict, as seen by a quote about Prime Minister Lloyd George. The Civil and Military Gazette said, "His latest declarations seem to point to an early acceptance of the patent fact that Ireland is in a state of war and that our soldiers must be allowed for their own protection to act accordingly."[19] The discussion in the newspaper was trying to prepare the public for some tough times ahead with the conflict. They also looked to the future and what would happen at the end of the conflict, once it did end, as they said, "At the moment all will support the Government in any measures necessary to restore the King's authority in Ireland, but when that consummation has been achieved, the labour will have been all in vain if we do not learn therefrom the lesson that the cult of political expediency is more criminal and more disastrous to a nation's welfare than the most repressive system of government that can be designed."[20]

This was a dangerous forewarning with the words that Lloyd George used. By portraying the Irish people as both proud and bloodthirsty, the British tried to show the public that their brutal mission of putting down the rebellion was somehow patriotic and righteous.

This would come back to haunt both sides.

CHAPTER 3

THE RISE OF THE IRA

In 1921, after centuries of contested British rule in Ireland, the island was divided into two countries. It was a compromise solution by Lloyd George, which smacked of desperation since the British never could crush the spirits of the Irish resistance. The Anglo-Irish Treaty was signed on December 6, 1921. The counties in the North were allowed to opt out of the Irish Free State, which they did and is one of the reasons you saw violence for many years afterward. The new state of Northern Ireland had an already built-in Protestant majority, which was close to 65 percent. At the time of partition, the Catholic population made up around 35 percent. Northern Ireland now had its own parliament and autonomy within the United Kingdom. However, Westminster was responsible for defense, foreign policy, and other concerns. London took a hands-off approach and left it to the Stormont administration. Stormont was what the parliamentary buildings in Belfast were referred to because of its location in the Stormont Estate area of Belfast. One of Northern Ireland's founders, Lord Craigavon, promised, "This is my whole object in carrying on a Protestant government for a Protestant people."[1] This laid the framework for Northern Ireland to unabashedly be biased toward its majority population in terms of who got the best housing and the prime jobs.

Protestants owned the best land and the largest companies, and they controlled industry and finance at the time. Basically, they controlled everything. It was similar to the white population in the United States. And just like the whites, the Protestants were determined to keep the resources in their hands.

Bernadette Devlin, one of the leading civil rights leaders in Northern Ireland, was asked about the 1921 solution in 1972 and said the following, which showed the connection with the United States: "The partition of Ireland was no more acceptable to farseeing Irishmen than the secession of [...] Southern states was to Abraham Lincoln. If you'd taken a plebiscite within the Confederacy in 1861, you would have found that a majority of Southerners preferred to split off from the United States. Lincoln put the good of the entire country ahead of regional sectarianism, and this led to (the) Civil War. In Ireland, too, we had civil war- between the government of the new Irish Free State and the militant Republicans."[2]

Tensions between those who are loyal to the British crown and those who want a United Ireland continue to this day. However, the Anglo-Irish Treaty did not completely end the violence. It settled on the partition of Ireland, establishing the Irish free state in the south, while the six counties of Ulster remained part of the United Kingdom. Eamon de Valera didn't support the treaty, and he ended up resigning as Michael Collins worked with the provisional government.

De Valera ended up being sidelined by hardline republicans and had to think of a way to make himself relevant again in the eyes of others. Years later he would do just that, using politics to reinvent himself.

De Valera could be a brooding figure and had bright blue eyes and thinning hair during his time in power. He was born in New York City to a Spanish father and an Irish mother. He ended up moving to Ireland when he was two years old and was raised by family members in the city of Limerick. He was educated at Royal University in Dublin. During his early days in Ireland, he was a math teacher. Over the years, De Valera became known as an activist and supporter of Irish independence from the United Kingdom. However, he saw the IRA as a guerilla, terrorist organization and he stopped supporting them after the Civil War in 1922. He continued his fight against them after he entered government in the early 1930s.

Exactly how did the Irish Republican Army become such a powerful organization? Between the years of 1841 and 1951, the Irish population went down by almost two million; many used emigration as an exit, which continues today, and created the political force in America that provided much of the power and money for Irish revolutionaries against England.

The young men and women who began their fight for independence some eighty years ago believed that if they wanted to be independent, they would have to fight for it and not wait for the people of England to determine their destiny. At the end of the Irish Civil War, the IRA was torn on the issue of the use of force. A number of IRA officers were against the treaty, and in 1922 the IRA occupied the Four Courts in Dublin. In June 1922, Ireland went to the polls and the pro-treaty group took close to 60 seats. However, days later,

The Rise of the IRA

republicans killed Ulster MP Henry Wilson, an outspoken opponent of an independent Ireland. Collins responded by attacking the republican-occupied Four Courts in Dublin.

The Irish Civil War continued with many casualties on both sides, but the anti-treaty group didn't have the support they needed to succeed.

Collins's decision to sign the Anglo-Irish Treaty essentially sealed his fate. It eventually led to his death at the hands of anti-treaty forces during the Irish Civil War. Collins was killed in an ambush near Bandon, County Cork, within a few miles of his birthplace in August 1922. Collins was with several officers from the Free State group, visiting the National Army's posts in South Cork and was on his way back to Cork City on some back roads since the main road was not passable.

Collins was accompanied by a bodyguard during his drive and there were well over 20 men in his group. A group of anti-treaty men attacked Collins's men and he was shot in the head. His last words before he died were like a presence that would haunt people like a ghost, "Forgive them. Bury me in Glasnevin with the boys."[3]

The fear throughout Ireland was that the death of Collins would usher in a new wave of guerrilla fighting in the country. A time when there would be attacks on both sides. One observer of the fighting said about his death, "It will put the clock of Ireland back five years."[4]

The funeral of Michael Collins was in Dublin and the procession was more than three miles long. Work was suspended throughout the country for the funeral. At that time, it was the greatest funeral that any Irish leader had ever seen. The funeral was not a military one, and no sound could be heard except the singing of the birds as the procession went past crowds of people who came out to see the event. They needed fourteen motorcars alone just to be able to carry all of the wreaths.

The war ended in May 1923.

The Guardian newspaper said this about the future of the country in August 1924, "The death of Mr. Collins may well mark a turning point in the conflict which is devastating Ireland and bringing a reproach in the eyes of the world upon her people."[5]

In August of 1924, Edward Isherwood, a young English driver, was taken from his house in Cork on August 29th by masked men. The men accused Isherwood of having driven Michael Collins on his journey that would see him assassinated. Isherwood was shot and left for dead and there was a card left on him which read, "Convicted spy. IRA. Beware."[6] However, that was not the end of the story. Isherwood had pretended that he was dead and was able to crawl for almost two miles to a nearby hospital. There are no records about what happened to Isherwood after that incident.

In 1926, Eamon De Valera found a way back to political power. He was greeted with all the pomp and circumstance, with the disappointment that happened during Easter Rising seemingly forgotten like ancient history. De Valera led the political party Fianna Fail, a party that he established. He went on to win power in 1932, and De Valera dominated Irish politics for the next two decades and then served two terms as the President of Ireland. De Valera's greatest achievement in the 1930s was to win the trust of British politicians and ignore the Anglo-Irish treaty, which basically made Southern Ireland a republic in all but name.

However, the bombing campaign of the IRA had roots as early as the 1930s. Random bombs went off during these times. With these bombings, the Offences Against the State Act, which allowed for imprisonment and detention without trial, became law on June 14, 1939. The IRA had been banned in 1936 and declared an unlawful organization, which put them in a shadowy light. This is when the police began to crack down on the IRA. Here, we saw the Catholic population deal with the beginning of blocked roads, checkpoints and other government measures to rein in the IRA. De Valera was part of the solution that crushed the IRA.

Bernadette Devlin told a story about an IRA attack in the city of Coventry, England on August 25, 1939, while her father was in town for a chance at a job. The attack was in the middle of the city and involved a timed bomb in the basket of a bicycle that was left parked on a busy street. It exploded and ended up killing several people. Nobody would give her father and the people he was with lodging because they were of Irish descent. Even back then, people in England would put signs in their windows: No Dogs, No Blacks, No Irish.[7]

Each community continued to be identified by its religion, and there was very little mixing between the two major religious groups. Schools, neighborhoods, workspaces and other gathering areas remained segregated. This was even seen in the name of 'Derry' and 'Londonderry'.

The last Irish Republican Army's last campaign in Northern Ireland ran from December 1956 until February 1962 before the Troubles began in 1968. The Unionists called it the "terrorist campaign" over those years. There were random incidents of violence throughout the country, with police in the streets. The Loyalists had created their own civilian militia, the B Specials in 1920 and they were created to fight the IRA.

During those six tumultuous years, there were approximately 300 major incidents in the country involving the IRA, and six police officers died. The campaign didn't fulfill its objectives, and the Nationalists saw violence at that time not the answer for what they were trying to achieve in the country. Unfortunately, it also impacted politics in a way that they probably didn't foresee, as the IRA's destructive tactics helped the Unionists retain power and control the Protestant vote and their allegiance to the group.

These people were committed to the armed struggle; they were revolutionaries in the vein of Che Guevara and others. They were not civil rights protestors or marchers. They drew comparisons to the Black Panthers at the time of the 1960s and 1970s. There is no doubt that the underground Irish fighters were trying to figure out how they could get their own army together to fight against the British one. The British Army was there and they were the target. It was almost too easy for the IRA to plan. The IRA was able to re-establish itself and its terrorist methods in 1969 and 1970. This was a result of growing frustration with the Unionist leaders and in the Catholic community.

The deployment of the British Army into Northern Ireland was another domino that pushed the IRA back into existence. The IRA saw this as a declaration of war in their country and believed the troops were an occupying force. This monumental change for the IRA changed the history of the country for years to come.

This was the beginning of the Provisional Irish Republican Army. The IRA had become almost moribund after the failure of the Border Campaign and its leadership had drifted towards socialism and favored participation in UK politics. The traditional republicans rejected both of these approaches. When the IRA failed to protect the Catholic community from sectarian attacks in 1969, the traditionalist republicans split from the 'Official' IRA to form the 'Provisionals'. They had been quiet for years but now they would fight for the North of Ireland. Their goal was to use force to defend nationalist areas and to eject the British from the six counties.

CHAPTER 4

STUDENT NONVIOLENT COORDINATING COMMITTEE

The 1960s was the time and decade when the Black population had gotten to the point where they were determined that they should have full, equal rights like every other citizen in the United States. Similar to the People's Democracy in Northern Ireland (the student-led civil rights group started in Belfast), SNCC (pronounced 'SNICK') was formed by Black college students. I am humbled to say that my parents were part of the student movement on their college campus of Livingstone College in Salisbury, North Carolina, in the early '60s. SNCC stood for the Student Nonviolent Coordinating Committee. For the first time in the US South, young people made a decision to enter the civil rights movement just like they did at Queen's University in Belfast. Before SNCC, a few groups of young people tried to involve themselves, but the efforts were mainly led by older people.

World War II had a huge impact on the creation of SNCC and other organizations that worked for civil rights for Black citizens. Many Black men fought in the war (I was lucky enough to do an interview with William Dabney, who was at the D-Day Invasion, and the story won honorable mention from Writer's Digest. He was from Virginia). Mr. Dabney and others were from the South and fought for democracy and against the racist policies of Adolf Hitler in Europe. He and other soldiers were able to enjoy being treated as equals in places like Britain and France. When they returned after the war, they and others were not ready to accept being treated like second-class citizens, and you slowly saw activists fight for rights such as voting. At the start of World War II, only two percent of eligible Blacks were registered voters in the South. They struggled with voting rights as the Catholics did throughout Northern Ireland.

23

24   GOOD TROUBLE

The young people were fighting against people and leaders who were staunch in their belief in white supremacy and the suppression of rights for Black voters.

In the early 1960s, young Black college students participated in sit-ins throughout America to protest the segregation of restaurants. One example was the protests that my parents conducted in the city of Salisbury to integrate places to eat there. Another example was on February 1, 1960, when Black students in Greensboro, North Carolina staged sit-ins that would defy segregation in restaurants and other public facilities.

My parents were both freshmen in the fall of 1962 when they marched in Salisbury, North Carolina. Dad's name is Forest G. Jones and Mom, at the time, was Betty Coates. My dad is known for his hearty laugh, stands about six feet tall and has never met a stranger. Mom is about five-two, loves to hug anyone and gave me my love for reading. Both ended up working in education.

Mom said about their marching, "We were influenced by Dr. Martin Luther King Jr. We had a very active NAACP (National Association for the Advancement of Colored People) on campus but I was not a member."[1]

Dad added, "We had a lot of people who were in the fight for equality. Stokely Carmichael came to campus (he was one of the Black Panthers). I went and marched that one time in Downtown Sailsbury and we were marching to integrate the lunch counters and movie theaters. A lot of the same stuff that SNCC was doing across the South."[2]

My parents were not directly involved as members of the NAACP or SNCC, but they did want to force change in the policies preventing them not being able to go to the movies or sitting at a lunch counter to eat their food in Salisbury as college students. Salisbury was a particular town—not a violent town for civil rights—but the Grand Dragon of the KKK did live down the road in Granite Quarry, North Carolina and the Klan was active in the area.

Dad explained his frustration at the segregation practices in the city, "It was funny. You could go in the stores, etc., and you could buy something to eat and take it out. You just couldn't sit and eat or drink. It was crazy. At the time we didn't think it was crazy because we were born into segregation and it was all we'd known for all those years!"[3]

Earlier in 1960, Ella Baker, a Civil Rights activist and a major force behind the US civil rights movement in the '50s and '60s, invited some other young Civil Rights leaders to Shaw University in Raleigh, North Carolina, in April 1960. People who attended that meeting included John Lewis and future Washington DC Mayor, Marion Berry. From that meeting of the students, SNCC was created. The group consisted mostly of mostly Black college students who participated in peaceful, direct action protests. Many of these were templates that the People's Democracy used in Northern Ireland. Baker said about the SNCC group, "The sit-in movement is bigger than a hamburger [...] [they] are seeking to rid America of the scourge of racial segregation and discrimination not only at lunch counters, but in every aspect of life."[4]

Baker, known now as the 'Mother of the Civil Rights Movement' was born in 1903 in Norfolk, Virginia. Her father worked on a steamship and was away often from the family, while her mother rented their place out to get some extra money. They left Norfolk after a race riot broke out in which whites attacked Black workers from the shipyard where her father worked. Baker was seven when they moved to North Carolina soon after the riot. She attended Shaw University in Raleigh, North Carolina. During World War II, she was the director of the New York City branch of the NAACP. She had worked in the South as a field organizer for the NAACP in the mid-1950s. Baker had said of her work in Civil Rights, "You didn't see me on television, you didn't see news stories about me. The kind of role that I tried to play was to pick up pieces or put together pieces out of which I hoped organization might come. My theory is, strong people don't need strong leaders."[5]

Just like the People's Democracy did, SNCC decided to keep its autonomy and not team up with other civil rights groups such as the SCLC (Southern Christian Leadership Conference), created in 1957 and led by its first President, Martin Luther King, Jr. Baker actually established the national office for the SCLC and had served as its executive director for a short time. King knew the importance of young people in the fight for equal rights, as seen by his words when he spoke on February 16, 1960 at White Rock Baptist Church in Durham, North Carolina. King acknowledged, "What is new in your fight is the fact that it was initiated, fed, and sustained by students."[6]

SNCC conducted a number of major civil rights events throughout the decade of the 1960s. One of the earliest of these events was the Freedom Rides in 1961. This was when SNCC members rode buses throughout the US South to uphold the Supreme Court ruling that said interstate travel could not be segregated. This was a very important stance that SNCC took because the South was known to have 'sundown towns'. The term sundown town originated from the numerous signs that were posted on the roads at the limits of such towns warning Blacks: "Don't Let the Sun Go Down on You in [...]"

The SNCC members faced violent acts from hate groups such as the Ku Klux Klan and law enforcement. I remember my father telling me about their marches in Salisbury and that the KKK was on one side of the street of the marchers, with the police standing on the sidewalk protecting the KKK, not

26   GOOD TROUBLE

on the street where the marchers including my mother and father were at the time, in the fall of 1962.

Dad explained, "We met one afternoon at one of the dorms on campus and went downtown on Main Street. The only thing I remember about the march was that the students were marching up one side of the street and the Ku Klux Klan were marching up the other side of the street in their hoods and regalia. And, the policemen were over there with the Klan. All of them had guns and here we were—young, dumb students walking and singing 'We Shall Overcome'."[7]

This sounded similar to what happened in other places in the South and in Northern Ireland, as you will later read about the police and their priorities with these marches.

Dad admitted, "We were lucky that nobody got hurt. No violence whatsoever. We just marched on back to campus."[8]

My mother said the following about that time, "Early in the 1960s, was the beginning of the nonviolent protests which was mainly being led by Dr. Martin Luther King, Jr. Inspired and motivated by Dr. King, some students at North Carolina A & T University started the sit-in movement on college campuses when some students sat down at a lunch counter of a five-and-dime store and ordered something. They were not served and were arrested and then released from jail. This act quickly spread to other Black colleges around the country. Many of us organized and led marches and sit-ins."[9]

Being freshmen in 1961, my parents mentioned that there were some very outspoken leaders in their class who wanted Livingstone College to join the protests. They began and continued to hold marches during the day and held candlelight ceremonies in the evenings. Those actions led to organized daily sit-ins at lunch counters, which were conducted by several young men at the school. Every day, a number of the girls would sign up in small groups of three or four to walk two or three blocks to the local movie theater and attempt to buy tickets for the lower level of the theater. Black people could only buy a ticket for the balcony of the theater.

A funny story that I laughed at was when my mother told me the story about their attempt to integrate the local movie theater in Salisbury. Mom said, "We integrated the theater. We went as a group one afternoon that fall in 1962 and tried to buy tickets but they wouldn't sell to us. But they sold to one girl. She bought her ticket, went inside, sat down and turned around and came back out and said to the ticket taker, she'd just integrated the theater."[10]

What the ticket taker didn't realize was that the girl was a student at Livingstone. A student who was very light-skinned, but she was Black. The ticket taker was stunned, and the college kids, including my mom, still laugh when they tell that story today. Mom said when they went back to campus, they told everyone what had happened. Mom said it was like something going "viral" today, the way it spread throughout the campus.

Mom said, "That ended our attempts to further integrate the theater because we had accomplished our goal."[11]

I'm so proud of my parents for both marching. Even though it was just one march, it did force change in downtown Salisbury. Overall, they both agreed that it was a decent city, and the white people, Klan included, did leave them alone. Mom and Dad agreed that the city didn't want any trouble like what was happening in Greensboro, North Carolina, and other places across the South.

Dad later admitted, "My parents said if you get arrested, we're not getting you out. I was afraid of getting arrested."[12]

Mom added, "A lot of kids got arrested trying to integrate the lunch counters and the NAACP would get them out so they wouldn't have to stay overnight."[13]

***

In 1962, SNCC started a voter registration campaign throughout the US South to get as many Blacks registered as they could. SNCC knew that this was key to true equal rights, the power of the vote. The same thing was seen in Northern Ireland with their slogan: "One Man, One Vote." Voting for Blacks in the South had been repressed since the late 1890s, when Black citizens were killed or severely injured if they voted or even tried to vote. Also, officials would make Blacks take bogus literacy tests to be able to vote or create crazy scenarios as making Black voters guess how many jelly beans were in a glass jar to be able to vote. Anything was being done to keep the Black population from voting.

Just like the People's Democracy in Northern Ireland, there were factions within SNCC that wanted different things. Some wanted direct actions such as protests which would definitely agitate the Southern whites. Others wanted a simple goal of registering as many Black citizens as they could. Even politically, President John F. Kennedy at the time stated that he thought voter registration efforts would be better than direct action, which could incite violence throughout the South. Ella Baker helped SNCC with this so they could avoid a split in the group. She knew deep down that you couldn't truly have one without the other in terms of direct action and mass voter registration. She created two wings in the group, which would focus on one or the other goal. However, as one SNCC leader admitted, "If you went into Mississippi and talked about

28   GOOD TROUBLE

voter registration they're going to hit you on the side of the head and that's as direct as you can get."[14]

This was an important moment for the organization as SNCC not only conducted sit-ins but also did Freedom Rides throughout the US South. They went into rural communities and risked their lives and the lives of people they talked to, to fight for the right to vote.

This was seen when SNCC went into Jackson, Mississippi, in June 1961. Members of SNCC attempted to get Black citizens in town to register to vote through the Freedom Rides. They also took a chance in terms of being arrested or worse. The students, again, were a huge positive in this approach in Jackson, as seen this by this report at a SNCC meeting in July. The report mentioned, "The group has been active in Jackson recruiting people to join the freedom rides and has received considerable support from the young people of the community. Thirty-six Jackson citizens have gone to jail. Since the establishment of the group in Jackson, interest has increased on the part of individuals and groups in Mississippi for direct action against segregation. The problem remains one of lack of leadership and of fear, but the group feels the prospects are good for the development of a stronger protest in that city."[15] This was both brave and dangerous, given the history of Mississippi. This was the state where, in 1955, 14-year-old Emmett Till was found murdered and brutally beaten because he was flirting with a white woman in Money, Mississippi. The group of students was greeted with both veiled threats and violence during their work in Mississippi. Unfortunately, the federal government did little to help the students; many think it was because President Kennedy at the time didn't want to risk re-election on the civil rights movement.

Just like in Northern Ireland, threats and violence throughout the South were used to keep Black people from trying to register to vote. In 1964, the hot summer months were known as 'Freedom Summer'. That summer more than most in the past, was extremely violent and bloody.

The numbers that summer, in terms of violent acts, were staggering. More than 80 SNCC volunteers were attacked and beaten severely. There were 37 churches that were either bombed or burned. Thirty Black homes and businesses were either bombed or burned.[16] The worst of the events in that summer of 1964 was the disappearance of three civil rights workers in Philadelphia, Mississippi: Michael Schwerner, James Chaney and Andrew Goodman, who were twenty-four, twenty-one and twenty years old respectively. Their bodies were found two months later after their disappearance underneath an earthen dam. Theories proliferated about who could have been responsible for the deaths of the three civil rights workers. It was revealed later through FBI informants that the Klan had colluded with law enforcement to lure the workers out to a road, kidnap them and eventually kill them.

In the eulogy for James Chaney, civil rights leader Dave Dennis said, "I blame the people in Washington DC and on down in the state of Mississippi just as much as I blame those who pulled the trigger [...] Another thing that makes me even tireder though, that is the fact that we as people here in the state and the country are allowing it to continue to happen [...]"[17]

These were examples of the widespread terrorism that Black and White citizens endured in the US South when they were trying to get equal voting rights for Blacks, very similar to the terrorism that citizens faced during the Troubles in Northern Ireland on both sides.

The silver lining to the Freedom Summer of 1964 was the impetus by President Johnson to get the Civil Rights Act signed on July 2, 1964.

CHAPTER 5

1963 MARCH ON WASHINGTON

On August 28, 1963, people from all over the country went to Washington, DC, to gather at the National Mall. One of those people was my mother, only 19 years old at the time. Their goal was to demand that the United States finally fulfill the country's mantra of life and liberty for all. The American Dream had not been realized by the Black population in the country.

There were some people who were there to protest and some who were there to simply see and hear Dr. Martin Luther King, Jr. There were college students, middle-class people, poor people, people from all walks of life. Numbers are different depending on whom you talk to, but most people say that there were approximately 250,000 attendees at the march. The official title of the march was '1963 March on Washington for Jobs and Freedom'. At the time in August 1963, the country was only fifty years removed from women getting the right to vote, less than twenty years removed from the military being integrated and nine years since the ruling of *Brown vs. Board of Education* desegregated public schools. Interestingly, on a side note, about ninety miles from me, Prince Edward County closed their schools rather than have Black children go to school with white children.

President Kennedy at the time had every intention of introducing civil rights legislation because of what he had seen throughout the South in terms of violence. However, he was met with resistance from various political leaders across the Southern states. With that resistance, he backed off the original idea of bringing up the legislation for civil rights to Congress. However, these days were different because many Black Americans were not going to be easily swayed from fighting for their rights. Birmingham, Alabama had the ugly nickname of 'Bombingham' because of the amount of bombings the city was

GOOD TROUBLE

experiencing due to the Ku Klux Klan. One of the civil rights leaders at the time, Bob Moses, testified in the summer of 1963 in front of a House subcommittee on the civil rights bill and said that the situation he had witnessed in Mississippi would get, "ten times worse than Birmingham" if the federal government did not intervene and do something.[1]

When the March on Washington had first been brought up to civil rights leaders, SNCC leaders didn't want to be a part of it. They saw this as a march that would be conservative in its tone and, at the same time, a compliant gathering that would be pushed to be like this by the federal government and President Kennedy. However, this march was going to be different, the leaders of it would demand that. Leaders like John Lewis wanted to do sit-ins and antagonize the congressmen in Washington. By any means necessary, they were thinking.

There was one Civil Rights leader who was deliberately not invited to the march. That leader was Malcolm X, who was part of the Nation of Islam at that time. Many people respected Malcolm, but they didn't agree with his radical ideas of fighting White people and not working with them. SNCC and the other leaders did not view him as part of their movement and therefore he wouldn't be a part of the March on Washington.

The march scared many people throughout the nation; some believed that it would be a radical, in-your-face march, and the thought of possible violence put a cloud on the event for some. However, many people also thought the march wouldn't go far enough in terms of pushing the envelope for civil rights. There were some main points that SNCC and the other leaders wanted to push through: public desegregation, voting rights and better housing, all driven by a piece of civil rights legislation. The last two points were the same things that the Catholics would be protesting for, six years later in Northern Ireland.

The program for the March on Washington said the following:

"March on Washington for Jobs and Freedom- August 28, 1963"

1. The National Anthem- Marion Anderson
2. Invocation
3. Opening Remarks- A. Philip Randolph
4. Remarks
5. Remarks
6. Tribute to Negro Women, Fighters For Freedom- Mrs. Medgar Evers
7. Remarks- John Lewis, SNCC
8. Remarks
9. Remarks

10. Selection
11. Prayer
12. Remarks
13. Remarks- Roy Wilkins, NAACP head
14. Selection- Miss Mahalia Jackson
15. Remarks
16. Remarks- Revered Dr. Martin Luther King, Jr.
17. The Pledge
18. Benediction

"WE SHALL OVERCOME"

The Washington Post had the following headline for Wednesday, August 28, 1963: "All's Set for March of 100,000 on DC." The other headline from the *Post* on Thursday, August 29, 1963, said: "200,000 Jam Mall in Mammoth Rally in Solemn, Orderly Plea for Equality."

My mother Betty Jones (Betty Coates at the time) was one of those people at the march. She had just finished her sophomore year at Livingstone College and took a bus up from her hometown of Hickory, North Carolina. She showed me a picture of what the crowd looked like and showed me the area she was at—it was way, way in the back near the reflecting pool.

She talked about how the day went, "The woman who spearheaded the trip to Washington was a member of the NAACP in Hickory (North Carolina) and I was a rising junior in college. She picked people who were out of school in the summer to go to the march."[2]

The crowds were starting to arrive on buses from all over the country. They started up Independence Avenue and Constitution Avenue toward the reflecting pool and the Lincoln Memorial. It is pretty neat to know that my mother was one of those people in that crowd. Some people marched over three miles to get to the location of the speakers. Everyone wanted to be at the mall where all the action was taking place. As one person who attended the march said, "[…] are people who walked to DC, because, no matter what, they were going to get there. And they did not have the money. They did not have the wherewithal. They slept by the side of the road. That was the level of determination."[3]

The weather was surprisingly warm but not the stifling humidity that could sometimes envelope DC during that time of the summer in August. My mother even said that it actually felt good that day on the mall. John Lewis said about the day, "DC was typically broiling at that time of year. But this day was amazingly balmy-eighty-four degrees, clear skies, a slight breeze. God could not have made the weather more perfect."[4]

34 GOOD TROUBLE

Because there were some who were afraid of what could happen at the event, there was security throughout the area. That included uniformed police dressed in riot gear and military officers everywhere you looked. William Vodra was at the event as a 19-year-old and said about what he saw, "These were older people: 40s, 50s, 60s. The men were all in suits and ties, and many wore fedoras. The women were dressed for Sunday service, and people were then marching down toward the Lincoln Memorial. So I grabbed and sign and walked on down with the crowd."[5]

As the crowd marched, you could see them with signs in their hands which read, "We demand jobs for all now!" and "We demand voting rights now!"

The different signs, most of them with a white background and black ink, mentioned the following:

'Integrated Schools Now'
'Century Old Debt to Pay'
'We march for effective Civil Rights Laws now'
'We march for higher minimum wage for all workers'
'We march for an end to police brutality'
'Civil rights plus full employment equals freedom'
'We march for first class citizenship now'
'USA'
'We demand an FEPC law now'
'UAW says God of justice, God of power, can America deny freedom in this hour?'
'We march together- Catholics, Jews, Protestants-for dignity and brotherhood of all men under God now'
'We demand an end to bias now'

My mom explained what they were thinking when they arrived, "Everybody knew what they were going for. The biggest thing was that we knew Rev. Martin Luther King, Jr. was going to be there. That was what was most exciting. It was a long trip from Hickory."[6]

Before the program got started, musicians played as the crowd continued to gather on the mall, with thousands relaxing by the reflecting pool, many women sticking their feet in the water to cool themselves off. The musical program included performers like Joan Baez, Bob Dylan, the SNCC freedom singers and others. It was also announced to the crowd that on that same day around noon that W. E. B. Dubois had died in Africa. Dubois had been one of the original civil rights leaders in the early part of the 20th century.

My mother said the atmosphere was electric. "It was amazing. You got there and saw all of the people. It was just mind-boggling to see just how many people were there. It was an all-day thing."[7]

Aaron Bryant, a curator at the National Museum of African American History and Culture said, "I think that people don't really understand that the March on Washington wasn't just a celebration. It was a protest march."[8]

Like my mother and others, the majority of people who came to the March on Washington came to see Reverend King speak. Geneva Green was thirteen at the time and talked about when King got up to speak, "When Martin Luther King started speaking, there was a hush over the crowd, and we as children could not figure out what was going on. But we stood there, and we listened, and we watched the looks on people's faces as they looked toward him and were listening to what he was saying."[9]

My mother said she was too far away to hear any of the speakers. However, the ones who could hear Reverend King speak were mesmerized by what he said as he stood at the steps of the iconic Lincoln Memorial.

King mentioned the following in his famous speech:

"I am happy to join with you today in what will go down in history as the greatest demonstration for freedom in the history of our nation...100 years later the Negro is still not free [...] 100 years later the Negro is still sadly crippled by the manacles of segregation and the chains of discrimination [...] 100 years later the Negro lives on a lonely island of poverty [...] There will be neither rest or tranquility in America until the Negro is granted his citizenship rights."

By nightfall, King gave his words that live on today, "We will be able to speed up the day when all of God's children, Black men and White men, Jews and Gentiles, Protestants and Catholics, will be able to join hands and sing in the words of the old Negro spiritual, Free at last, free at last, Thank God Almighty, we are free at last." The program was done after those famous words. John Lewis was impressed with King's speech even though he didn't think it was his best, "But considering the context and setting and the timing of this one, it was truly a masterpiece, truly immortal. Dr. King spoke from the soul [...] and anyone who saw it—anyone who sees it today—could feel it."[10]

What a historical day. One positive was that television was getting popular at that time. That would also help the millions who would see and hear bits and pieces of the march. It was a day that my mother still talks about and she's now eighty years old. She didn't realize how big it would be but looking back now, she is proud that she was there that day.

Janus Adams was there that day and said, "It's little wonder that J. Edgar Hoover called the Nobel Peace Prize winner Dr. King the most dangerous man in America. We were all dangerous that day. It was dangerous to face down the doctrine of White supremacy."[11]

It was an important moment in not just Black history but American history overall. It was a moment that the Black population had waited for since the deliberate shutdown of the promising Reconstruction period after the Civil War and the introduction of Jim Crow rules for Blacks. As you'll see in the rest of the book, the thousands of people who were there at the march, including my mother, headed in all different directions, but they all continued to march through the '60s, toward changing the path of the United States for Black Americans.

My mother still talks about the march today, more than 50 years later. "I did not know the impact that it would have later. As I grew up, nobody talked about it a lot the way they do now. Looking back now, I'm amazed that I was a part of it."[12]

Immediately after the march, the civil rights bill from Kennedy died in the subcommittees.

President Johnson signed the final version of the civil rights bill less than a year after the March on Washington on July 2, 1964. This bill outlawed segregation in public places, such as schools and swimming pools, as well as in businesses, such as hotels and restaurants. It also banned discriminatory practices in employment.

Martin Luther King III recently said about the march, "And so, even though there were great losses, there were also great gains."[13]

Walter Naegle, the partner of Bayard Rustin, one of the architects of the march, said the following: "Some of the major things that they set out to accomplish during the march, they were accomplished. I mean, we won. And that's a reason to celebrate" (Post, 8/25/23).

Sixty years later, the legacy of the March on Washington still lives on through the people who were there and the people it influenced.

Little did they know, this was only the beginning of the movement.

CHAPTER 6

THE COURAGEOUS EIGHT

As a former history teacher, I had to admit to one of the people I interviewed who had a connection to the Selma to Montgomery march that I had never heard about the Courageous Eight.

Carolyn Doyle King was 18 at the time of the march and participated in Bloody Sunday and the march from Selma to Montgomery with both her mother and her father. I was able to do a phone interview with her in April 2024. Mrs. King is now 78, and her mind is still sharp as a tack. We talked for thirty minutes and her memories of those events are still fresh in her mind, as I could tell as we chatted.

Mrs. Doyle said the following about the thoughts during that time, "It wasn't about one person. We were a unified group of people. Many of them would meet at my home to strategize and plan for the movement."[1]

The unified group Mrs. Doyle King referred to was known as the 'Courageous Eight'. The Courageous Eight (also known as the Dallas County Alabama Voters League) were Black leaders who advocated for voting rights, equality and justice during the 1960s in Selma and Dallas County, Alabama. The Eight believed in peaceful protests and were the ones who worked behind the scenes for the Selma to Montgomery march. They were also the ones who made the decision to invite Martin Luther King, Jr. to become the front face of their fight for rights. The eight individuals were Reverend Frederick Douglas Reese (began teaching in Selma and then was the pastor of Ebenezer Baptist Church, he was seen as the leader of the Courageous Eight), Ulysses Blackmon (taught at several institutions in Alabama and was a Korean War veteran, he also served as the treasurer for the Courageous Eight), Amelia Boynton-Robinson (worked for the USDA in Selma, she worked with Rev. Reese to

37

conduct voter registration drives in Selma, she and Rev. Reese invited Dr. King to lead the work for voter registration, she marched and was attacked on Bloody Sunday), Ernest Doyle (Mrs. Doyle King's father), Marie Foster (worked as a dental hygienist in Selma, she helped teach Black citizens how to pass the literacy tests put out to bar them from voting, one of the marchers attacked by billy clubs on Bloody Sunday, walked 50 miles in five days as part of the Selma to Montgomery march), James Gildersleeve (World War II veteran, served as the Principal for the Selma Lutheran School), Reverend J. D. Hunter (editor of two Black newspapers in Selma, President of NAACP, he held civil rights meetings in the basements of various churches to encourage Blacks to vote), and Reverend Henry Shannon (WWII veteran, and lifelong pastor).

During the 1950s, Boynton-Robinson and her husband, Sam Boynton, created their own company, an insurance one, which insulated them from losing their livelihood because of their involvement with the NAACP and the Dallas County Voters League. The Boyntons had been attempting to get Black people to vote in the area since the 1930s. Foster, who was a dental hygienist, was a member along with Gildersleeve, who was nicknamed "The Preacher" because he talked to anybody, and Rev. Reese were members.

In 1963, SNCC and the Dallas County Voters League began planning for a nonviolent movement that would include marches and sit-ins to fight for voting rights. The DCVL was the group that was trying to get Blacks registered. At the time, that was the most militant thing going on in the area. This would continue for a couple of years when they started thinking about getting King back to Montgomery, the place where he had been a preacher before leaving for Atlanta. Rev. Reese was the one who wrote to King to ask him to come and help them in Selma to get voters registered.

Few historians know that the Selma to Montgomery march would have never taken place if it weren't for these brave eight individuals. Many people do not realize that in 1956, the NAACP was banned in the state of Alabama. This forced the members to go underground to hold their meetings about voting rights. There was even a state injunction that went into effect to ban three or more Negroes from meeting in Selma or Dallas County to discuss civil rights or voting rights. Alabama was determined not to give in to the civil rights movement. In 1964, Selma's NAACP chapter was reinstated. This was also the time when they invited Dr. King to get involved. They decided that a steering committee for the Courageous Eight would reach out to King. They first invited Dr. King to speak at a rally in Selma on January 2, 1965.

Mrs. Doyle King's father (Ernest Doyle) was a veteran of World War II, and he was the NAACP president for 15 years.

The Courageous Eight

Mrs. Doyle King explained what happened, "Dad kept the Selma NAACP together himself. When Dr. King came to Selma, they had already organized everything, doing the work and scouting the path. My dad was President and worked behind the scenes to help organize the march in Selma. He made sure to organize so that not all of the leaders would be out in front, just in case someone was shot and they would still have key leaders left."[2]

Mrs. Doyle King said about her parents and the group, "A lot of them were veterans who had been to Europe and were exposed to what it felt like to be treated as full citizens. This spearheaded their fight for equal rights back home in Alabama."[3]

A huge issue in Selma was that most of the adults who could vote were barely able to read and write. Only about a third of the Black population were literate at that time. The Dallas County Voters League formed literacy classes for adults. However, there continued to be problems such as literacy tests and other bogus tests such as questions for prospective voters that made no sense at all, created only to disqualify Blacks from voting.

The Courageous Eight became known as "The Crazy Eight" to some because they continued to push the envelope when it came to trying to get more Blacks to vote. This was despite groups such as the "White Citizens Council" and others warning them to stop.

The DCVL would have to move their meetings continuously because of the danger they were flirting with in terms of meeting together. At these meetings, they would plan and strategize, such as where they would march and their courthouse visits to help with voter registration. James Gildersleeve was the President of the DCVL at one point. However, he eventually gave it up because of friction between moderate and more militant wings in the civil rights movement in Selma. But, the danger was always there for all of the members of the Courageous Eight.

Mrs. Doyle King told me one harrowing story about her father, Ernest Doyle. One night, Mr. Doyle was kidnapped by three members of the White Citizens Council. They drove him miles outside of town, and one of the men asked, "What should we do with him?" Mr. Doyle no doubt thought he was going to be killed. This same thing had happened to hundreds of Black men over the years, with bodies ending up in the Alabama River, never to be identified. Incredibly, one of the men in the car said, "Let him go." And they did. Only by the grace of God and divine intervention of some sort did Mr. Doyle survive that frightening night. It is a story that both Mrs. Doyle King and her daughter, Dr. Shannah Gilliam, told me and to this day, they cannot believe that he survived that ordeal.

Mrs. Doyle King explained how important voting rights were for the Courageous Eight, "They wanted the right people in office because they knew life would be better for them all. Because of that, they were willing to risk their lives."[4]

Mrs. Doyle King mentioned the time when the Klan visited their neighborhood one night. They both said that all of the Black households turned their lights off, and all they could see were the cars, each filled with four men in their white Klan regalia. All of the lights were on in the cars so everyone in the houses could see that it was the Klan, and they were making it known that they were still in power, regardless of the neighborhood they drove in. Long lines of cars paraded down the street. Mrs. Doyle King said, "This was an effort to frighten the Black folk."[5]

That particular night, Ernest Doyle walked out of the house while the cars went down the street. He walked to the edge of the street in the dark. Mrs. Doyle King and her mother were worried that he wouldn't come back. When he finally walked back into the house, he announced to the family, "I won't let anyone know I'm afraid."[6]

Mrs. Doyle King explained how she and her mother felt every time her father left the house. "We didn't know if he'd be back each time he left the house."[7]

Dr. Gilliam talked to me about her grandfather's mission with the Courageous Eight. "He didn't think what he was doing was heroic. They were basically standing up for what they knew was right. They just didn't want to be treated like second-class citizens. They wanted the right to vote in a country that they had fought for. For them to come home after World War II and be treated poorly, that was something they just couldn't abide."[8]

Mrs. Linda Gildersleeve-Blackwell talked to me about her parents, in particular, her father, Mr. James Gildersleeve. Both of her parents were raised in the same rural area in Alabama, between Selma and Mobile, named Vineland. Vineland was a farming community, and Mr. Gildersleeve's grandfather owned over 500 acres. They ended up building a Lutheran school, which housed a one-room schoolhouse and a church.

James Gildersleeve saw injustice firsthand when he was young. One night he was running errands with his father and his brother, George. They were all at one of the local filling stations to refuel their car. There are not many details about what happened, but the owner of the white filling station claimed that the elder Gildersleeve tried to drive off with the nozzle still in his car. The owner pulled out a gun and shot James's father. His father was taken to the hospital to get medical treatment. A few days later, James found

The Courageous Eight 41

out while he was at school that his father was about to die. He immediately ran out of the school, which was miles from the hospital, to go see his father one last time. James arrived there just in time as his father had one request; he asked James to take care of the family. He was forever shaped by that tragic incident.[9]

As James Gildersleeve got older, he ended up working in the Lutheran school, and his wife taught at the same one-room schoolhouse at the Lutheran school. Both knew the importance of the voting rights registration struggle. His daughter explained, "Their whole focus was that the Blacks needed to know their rights for all services when it came to voting."[10]

Gildersleeve was trying to educate the Black citizens on how to vote because many of them in the area were illiterate. He taught the voters to look for the rooster and the donkey. The rooster represented Democrats and the donkey meant Republicans. Even if they couldn't read, they could figure out that part by what they saw on the ballot. Gildersleeve and others would recommend that they vote a straight Democratic ticket since it would be difficult to explain to people on how to do a split ticket. Unfortunately, that meant you had some good with bad, but for the Black voters, it was the easiest thing for them to do as they would mark an "x" by the rooster. Gildersleeve and others in the Courageous Eight knew the importance of voting.[11]

All of the work that Gildersleeve did behind the scenes, like the others, put his life in danger as well. There were many times that he would get phone calls in the middle of the night. These were Klan leaders who were trying to get him to come out in the middle of the night, telling him that he had won money or a prize. For that money or prize, he would need to come down to the local Firestone station and collect his prize. This was all a trap, a trap that he never fell for—a trap that could have cost him his life.

Because of that, Gildersleeve carried a pistol under his driver's seat at all times. He kept shotguns in his house and taught his kids how to shoot them just in case they did have an intruder in the house. Danger was all around the Courageous Eight, and he knew that the phones were tapped. Back then, they had party lines as well, where basically everyone could hear everything. He would often tell people, "I'm non violent until you challenge me. I'm going to protect me and my family."[12]

Linda Gildersleeve Blackwell said about that dangerous time, "It was a volatile time and a very scary experience, people need to understand that who look back at that time and think it was glorious. When I was 10 years old, I told my father that he needed to get life insurance so we would have money to live on if he died. It probably shook him to his soul for me to tell him that but I

42   GOOD TROUBLE

saw what was going on. There were killings all over and you didn't know when someone would come after you."[13]

As the Dallas County Voters League continued to work behind the scenes, the decision was made to invite Dr. King back to Selma in January 1965 for a jolt in the arm of the civil rights movement there. There were some people who didn't want King there, but people like Rev. F. D. Reese knew it was the right thing to do and how much it would help the movement. He also knew that King would only come if he was invited.

Mrs. Gildersleeve-Blackwell said, "When Dr. King was there and we had those meetings, people were so fired up and ready to hit the streets and do whatever it took. It was a rally call; every week we had meetings to prepare. When Dr. King came, it took the movement to another level."[14]

Rev. Frederick Douglas Reese was a Baptist minister in Selma and an educator. Years later, he also became a successful politician at the local level for the Selma City Council. Not many people immediately think of Rev. Reese when they talk about the civil rights movement, but they should. Reese was the leader of the Courageous Eight and the President of the Dallas County Voters League, starting in late 1961 and early 1962.

When Rev. Reese became President of the DCVL, there were only 100 members at the time. The group grew to over 2,000 members under him. In late 1964, Reese was the one who spearheaded the letter to Dr. King to invite him to come and help in Selma with the voter registration effort. Browns Chapel, the church where the marchers left for the Selma protest, was the only church that agreed to have Dr. King come and speak.[15]

I interviewed the grandsons of Rev. Reese, Marvin Reese, Jr. and Alan Reese, Sr., over the phone. They were both a pleasure to talk to and now they are leading an organization to continue spreading the work that their grandfather did for voting rights. Marvin Reese, Jr. said the following about what happened when Rev. Reese invited Dr. King to speak: "My grandfather actually had the right to vote and it was important to him because he knew what the numbers of registered voters could do. At the time of Dr. King's invite, there was an injunction for no mass meetings or having three to five Black people together, which means they were congregating. My grandfather called the other churches for King to come speak and nobody called him back except Browns Chapel. When he announced to the community at Brown Chapel that Dr. King was coming, he was booed by the other clergymen. SNCC and the other groups didn't want him coming. My grandfather simply said Dr. King would be there on January 2, 1965, to speak."[16]

Rev. Reese did what he thought was right. He believed that inviting Dr. King would only magnify the fight that was taking place in Selma for voting registration rights. He, like the others, knew it would be dangerous for what they were about to do as well. However, if it wasn't for people like Reese, the national leaders would not have converged on Selma to help with the movement.

Marvin Reese, Jr. said about the danger that his grandfather faced during those times, "The Ku Klux Klan put a bomb on the house where my grandfather lived and luckily it didn't detonate."[17]

Bravery is a word that is used quite often, but sometimes we don't know what true bravery is. The Courageous Eight showed everyone what true bravery meant. It is a shame that more people don't know about them. They've been overlooked for years, and one wonders what would have happened to the civil rights movement if it wasn't for them.

Dr. Gilliam still is amazed by what her grandfather did. "He wasn't even considered a whole man. I respect the dignity with which he carried himself, even in light of the public nullification of his humanity."[18]

All of the Courageous Eight have now passed on. However, it was a pleasure to talk to their relatives and learn more about their impact on the Civil Rights movement as a whole, particularly Bloody Sunday and the Selma to Montgomery march for voting rights. They marched for freedom, justice and equality for all.

They risked their lives and some of them lost their ability to survive financially or were blacklisted in the state of Alabama, all for the right to vote and to create a fair society for Black citizens.

Ernest Doyle said how he and the Courageous Eight felt about the movement, "Only death can stop us."[19]

CHAPTER 7

SELMA TO MONTGOMERY MARCH

This was the march that set in place the Civil Rights Movement. It was televised for all to see. The entire world saw the hate that was occurring in the South at that time. It is always amazing to me how history tends to repeat itself—seeing the same type of frustration with Blacks wanting equal rights like we did right after Reconstruction in the early 1870s, where in a state like South Carolina, there was a systematic process by the Klan to suppress voting and terrorize anyone associated with equal rights for the Black population.

To understand what the marchers were fighting for, one had to understand the landscape in Selma and the state of Alabama overall. Black citizens in Alabama for decades since after Reconstruction (the failed government that the United States had after the Civil War) had basically no legal rights. Just like the Catholics in Northern Ireland, the Blacks were subjected to violence and discrimination by the police, the courts and the state of Alabama. Most Black people in Alabama worked in sharecropping, tenant farming and menial services such as maids. This way of living, in addition to voter disenfranchisement and racial terrorism, made the state of Alabama a dangerous place for a Black person, male or female.

Selma itself was like Derry and Belfast in Northern Ireland—a place where thousands of poor, Black people lived. In Derry and Belfast, thousands of poor Catholics lived. In Selma, people could not register to vote because of the color of their skin. Barely 2 percent of Blacks were registered to vote. They had to pass a 'literacy test' or count how many jelly beans were in a jar.

An example of the literacy test that many Blacks used to have to take looked like the following that was used in Louisiana in the early 1960s:

45

46   GOOD TROUBLE

The State of Louisiana

Literacy Test (this test is to be given to anyone who cannot prove a fifth grade education)

Do what you are told to do in each statement, nothing more, nothing less. Be careful as one wrong answer denotes failure of the test. You have 10 minutes to complete the test.

1. Draw a line around the number or letter of this sentence.
2. Draw a line under the last word in this line.
3. Cross out the longest word in this line.
4. Draw a line around the shortest word in this line.
5. Circle the first letter of the alphabet in this line.
6. In the space below draw three circles, one inside (engulfed by) the other.
7. Above the letter X make a small cross.
8. Draw a line through the letter below that comes earliest in the alphabet.
   Z V S B D M K I T P H C
9. Draw a line through the two letters below that come last in the alphabet.
   Z V B D M K T P H S Y C
10. Cross out the number necessary, when making the number below one million.
    10000000000
11. In the line below cross out each number that is more than 20 but less than 30.
    31 16 48 29 53 47 22 37 98 26 20 25
12. Draw a line under the first letter after "h" and draw a line through the second letter after "j"
    a b c d e f g h I j k l m n o p q
13. In the space below, write the word, "noise" backwards and place a dot over what would be its second letter should it have been written forward.
14. Draw a triangle with a blackened circle that overlaps only its left corner.
15. Draw a space below, a square with a triangle in it, and within that same triangle draw a circle with a black dot in it.
16. Spell backwards, forwards.
17. Print the word vote upside down, but in the correct order.
18. Place a cross over the tenth letter in this line, a line under the first space in this sentence, and circle around the last the in the second line of this sentence.
19. Draw a figure that is square in shape. Divide it in half by drawing a straight line from its northeast corner to its southwest corner, and then

Selma to Montgomery March 47

divide it once more by drawing a broken line from the middle of its western side to the middle of its eastern side.

20. Print a word that looks the same whether it is printed frontwards or backwards.
21. Write right from the left to the right as you see it spelled here.
22. Divide a vertical line in two equal parts by bisecting it with a curved horizontal line that is only straight at its spot bisection of the vertical.
23. Write every other word in this first line and print every third word in the same line, (original type smaller and first line ended at comma) but capitalize the fifth word that you write.
24. Draw five circles that one common inter-locking part.

There were 30 questions in all. Remember, you had to finish this in ten minutes and one mistake would disqualify you from voting.[1]

My grandfather on my father's side, Forest Vaughn Jones, was born in Walkertown, North Carolina and lived close to Kernersville, Winston-Salem, and Walnut Cove, North Carolina. For years he worked at the world-famous R. J. Reynolds tobacco plant in Winston-Salem, North Carolina. My grandmother and his wife, Frances Taylor Jones, was born in Kernersville, North Carolina. My grandfather used to tell stories of how they would use either jelly beans or marbles to count in Walkertown, North Carolina. Prospective voters would have to guess how many jelly beans or marbles were in the jar. If they guessed right (which they never could), they could vote. If not, which was always the case, they couldn't vote. When my grandfather would go to vote, luckily he would not have any trouble. To put this into context, he was so light skinned that people thought he was white. This actually helped him when he lived in Buffalo, New York in the late 1920s and early 1930s and passed as a white man up there to be able to work as a doorman at a prominent hotel. However, people also knew him in the small town of Walkertown and didn't bother with him. My dad never could figure out why this was the case. My grandmother would always ask him if he had any trouble when he returned from voting. He never had any issues.

I interviewed Reverend E. T. Burton at his home in Roanoke, Virginia. Rev. Burton had been in charge of Sweet Union Baptist Church for over 50 years. He is now 96 years old and in great shape, both mentally and physically. He still walks without any aid and has a great laugh. His small but loud dog (looked like a Shih Tzu, but I'm not a dog expert) greeted me at the front door of his assisted living facility. After he told me it wouldn't bite, he showed me in

48   GOOD TROUBLE

and told me about how difficult it was to vote in Virginia in the late 50s and
early 60s.

Rev. Burton said, "The state of Virginia had the blank paper registration.
That meant when you went to the registrar's office to sign up you were given a
blank sheet of paper and you had to know what to put on the paper. You had
to also pay the poll tax which was $1.50, a lot back then. That eliminated some
people. You had to go to somebody who knew what to tell you to put on the
paper or you wouldn't be qualified to vote, it was like a registration form that
they have now."[2]

In Selma, at the county courthouse, they would sometimes put up a sign
saying the place was closed when it wasn't. Blacks would go there day after
day to register, standing in line to no avail. Some were beaten and some were
arrested while they stood there, just to register to vote. In Dallas County and
Selma, only 300 Black citizens were registered to vote out of 10,000 Black citizens who were eligible in the early 1960s.

James Gildersleeve said that when he went to vote, he would be asked how
many bubbles were in a bar of soap. He would give it right back to them, give
them a number, and say, "If you don't think that's the right answer, count
them!"[3]

James Gildersleeve's daughter said about the push to get people registered,
"The people in power fought tooth and nail to keep people from getting registered to vote. Domestic workers could lose their employment. Luckily, preachers and teachers enjoyed independence from that stress since they weren't tied
to their employers."[4]

The marchers knew they had to take on a grassroots approach to overcome the harsh legacy of Southern segregation and prejudice in the streets
and in politics. They were fighting for voting rights and equality, just like the
Catholics did.

The idea of marching to Montgomery, Alabama started after a violent
attack on civil rights marchers in Marion, Alabama two weeks earlier. A young
Black man named Jimmie Lee Jackson was shot to death by a state trooper. At
Jackson's funeral, sympathizers said, "Goddamn it, we ought to carry his body
over to George Wallace in Montgomery."[5]

Jackson's killing created a feeling among Civil Rights protestors that there
needed to be something more to do. That something more to do was the plan
to walk from Selma to Montgomery to force Governor Wallace to give Blacks
the right to vote in the state.

Courtland Cox said this about the Selma to Montgomery march, "It was a
high point, highly visible."

Selma to Montgomery March

[6] At the time, Cox was twenty-two and a leading SNCC representative at the March on Washington. Now, Cox is eighty-two and chair of the SNCC Legacy Project.

Aaron Bryant said, "You had one group coming out of the 1950s dealing with civil rights issues, but then you have a younger generation, represented by people like John Lewis, for example, who had very different ideas about how to bring about social change."[7]

***

On Sunday, March 21, 1965, the city of Selma, Alabama, was displaying feelings of anticipation and fear as plans were carried to fruition for the Alabama Freedom March to Montgomery, Alabama. It was a breezy day with clear, blue skies on the horizon. The march was scheduled to begin at 10 a.m. that Sunday morning. Hundreds of marchers went into the city of Selma, which under normal, everyday circumstances had a population of just over 28,000.

It was just past twelve-thirty in the afternoon when the leaders gathered at Browns Chapel. There were a number of marchers already gathered behind the church on the basketball courts and fields, approximately five hundred of them. Many of the SCLC (Southern Christian Leadership Conference) members were practicing with the marchers on what they would do to protect themselves if they were attacked by the Klan. Knowing how to kneel and protect their bodies and heads would be key to possibly avoiding a horrible injury.

John Lewis and other leaders of the demonstration expected between 4,000 and 5,000 people from all over the United States to join in the march from Selma. The march was expected to take up to four days, which would put their arrival in Montgomery that Thursday, where the leaders believed they'd have up to 20,000 in the caravan march with them. The marchers were lured to Selma by a tantalizing prospect—a chance for equal rights for the Black population in the South.

People who were involved in the march knew that what they were about to do had the potential to be a part of an important historical moment in time. All of the participants knew that the armed forces of the United States would be there and that their job would be to protect the marchers. Everyone knew that the chance for violence at these marches was always there; however, violence was not expected at this particular one. More than 4,000 troops were prepared to provide protection for the marchers.

On Saturday, March 20, 1965, the first wave of federalized Alabama National Guardsmen moved into the city. There were close to 1,900 in the first

GOOD TROUBLE

group. The troops spent the night in the National Guard armory, which was a few miles from Selma on State Highway 22. There were also two battalions of military police, totaling over 1,000 that were at the bases in the area. Another army unit of close to 1,000 troops was on standby at Fort Benning, Georgia. Some of them were on their way to Selma as well.

The 720th military police battalion of Fort Hood, Texas, was at the Craig Air Force base east of Selma on US Highway 80. This was also on the path of the route for the march. The 503rd military police battalion of Fort Bragg, North Carolina, was flown into the Maxwell Air Force base near Montgomery, Alabama. The 503rd was primarily for riot control. Each of the battalions had over 500 troops. President Lyndon B. Johnson said the following about the precautions being taken, "100 agents of the Federal Bureau of Investigation and 74 to 100 marshals were in Alabama with more marshals on the way."[8]

All of the military troops that were mobilized by President Johnson fell under the command of Brigadier General Henry V. Graham. Graham was in charge when the Alabama National Guard was mobilized by President John F. Kennedy in 1963 when the University of Alabama was integrated.

The march was scheduled to begin at 11 a.m. Eastern Standard Time. It would start from the Browns Chapel Methodist Church. Most of the participants didn't think it would start on time since the starting time for the march had already been changed twice. The huge number of visitors to the city of Selma, many of them being students and White ministers didn't end up staying at hotels and motels in Selma. Most of those had already been taken up by news reporters and members of the federal government.

The visitors mainly stayed in the homes of the Black citizens in the city and in the Black churches. The planning for the march had been quite extensive, with the Black community in Selma helping out with food, shelter, bathroom facilities and security for the marchers. This included portable metal toilets that had been installed on flatbed trucks, a kitchen that was installed in the basement of the First Baptist Church where food would be prepared and transported to the marchers by bus and car.

The front room of the First Baptist Church had been used as the headquarters for the Selma to Montgomery march. Organizers could be seen shuffling back and forth from the outside, giving out instructions for the march.

President Johnson made an announcement to the press that a 75-bed hospital was being created near Selma to be ready for the march. The hospital would have five doctors and forty-three medical helicopters. President Johnson said the hospital would be for both marchers and the military troops.

Reverend Hosea Williams was the official director of the march. He was part of the Southern Christian Leadership Conference. He believed that the five-day march would cost well over $30,000. The march would last 54 miles from Browns Chapel to the Capitol building in Montgomery. The march would go through some of the most rural countryside in the state. The only true town that was in between Selma and Montgomery was a place called Lowndesboro. The procession would go down to no more than 300 marchers when it reached the Lowndes County line, which was about twelve miles east of Selma. From there, the highway narrowed from four lanes to two. The other marchers would rejoin the march once the highway turned into four lanes again, which would be a few miles near Montgomery.

There would be many different organizations that would take part in the march from Selma to Montgomery. Shirley Mesher, who was a member of the Congress of Racial Equality and had been appointed the official spokesperson for the marchers, said of the participants: "Representatives of all the major civil rights organizations and several religious groups would lead the march."[9]

There would be a prayer service on Sunday morning at 8 a.m. at Browns Chapel Methodist Church. At 9:30 am, the Reverend Martin Luther King, Jr. would conduct a sermon before leading the marchers across the Edmund Pettus Bridge and out on US Highway 80. Rev. King was the president of the Southern Christian Leadership Conference (SCLC). Dr. King was expected to also walk all the way to Montgomery with the marchers.

The purpose of the Selma to Montgomery march was to present petition to Governor George C. Wallace. The petition would state the grievances of Blacks in Alabama. The main grievance would be the issue of voting rights. Voting rights were also the main issue for the Burntollet Bridge march for the Catholic civil rights marchers.

Governor Wallace was not expected to be at the Capitol when the marchers would arrive there to present the petition. Wallace tried to ban the march but was overruled by a federal judge. Judge Frank M. Johnson said the following about the march, "The people had a right to demonstrate for redress of grievances."[10]

However, the day before, Dr. King had proposed to postpone the march until Monday. John Lewis and the others didn't find out until the day of the march, that Sunday. Hosea Williams and others were visibly upset when they were told about this. Andrew Young, another young civil rights leader, was seen at the church that Sunday and had been sent to give the message from Dr. King. The problem was the people were already there, ready to march. Lewis and the others felt like they couldn't postpone it.

GOOD TROUBLE

Lewis had later found out that there were other issues that made King not come to Selma that day. As he later remarked, "The most serious being a death threat, of which there had been several during the previous two months. Dr. King was initially leaning toward still coming, but his staff talked him out of it."[11]

What followed on Sunday, March 21, 1965, just like the Belfast to Derry march in Northern Ireland, would forever change the future for the Civil Rights movement in both the United States and Northern respectively.

CHAPTER 8

THE PEOPLE'S DEMOCRACY IN NORTHERN IRELAND

The People's Democracy at the heart of the matter started out as a student movement, very similar to SNCC (Student Nonviolent Coordinating Committee) in the United States at the time. In 1968, the People's Democracy was a big part of the Catholic Civil Rights movement in Northern Ireland. The late '60s and early '70s were just as turbulent in Northern Ireland as the '60s were for the United States. One of the problems was that Parliament at Westminster did not give much attention to what was happening in Northern Ireland. Richard Rose said about this, "In the five years preceding the disorder of 1969, the Commons devoted less than one sixth of one per cent of its time to discussions of Northern Ireland questions; most of this talk concerned matters of trade, not the matters that affected allegiance to the regime."[1] Because of that, the Unionists controlled the Catholic population without any tampering from Westminster and for the most part, the Catholics fell in line and didn't try to rock the boat at all. Usually, if any complaints came from the Catholic community, they were largely ignored by the Unionist power base. This basically described the way Northern Ireland politics had been conducted between the years of 1920 and 1968.

All was quiet politically for the most part until the late 1960s. We saw this same inertia in the Black community in the United States in the early to mid-1960s as well. However, poverty still impacted mainly Catholics during the early twentieth century, just like the Blacks in the United States, as Northern Ireland saw numbers struggling with bad health, inadequate housing and schools. The other issue is that Northern Ireland saw the rise of Reverend Ian Paisley and the extremism that he produced. Riots broke out in 1964 and

53

54   GOOD TROUBLE

1966 between Paisley's followers and the UVF (Ulster Volunteer Force), a name taken from illegal groups started by Unionists in 1913 to fight against the Catholics and the Catholic population. The turning point for Northern Ireland was in 1965 when the first debate on Anglo-Northern Ireland relations happened. The Labour Party won in 1966 and Gerry Fitt's victory in West Belfast forced an enquiry into relations in Northern Ireland. Three Parliament members visited the country that year and reported back, "how near the surface violence lies in current political life."[2]

In the mid-1960s, changes were occurring throughout Northern Ireland in politics. Catholic communities were seeing more signs of Protestant extremism and the Catholics were wanting equal rights in their country. The situation mirrored what had happened in the United States, especially in the South. The Catholic population saw their religious apartheid as very similar to the racial segregation throughout the US South. They wanted the rights that all citizens had, just like the Blacks in the United States. One observer in 1966 saw what was on the horizon when they said, "Many Catholics exhibit a mere hopeless antagonism to the present situation but there are signs that this is changing to a more active self-respect. It is not ridiculous to envisage a Catholic Civil Rights movement in the not too far distant future."[3]

Another peek at what was on the horizon was the new groups that popped up in Northern Ireland to pressure the government about housing and equal rights in the country. One was the CSJ (Campaign for Social Justice in Northern Ireland) which was created in 1964. They publicized issues such as gerrymandering and work discrimination in Derry. Some of their pamphlets that were given out to people said the following about their purpose, "[. . .] for the purpose of bringing to light of publicity to bear on the discrimination which exists in our community against the Catholic section of that community representing more than one-third of the population."[4]

Protestant families for years had been given priority to houses over Catholic families. There were hundreds of Catholic families on a waiting list for housing, some on the list for more than ten years. This practice of unequal housing forced Catholics into low-quality housing and segregated the Catholic community from the Protestants.

Just like many of the organizations in the United States for Black civil rights, these organizers focused on nonviolent methods and direct action. They did not agree with the goals of the IRA at the time. Their focus concentrated on housing and employment, not Irish unity, but on what could help the Catholic society as a whole. However, when it became obvious that progress was not being seen, a group of students at Queen's University in Belfast began to lift the idea of political agitation.

Here is where we see the beginnings of the People's Democracy. Queen's University was the place where the Civil Rights campaign got a foothold since it was a student movement. The majority of its members were students, and they did establish a connection with student movements such as SNCC in the United States. There is no doubt that in both Northern Ireland and the United States, the student protest movement was a by-product of the 1960s. In 1968, the People's Democracy started, and they borrowed much from the movements in the United States such as sit-ins, sit-downs, pickets and marches.

Eamonn McCann was there at the start of the group and said the following, "People's Democracy had a loose membership, you just showed up. We sat around talking about the plight of the working class and how we could get them to rise up. What emerged from this were the students in Belfast from Queens University who became involved."[5]

October 1968 is when the group officially started. In February 1969, it became a well-oiled organization and one that the higher-ups in government knew they had to deal with. The movement was now seeing light. The activists such as Bernadette Devlin and John Hume were determined to upturn the apple cart and demand civil rights and social justice.

The first organized march for the group was on October 5, 1968. The march was to be in Derry. The city of Derry at that time was seen as the hotbed of Unionist rule with high unemployment, gerrymandering and discrimination across society toward Catholics. Unemployment was a huge issue as companies would often hire Protestants before Catholics.

The march had over 2,000 people attend, even though the minister of home affairs refused to accept the route for the march. The march went ahead anyway and included members of Parliament. Unfortunately, it ended with a dangerous riot when the marchers tried to ignore the ban. Just like a scene from Alabama or Mississippi, the police riot squad cornered the crowd in a narrow street. They beat many people with batons and used two water cannons on the marchers. After it was over, 77 civilians were injured, along with 11 police officers. Rioting continued in the Catholic west side of Derry and the Bogside into the next day. The violence handed out by the RUC was caught on film by cameramen from the Republic of Ireland. These horrific scenes were broadcast all over the world. This created a storm of criticism toward the heavy-handedness of the policing of the situation.

As Bernadette Devlin said about the whole situation in front of them, "And as far as I was concerned it was one of those peaceful civil rights marches, go

56 GOOD TROUBLE

along, make your protest and go home. The police brutality did something much more important than focus the attention of civilization on Northern Ireland. It awakened the people of Northern Ireland, particularly the students. I know what it's like to live in an unbalanced society because the more you become involved in it, the more you realize that the whole problem is much bigger than a few bigoted members of the government. It's the whole system that's wrong."[6]

This could have been said for both the United States and Northern Ireland at the time. The events of March 5, 1968, would fuel the goals of the People's Democracy, even though there weren't many set rules when it came to the group.

"There were no rules. These were left wing students. The People's Democracy was a direct reaction to what was happening on the streets with the police. And what do university students do? Call a meeting. After the meeting, three days later they wanted to change the name again," McCann laughed.[7]

The British government still had not shown a lot of interest in the goings-on in Northern Ireland, but Prime Minister Harold Wilson threatened Stormont with strong condemnation of the events. He said, "[...] (we may have to) propose a radical course involving the complete liquidation of all financial agreements [...] if swift changes were not made."[8]

The People's Democracy thought that they could have the same effect in Northern Ireland as the Blacks did in the US South during their civil rights movement. A movement for the Blacks that still was not fulfilled.

However, just like what was seen in the United States, things would get worse with more protests before they would become better.

CHAPTER 9

JOHN LEWIS

John Lewis was one of the most revered Civil Rights leaders in the history of the United States.

Lewis was born in 1940 in segregated rural Alabama near the town of Troy on a sharecropping farm owned by a White man. His parents ended up owning their farm after they purchased 110 acres of land. Lewis was the third of ten children. He would leave school at harvest time to help pick cotton and corn. Their house had no plumbing or electricity, and they had to use magazine pages as toilet paper when they used the outhouse.

Troy had a population of close to 7,000 and was about fifty miles south of Montgomery. The place where he grew up was so small that it was difficult for people to find it on the map of Alabama. Martin Luther King Jr. would call the town of Troy and its surrounding areas, the Four Corners of Alabama.

As a young child growing up in rural Alabama, Lewis could plainly see the Jim Crow laws of segregation and racial discrimination all around him. He attended school in a one-room church all the way up to sixth grade. The books that they used were routinely sent down to them, used by the White schools across the state. Even today, you will hear stories from people who grew up in Jim Crow Alabama about the awful state the books were in that they used, many in tatters.

Lewis would see the usual signs around his town—COLORED ONLY, COLORED WATER FOUNTAIN. He told one story of a store in town that had a shiny, new fountain for White people to drink out of and an old, rusty spigot for COLORED ONLY.

Lewis' nickname from his family was "Preacher." He was inspired by listening to a young Martin Luther King and reading about the bus boycotts

58   GOOD TROUBLE

in Montgomery, Alabama that King helped with. Lewis went to Nashville to study theology and while there, he started his protest work such as sit-ins to protest the refusal of restaurants to serve Black people at their lunch counters. His leadership with this evolved into SNCC (the Student Nonviolent Coordinating Committee).

Lewis's bravery in Nashville was noticed by many people, including reporters who were impressed by the guts of the 20-year-old young man. A reporter for the Nashville Tennessean said about Lewis and his team, "The protests had been conducted with exceptional dignity [...] courteous young Black people [...] seeking the most elemental of rights, while being assaulted by young White hoodlums who beat them up and on occasion extinguished cigarettes on their bodies."[1]

Lewis's work was fruitful as Nashville became one of the first major Southern cities to desegregate public facilities. Lewis's parents were not fans of him being arrested and couldn't understand why he just couldn't let things be in the Deep South. Lewis used Martin Luther King as a guiding light as he said his goal was to "get into trouble, good trouble, necessary trouble."[2]

One of John Lewis's greatest quotes was almost a premonition of what he would find on the Selma to Montgomery march in 1965 as a 25-year-old young man. Lewis said, "If there was anything I learned on that long, bloody bus trip of 1961 [...] it was this—that we were in for a long, bloody fight here in the American South. And I intended to stay in the middle of it."[3]

When Lewis arrived in Washington in August 1963, he eventually became the youngest speaker for the event at age 23. His speech punched holes in the civil rights bill for what he and other young leaders saw as opportunities for improvements for Black people as a whole. Lewis was careful with his speech so as to not to offend the old guard but still bring up concerns. However, this did not happen without some people around him being very worried about his speech.

It is truly amazing that Lewis was even picked to speak at the March on Washington. Just a few weeks before, he was leading SNCC on their sit-in campaign. He was one of the up-and-coming faces among young leaders forging the nonviolent movement for civil rights. Lewis was also rising at a time when there was a militant arm in the civil rights movement with Malcolm X and others who believed in equal rights by "any means necessary." This was very similar to the People's Democracy in Northern Ireland and the far-left wing that wanted more from them in the Catholic fight for civil rights. Some of SNCC's leaders were even doubtful of the impact that the March on Washington would have. Lewis said about them believing it would end up being, "a lame event, organized by the cautious, conservative traditional power structure of Black America."[4]

On June 22, 1963, Lewis met with President Kennedy at the White House. The purpose of the meeting was for the President to persuade them to not go through with the march because of the simmering tensions throughout the nation that summer. Dr. King and the others didn't budge, and President Kennedy ended up going along with their plan for the march and gave them his support. Another positive was that SNCC was part of the meeting, and Lewis would be the speaker in the spotlight for them. He also knew this was a chance to move the needle in terms of what he and others wanted from the Civil Rights movement.

Lewis took his time on the speech and wrote that SNCC, "cannot wholeheartedly support the administration's civil rights bill [...] (it was) too little and too late."[5] Friends took a look at the speech; some thought it went too far, and others thought it didn't push things enough. On the Tuesday before the march, one of the march's organizers said parts of the speech needed to be amended. Lewis agreed to do so, reluctantly.

That Wednesday, the day of the march, Lewis believed he had the speech right where he wanted it.

Lewis took a look at the crowd before he spoke and couldn't believe the size of the sea of people that he saw. He said about the crowd, "I don't think anyone who was there that day would argue that the official figure was one of the great undercounts of all time. And the striking thing about this ocean of people was this was truly a human rights demonstration. Four out of five people there were Black, but there were Whites as well. And a sprinkling of Asians, Hispanics and Native Americans. Protestants, Catholics and Jews. Liberals and Labor. Hope and harmony—that was the music of the day, that was the message."[6]

John Lewis was making changes to his speech right up until he got on the stage to give it to the thousands of people on the mall. Courtland Cox, a colleague of Lewis, said about the controversy over the speech, "[...] brought Philip A. Randolph to us, and Randolph pointed out that this was something that had been in the works for over 20 years, to begin to deal with the discrimination in the United States and make a big statement about it. And he would really appreciate it if we made the changes."[7]

Cox explained that he and Lewis made the appropriate changes backstage, so the speech would not add any controversy to the March on Washington. Lewis cut the words in the speech that mentioned President Kennedy's bill being "too little, too late."

Lewis began his speech, and admittedly, he felt nerves until the crowd cheered and hollered, which loosened him up quite a bit. His closing words were powerful as he said, "We will not stop [...] the time will come when we will not confine our marching to Washington. We will march through the South...but we will march with the spirit and love and with the spirit of dignity that we have shown here today [...] we shall splinter the South into a thousand pieces and put them back together in the image of God and democracy. We must say, "Wake up America. Wake up!" For we cannot stop, and we will not be patient."[8]

John Lewis's speech went ahead, and he did edit it with the suggestions of the older Black Americans at the time. However, the tone of the speech still rubbed some leaders the wrong way, such as NAACP head Roy Wilkins, Attorney General Bobby Kennedy and the head of the National Council of Churches, Reverend Eugene Carson Blake.

Years later, Lewis still appreciated the March on Washington and what they had accomplished on that day. "What raised my heart," he said, "was to see hundreds and thousands of young White people walking the streets hand in hand with young Negroes."[9] The march also forged the momentum to pass the 1964 Civil Rights Act, which banned public discrimination in most areas of public life.

However, the battle for civil rights was not over. John Lewis's legacy would be cemented two years later on the Edmund Pettus Bridge in Selma, Alabama.

CHAPTER 10

BERNADETTE DEVLIN

There is a beautiful mural of a young Bernadette Devlin on the side of a building in the Bogside in Derry. It was one of the first things I noticed when I did my first-ever tour there in Summer 2022. The blue and gray mural shows Devlin at 21 years old at the barricades in August 1969. That mural shows the determination and guile of a young girl who wouldn't settle for the status quo for herself and the Catholic population in her country.

Her story is quite remarkable: she slapped the Home Secretary for his flippant remark about Bloody Sunday in 1972, was shot nine times in a home attack by a Loyalist paramilitary group and survived, and was banned from entering the United States in 2003 because she was called a national security risk due to her criticism of America's role in their war with Iraq.

Bernadette Devlin was just another 21-year-old psychology student at Queen's University in Belfast, Northern Ireland, until she was elected as a Member of Parliament in the House of Commons for Mid-Ulster. Devlin had been elected the youngest MP since William Pitt won his seat in 1781, also at the age of twenty-one. That record lasted until 2015. She talked about her moment in government and what she wanted, "In this movement, which is still struggling to free our people from the bonds of economic slavery, I am only one among hundreds of my generation. We were born into an unjust system; we are not prepared to grow old in it."[1]

Devlin was described as both warm and intense, but also self-mocking. She had long, brown hair and light gray and green eyes with a thick Derry accent and a small gap in her front teeth. Devlin, who was just barely five feet tall, had built her reputation as one of the top leaders in Northern Ireland's tumultuous civil rights movement.[2] Her eyes were bright when she talked and her smile was wide. Devlin was put into office primarily because of her fight for the rights of the Catholic minority in her country. She constantly demanded that the Protestant-dominated government help Catholics with jobs, housing and local voting rights. The comparison in the United States would be with the young John Lewis, who spearheaded the Selma to Montgomery march.

Devlin was one of five children and was born in Cookstown, County Tyrone. The area was a small farming community, originally a plantation, settled by the Presbyterians that the British sent over in the seventeenth century. Ironically, she was born on April 23, 1947—the same April 23 when the Easter Rising occurred in 1916. Her father was a carpenter, a man who was vocal about a United Ireland, and died when she was nine from a heart attack. At that time, Cookstown was the same as it had been for over three hundred years. At one end was Old Town, a Protestant area, and at other end was the Catholic area. I can understand this, remembering one of my first visits to Belfast, where I could tell which area I was in just by looking at the flags that adorned the streets.

She could see the comparisons in Northern Ireland to the United States early on, "Protestants still have a sense of settler superiority and expect the Catholics to stay in their place and not get uppity, pretty much the way [...] many White Southerners still feel about Blacks [...] And the Blacks, we were poor, virtually disenfranchised and very angry. We still are."[3]

Her father was labeled early on as a 'political suspect' when he applied for his work permit over the years. He had never committed a crime or been in jail but years before, he did take soup to a man being held on charges in prison for alleged Republican connections. Because of that one soup visit to jail, he couldn't find a job. Even the Catholics there wouldn't give him a job because of fear of repercussions. He was forced to go to England for work because of those unjust circumstances.

Devlin was a proud Irish girl growing up, hearing stories from her father about Irish history. She remembered her first nursery rhyme, which fit in well with the politics at the time: Where is the flag of England? Where is she to be found? Wherever there's blood and plunder, they're under the British ground.[4] After her father died when Devlin was nine years old, she and her five siblings barely lived off welfare benefits. It wasn't a dirt-poor poverty but one where they scraped by to survive.

Devlin grew up seeing what it was like to grow up a Catholic in Northern Ireland as she described how finding work was so difficult, "You come to a factory looking for a job and they ask you which school you went to. If its name was 'Saint Somebody', they know you are a Catholic and you don't get taken on."[5]

Bernadette Devlin 63

Her mother died when she was nineteen, and it then became her purpose to take care of her family, and at the same time finish her studies at Queen's. Devlin was determined that after finishing up university, her goal was to improve life for the Catholic population in Northern Ireland. College was also the time when she got involved in politics, seeing all of the options that were out there for her: labour, tory, liberals and socialists. However, she struggled to find anything that she connected with in the political realm.

After her mother died, Devlin was traveling every day between Cookstown and Belfast to attend Queen's University. As a family, they were determined to stay together and not be broken up and sent all over the place. Government officials warned Devlin that nobody was over 21, and they had to leave their council house. After a lot of back and forth, they decided to let Devlin be the head of the household even though she was not old enough. She also saw how the rules were stacked against poor people when they needed benefits, like her family did in that situation. She commented, "Suddenly I saw that what plagues Northern Ireland isn't the difference between Catholics and Protestants but the gulf between the haves and the have-nots."[6]

Devlin also started believing that there needed to be some type of revolution in Northern Ireland with what happened to her and her family after the death of her mother. "I'd say these events crystallized my political awareness."[7]

One of her favorite Republican anti-Free State songs was the following:

Take it down from the mast, Irish traitors
It's the flag we Republicans claim
It can never belong to the Free Staters
For you've brought on it nothing but shame
Leave it to those who are willing
To uphold it in war and in peace,
The men who intend to do killing
Until England's tyranny cease.

The more that Devlin learned and read about her country, she started to believe that partition was not the main issue. She realized democracy was the answer, true democracy in a British state. She thought, "If they're going to make us British by law, we must be British by standard of living as well."[8] During 1968, Devlin began to drift away from the Republican line of thinking and leaned more toward the goal of nonpolitical social justice.

64 GOOD TROUBLE

Devlin, like others who were around her during that time, started to get frustrated with the usual 'don't say anything' way of life. "Don't rock the boat," the older generation would tell the younger ones.

It was amazing that such a young leader could be someone that many older people would follow as well. Devlin explained her courage with, "It comes from my Christianity. I do it because I believe it is my Christian duty. If there is less bigoted religion in Ulster and more Christianity, there would be far less problems. Christianity is love thy neighbor, but half the populations of Ulster hates the other half in the name of Jesus Christ."[9]

She had many death threats against her in the late '60s and early '70s, but she continued to travel without a bodyguard. Devlin explained her thinking, "I think about it from time to time, but it doesn't worry me. That's not mock heroics, just realism [...] My parents taught me to enjoy life rather than fear death. And living in a society that's characterized by violence and institutionalized brutality, you somehow come to accept the impermanence of your own life. If anyone's a product of her environment, I am."[10]

Devlin and her group were fighting in a country where, at the time in the late '60s and early '70s, the unemployment rate was double compared to the number of Protestants out of work. Very few Catholics owned any property, and even fewer had any type of political rights whatsoever. The Unionists/ Protestants owned the land and houses and the right to vote.

She explained the feeling in many areas in Northern Ireland: "To understand the present struggle in Ireland, you must see it from the perspective of 800 years of invasion, oppression, exploitation and genocide. Irish history is written in Irish blood."[11]

At the same time in Derry, the citizens were reeling from the Battle of the Bogside from August 12 to 14, 1969. This particular battle showed the world, through television and still photos, the violence that the Catholic community was facing. One famous photo captured Devlin; it shows her with a mask on, standing next to Paddy Coyle, the 13-year-old who was the subject of the famous 'Petrol Bomber' mural in the Bogside. Devlin felt a strong connection with the Black movement in America. Foley's article about her in 1970 mentioned, "Oppressed peoples differ, to be sure, but oppression itself very often seems to take the same form whether it is directed against the Irish or the Afro-Americans."[12]

With the violence spreading to Belfast, John Hume said, "If there is no solution, the alternative is too terrible for words. The alternative is Civil War. And what must be realized by everybody on all sides is that nobody gains from this. On one side, what use is One Man, One Vote if you're not there to exercise it.

And on the other side what use is it to maintaining a situation of privilege and power over a desert. The price of no solution is total destruction."[13]

As the rioting spread over a few days in both Derry and Belfast, the government in Northern Ireland called for the British Army to intervene. It was a situation eerily similar to the riots in Detroit in the United States. It was a shaky situation in the country as Devlin said, "Just how delicate this balance is was proved in 1968 when the civil rights movement's demand for simple justice put the country up in flames."[14]

Tom Wharton was part of the British Army and he admitted that he didn't know what was happening in Northern Ireland as he was stationed in Honduras at eighteen years old. He said, "We'd begun to get briefings about the riots that were going on and the killings in some places that had been going on."[15] Wharton didn't realize that the place where all of this was happening was indeed Northern Ireland.

In August 1969, British troops arrived to take over security duties in Belfast, the Bogside and other strategic points. I personally remember a friend of mine who currently lives in Dublin talking about this and saying that her aunt remembered when the troops arrived because it was the first time she'd ever seen a Black person face to face.

Wharton said of his arrival, "We'd been brought in to stand in the middle of this and to stop them from killing each other."[16] The residents were glad to see them, even though they didn't know what to expect from them. They hoped that it would bring some calm to the situation. Interestingly enough, many of the housewives would routinely bring tea, sandwiches and biscuits to the soldiers. Both sides would help out the soldiers with food, Protestant and Catholic.

Wharton continued about the treatment they received when they first arrived, "And the people on both sides were so pleasant. It was unbelievable. We were asking ourselves, why are we here?"[17] However, these were early days for the British troops on the ground in Northern Ireland. The Catholic population didn't realize what was ahead for them and the troops there. Many of the Catholics knew this was the start of something that would change Northern Ireland forever.

In April 1969, Devlin was speaking in the British House of Commons. She was giving her first speech as a Member of Parliament. Devlin went on to talk about British rule in Ireland and how people were living and surviving in Northern Ireland. She barely needed any notes or to take a breath. Devlin spoke for more than twenty minutes to an audience that was both surprised and stunned by the speech and the words in it. When she sat down, there were a few moments of complete silence.

Nobody said a word.

Seconds later, the House exploded with a roar of applause for the newly elected Bernadette Devlin.

Newsweek said, "One after another, MPs hailed her maiden speech as one of the best in the history of Commons."[18]

The date of the speech was April 22, 1969.

However, the applause would be short-lived. In the next fifteen months, she would be battling the police in the Bogside of Derry and behind bars.

At the same time, Bernadette Devlin would become one of the most influential leaders of the Catholic Civil Rights movement in Northern Ireland.

CHAPTER 11

JOHN HUME

John Hume is admittedly one of my favorite people in the Catholic Civil Rights movement. I saw how he used the Black Civil Rights movement in the States and borrowed what we did for the Catholics in Northern Ireland. His picture with John Lewis on the Peace Bridge in Derry is still my portrait on my Twitter page. It shows how close both groups of people are and how much we have in common. Hume was a Nobel Laureate for his peace work in Northern Ireland. He ended up in politics like Devlin-McAliskey, and he was seen as a driving force behind the end of 25 years of sectarian conflict in the country. Hume is also known as being one of the architects of the Good Friday Peace Agreement, which to this day is still seen as one of his crowning achievements. His actions and goals were influenced heavily by Martin Luther King, Jr. and his work with the Black Civil Rights movement in America.

Hume was born in Derry in 1937 and was the eldest of seven children. His father was a shipyard riveter, and both his parents raised the family on slim pickings since they were part of the state welfare service. The Hume family lived in one room in a house. He was well aware of the poverty in Derry during the 1940s and '50s, given the housing shortage there and the high number of unemployed people. Hume's father worked in a shipyard and when World War II ended, he never worked again; he was unemployed for over twenty years. One thing that influenced Hume in his older years was that the family had Protestant families on their street, and for years afterward, the families remained friends. The only issue was when the 12th of July or August Protestant marching season came around and Hume became well aware of the differences. After that, they all were friendly again.

68 GOOD TROUBLE

He won a scholarship to St. Columb's College in Derry for middle-class Catholic professionals and studied the priesthood before switching to History and French. In his 20s, he taught French and, at that time started to become a leader in the Civil Rights movement.

When Hume was asked years later about his greatest achievement, it wasn't the Civil Rights Movement, Nobel Peace Prize, or the Good Friday Peace Agreement. He believed it was his part in creating the Derry Credit Union. Because at that time, during the 1950s, the city's poor, majority Catholic neighborhoods lived in a difficult cycle of poverty, since most people were too poor to buy a home which could help with a bank loan, if needed. Hume and five of his mates from the Bogside put their money together—almost ten pounds—and founded Northern Ireland's first credit union in 1960. To this day, that was monumental as the Derry Credit Union now has more than 30,000 members and has issued over a million loans for individuals and families. Hume and his partners knocked on every door in the Bogside, asking people to start a savings account in the credit union that they had created.

Hume lived in the Bogside, and that made a big difference because he was working and living in the heart of where he grew up. He was a Bogside boy and always would be. After he set up the Credit Union, he turned his eye to politics due to issues in Derry, such as housing and voting rights. Despite the Catholic population being in the majority, Derry's city council was controlled strongly by Unionists. The reform of the council was one of the demands in the Civil Rights Movement that Hume worked with. As the situation became worse in Derry and throughout Northern Ireland, Hume joined with other Nationalists and founded the SDLP (Social Democratic and Labour Party). During the 1969 election, Hume called at every house to tell people they had a vote, and they needed to use it.

Hume grew frustrated with the Unionist government at their unwillingness to listen to the Catholic minority community and what they were asking for. He then chose to participate in the Civil Rights movement campaign. He was elected to the Derry Citizens' Action Committee as Vice-Chairman and tried his best to make sure that the protests he was involved in were peaceful. This enabled him to win a parliamentary seat representing the Foyle constituency in the city between 1969 and 1972.

Northern Irish Civil Rights leaders such as Hume had been critical of the People's Democracy for purposely countermarching to incite the Loyalist population by marching through their towns. However, he knew that any type of civil rights movement, especially by students, was better than nothing at all.

Another positive for the People's Democracy was that they also had members who were Protestant who had joined the fight for full Catholic equal rights.

Hume was a very astute politician, and he knew when it was time to force the hand of the government leaders. He always believed that dialogue with your adversaries was important and that conflicts could only be settled through conversation.

On January 22, 1972, Hume led a march against internment (the rule where you could be arrested if suspected of being involved with the IRA) on Magilligan Beach, a few miles outside of Derry. At this march, Hume led over 2,000 protesters on the beach, where internees were being held in a World War II army base that had been turned into an internment camp.

The marchers took the route to the strand as they all sang the "We Shall Overcome" song that had been sung in the US Civil Rights movement. There was barbed wire placed all along the beach, which blocked the path that the marchers intended to take. The series of barbed wire barricades stretched across the sand and didn't end until the edge of the water. The atmosphere was as tight as the barbed wire on the beach.

The British Army had its Parachute Regiment soldiers in riot gear protecting the area and refusing the marchers entry onto the British defense property. The Parachute Regiment was the elite of the British Army. Hume continued to ask the soldiers for permission to pass through.

Without any warning, the soldiers began to charge into the crowd with their batons and hit any protestor they saw. As the marchers attempted to flee the area, the soldiers continued to hit and kick them. The crowd panicked and ran across the sand to any safe area they could find. In the water, seaweed was everywhere.

Gerry Duddy (Julieann Campbell's uncle and the brother of Jackie Duddy who was killed on Bloody Sunday) was 11 at the time of the Magilligan Beach incident. I met Gerry at a hotel pub in Derry in March 2024 with Julieann. Gerry is now 67 years old, a former plasterer and a little over six feet tall. He still looks nice and slim for someone approaching 70. He was a friendly man who was a pleasure to speak to. We shared a Guinness and talked about everything civil rights.

Gerry talked about Magilligan from what he had heard from others who were there. "Magilligan was a protest march against what the army was doing. Magilligan was the week before the Bloody Sunday march. Hundreds got attacked, the same way they did on Bloody Sunday. The people had nothing to fight back with and got the shit beat out of them. They just laid into them, they

GOOD TROUBLE

tried to defend themselves but they had nothing. It put fear in people's minds and people out on the streets."[1]

As Hume tried to calm the marchers down, the soldiers fired rubber bullets and CS gas into the crowd to disperse them.

Julieann Campbell mentioned she had heard stories of how the rubber bullets had been used. People had told her that the bullets had been sliced open by the Army to put glass or razor blades in them to make them even more lethal than they already were. That also showed how vicious the Army had turned. She said that years later during an interview she did, the person said they had found a rubber bullet at Magilligan Beach and they kept it for years.[2]

Years later, Hume added about the day on the beach, "Whereas I had an idea that the army would be tough on the day and would behave wrongly, I had no idea that the army would start shooting at the marchers."[3]

Hume explained the situation on the beach by saying the soldiers were, "berating, brutalizing and terrorizing demonstrators."[4] Sadly, this foreshadowed what would happen later that month in Derry during the infamous Bloody Sunday event. Before Bloody Sunday, Hume voiced his concern over the violent nature and deep hatred by the parachute regiment by saying about them dealing with protestors, "someone will be killed."[5]

Julieann Campbell said about the incident on the beach, "It was a week before Bloody Sunday. Even today people think it was a practice for what would happen on Bloody Sunday."[6]

Gerry Duddy and others believe that John Hume had an inkling that the repeat could happen the next week on what would become known as Bloody Sunday. "John Hume was warned off about not attending the Bloody Sunday march. That's what people say. He gave us great help over the years but he got scared. Scared of what he saw at Magilligan Beach and what happened."[7]

For years, Loyalist and Republican paramilitaries were opposed to Hume's determined efforts to achieve a peaceful settlement in Northern Ireland. During these years, it is incredible to think that Hume never carried a weapon on him. Even though his family, who were raised in Derry and walked to and from school, would often see graffiti on the walls that were personally insulting to Hume. The home of Hume had been defaced over the years as well, with paint and other items.

There was no doubt that the IRA hated John Hume and what he stood for at the time. One has to remember, during this time, the IRA didn't want any concessions made to the Unionists. Journalist Eamon McCann remarked about how Hume was seen by them, "They hated him […] that is not too strong a word to say. The people who would become the Provos- Provisional Sinn

Fein or the Provisionals at the time- hated John Hume [...] I mean the Provos don't like to be reminded of this. They attempted to kill John- they attempted to kill his family. There was one occasion they threw petrol bombs at John's house in West End Park. The entire front of the house was engulfed in flames, the entire front of the house. It was a serious attempt to kill the Hume family."[8]

Ironically, it was Sinn Fein that Hume worked with to create the peace agreement, specifically Gerry Adams of Sinn Fein at the time. Hume even admitted that he would leave politics forever if the deal with Sinn Fein couldn't be worked out. While they worked on the agreement, the horrific bombing in October 1993 on the Shankill Road in Belfast, a predominantly Protestant stronghold, killing ten people including two children.

As horrible as the bombing was, pressure intensified on Hume as Gerry Adams was photographed helping to carry the coffin of the bomber. Adams almost had to do that since the bomber was part of the Republican movement at the time. Hume's wife even begged him to stop the talks with Adams, seeing all of the hateful messages that he and the family were receiving on a constant basis. However, Hume would not give up as he stated he'd do, "everything in my power to bring this to an end."[9]

There was a retribution bombing by the UDA one week later after the Shankill bombing at the Rising Sun bar, located in the village of Greysteel. Eight people died in the attack.

Again, Hume continued to work for peace. He was determined, and possibly, stubbornly not to give up.

Tony Blair became prime minister of the United Kingdom in 1997, and his introduction to the peace talks gave a breath of fresh air to the situation. He talked about Hume:

"He would explain the pressures that were on him, pressures from within his own party. A lot of people within his own party were actually quite irritated with what he was doing. In fact, angry [...] because they thought it was validating Sinn Fein without forcing them to change. So that again is where his own [...] the bigness of this character was very important. I mean, I never thought of him as an SDLP figure. I thought of him as John Hume, you know, as I say, he was a figure in his own right."[10]

To this day, the people of Northern Ireland on both sides are indebted to John Hume for the peace that they enjoy today. Or as many people said about him, "(he was) A father of the peace process and one of Derry's greatest sons."[11]

Hume no doubt was one of the most important Irish politicians of the last 50 years for both the North and South of Ireland, and his impact on Northern Ireland is still being felt today.

CHAPTER 12

EAMONN MCCANN

One of the leading figures today for equal rights and Civil Rights, not only in Northern Ireland but around the world, remains Eamonn McCann. McCann was born and raised in Derry and continues to live in the Bogside today. He was raised Catholic and attended St. Columb's College. McCann's life has been filled with a belief in socialism, but also a deep-seated belief in justice for all. He also admittedly, as a young student, was excited by the spectacle of rebelling against the 'system'. His protests and work no doubt set the framework for the change that people in Northern Ireland enjoy today.

I met with McCann for an interview in June 2024 at bar Sandinos one afternoon with Julieann Campbell. Just before 4 p.m., upon my entry I saw McCann speaking with another gentleman, and as I didn't want to bother them, I went back outside to wait for Julieann. When she did arrive, we walked in together and waited at the bar as McCann wrapped up his conversation with the man. Julieann and McCann gave each other a warm embrace, and I shook hands with the legendary figure. It felt like meeting someone who had seen everything over the years in Derry.

Eamonn McCann still looks youthful for 81 years old. He's slim and bald now and was wearing a t-shirt that read "TRAMP," a band that he was fond of, along with a black puffer jacket and black-rimmed glasses. He walked with a black cane, a remnant of a recent health battle he had endured. The three of us took a table in the far corner that was next to the door that led upstairs. I went to the bar and ordered McCann a cup of tea and two beers for Julieann and myself. As I returned to the table, McCann was everything I thought he would be—a huge laugh, a great smile and gesticulated as he spoke to us. He had just returned from visiting relatives in Canada and said he felt good overall.

74 GOOD TROUBLE

One of the first things we spoke about was how hard it was to get in touch with Bernadette Devlin. McCann was nice enough to tell me, "I'll give Bernadette a ring this weekend even if it's for her to say no, she won't talk to you."[1] We all laughed at that comment.

McCann can still remember when he realized that he was different and where he lived gave people predetermined notions about him. When he announced on his first day at secondary school that he was from the notorious Rossville Street area in Derry, the priest responded, "Rossville Street, that's where you wash once a week."[2] McCann remembers that statement as clearly as today. "I was 11 years old, and I suddenly realized, I remember this being a flash to me, that we are looked down on."[3]

McCann's mother, Elizabeth, was from the parish of Warbleshinny in the County Derry countryside. There she attended a mixed (Catholic and Protestant) primary school, which was rare in those days and even today. His father, Edward, was a fan of Dr. Noel Browne, who attempted to get the Mother and Child Scheme into the Republic of Ireland. His father also idolized Aneurin Bevan, the person who created and led the National Health Service. His father was heavily involved with the trade union movement and that was a huge influence on McCann. It helped fuel his political activism with an eye on not only Northern Ireland but the world view. This also impacted his time during his university years.

Speaking about his father's influence, McCann said, "I knew through my father that the Tories (Conservative form of government in the UK) had opposed the National Health Act and he would never forgive them for that [...] those were the issues, not partition, even though of course we were against discrimination [...] I got that at a very early stage, and I've never lost it, and I wouldn't, not just out of fealty to my father, but just that it became ingrained upon me."[4]

McCann attended Queens University and was one of the first founders of the People's Democracy group in Belfast. He ended up leaving the university without graduating. McCann said he was asked to leave because he was seen as a troublemaker at the school.

In 1968, McCann became known as an incredible speaker who became one of the leading faces of the Civil Rights movement.

He still remembers the first time he saw a riot back in 1951.

"The first riot I ever saw was when I was eight years old. It was in Derry on St. Patrick's Day. There was a parade and flags, the whole nine yards. I still remember that to this day."[5]

Eamonn McCann

This was at the time when there was an unspoken rule that Catholics were not allowed to march inside the Derry walls. It was amazing that McCann still could recollect to this day the details of that first riot he saw. It showed the impact that it had on him. He also remembered the humor that even a riot could bring.

"I remember there was a veggie shop. Fresh fruit, veggies daily the sign read. When the battle started, people took potatoes and turnips and hit a few cops in the face. Nobody got hurt, but it was quite funny for me at the time as a young boy," McCann laughed.[6]

His introduction to the Civil Rights movement happened by accident. In 1968, he bumped into a man named Dermie McClenaghan, someone who would become a friend for years.

McCann explained what happened on that fateful day in January 1968.

"I discovered the civil rights movement in the North by accident when I was walking along Rossville Street where I was born and met my friend, Dermie."[7]

McCann asked him, "What's happening here?"

McClenaghan was on his way to block a road with a caravan in protest at the local authority's refusal to give a local Catholic family a house. McCann said, "I was asked to help, I agreed and off we went […] What else would I say? And then just one thing led to another."[8]

McCann hadn't seen any of his friends for well over a year and a half because he had been working in London, England. He explained that he loved London and the job he had as a tree trimmer.

He explained what that experience did for him in his later years, "I had a good job in London and I got on well with all the people I worked with. I was the only person who wasn't a Londoner. That experience cured me of my anti-English bias that I ever had because they were lovely people."[9]

McCann explained that the only reason he came home to Derry in 1968 was to see his sister because his mother said she would be coming home for ten days.

The protestors told the police that they were not moving the caravan until their demands had been met—housing, votes, jobs.

McCann said, "This caused great consternation for two weekends in a row. The authorities began to get very angry at that."

That was the beginning of marching and protesting for Eamonn McCann.

He explained, "We organized marches, demonstrations, occupied the city chamber, blocking traffic and so forth. This helped us. It made us notorious.

We had riots, people threw stones and in those days we were getting a lot of attention. Even the bishops were making statements condemning our actions. The priests didn't like me at all. They saw me as a loudmouth."[10]

That event led to more protests from McCann. He was arrested in the summer of 1968 following a sit-down on Derry's Craigavon Bridge, something that the young leaders of SNCC in the United States would do as well as a protest for civil rights.

"I was living with a girl from Nottingham at the time in London. She was a beautiful girl. Almond eyes, soft skin. I was in love with her, I really was."[11]

It can be plainly seen, as McCann told that story about one of his past loves, that there was no doubt he had been a handsome man and probably had a way with the ladies. He has that type of personality.

McCann said, "I started coming back to Derry over long weekends. I was involved with trade unions in London. And this went on for about six months."[12]

He has seen so many changes during his lifetime, which includes Northern Ireland being transformed. He reminds me of my parents with the changes they have seen. For him that includes seeing the country change from one deep with sectarian divides, including discrimination, housing and voting through the Civil Rights movement, the Troubles, to Stormont being the place to share government between the religions.

As this book ends, as Bloody Sunday ended on January 31, 1972, he was present during that horrible event. Even as he prepared for the 'Fight For Gaza' appearance in Derry in Spring 2024, McCann said that he still enjoys "going against the established order of things, and taking joy in that."[13]

Today, McCann continues to fight for the rights of all people. He won an election in 2016 as a People Before Profit representative at the age of 73. He had been running for a spot throughout his life and lost back in the early '70s to another Derry man, John Hume.

McCann gave clarity to what he did, "One of the things I've got from marching is that it's in numbers that people get a sense of their own power. The most radical changes of mind that I've observed in my time have happened in the context of the lower orders rising up, and I would hope to see that again. All history shows nothing significant can be achieved without solidarity from the lower orders. That's what changed the world, not anything else."[14]

As you will see in the book, Eamonn McCann was central to the Civil Rights movement and the future of Northern Ireland. Julieann Campbell said of McCann, "He's one of the finest orators and he can tell a story."[16]

A man who was present at the landmark moments of Northern Ireland history: Duke Street, Burntollet, the Battle of the Bogside and Bloody Sunday.

CHAPTER 13

SELMA TO MONTGOMERY MARCH—BLOODY SUNDAY

There are not many people still alive who witnessed the historic Bloody Sunday march in person.

Richard Smiley is one of those people. He is also one of the few who marched all the way from Selma to Montgomery when the marchers completed the five-day, 54-mile march. Smiley was 16 years old on Sunday, March 7, 1965. He is in his 80s now and lives in Tampa, Florida, but the memories of that day and the days afterward are still strikingly fresh in his sharp mind. I talked to Mr. Smiley in a phone interview in May 2024, and he explained to me why he felt he had to march and take part in the movement at such a young age. I was spellbound as I listened to his story. Selma honors people like Smiley each year; they call them the "Foot Soldiers." Sadly, each year there are fewer and fewer of them left.

Smiley traced his interest in the civil rights movement back to 1964 when he was 15 years old. He had been bouncing around living-wise and ended up in a foster home. He was not attending school the way he should have been and kept getting picked up for marching and was arrested a couple of times as well. The couple of times turned into more and more arrests as he eventually dropped out of school at the age of 15. In his mind, dropping out of school and marching was something that he didn't choose to do but he had to do. He believed he needed to be there with his Black brothers and sisters to fight for equality and voting rights. An incredible stance for someone so young at that time.[1]

Smiley said about his early days, "Even before Bloody Sunday we were going to jail every day. We boycotted the high school. We marched every day."[2]

He told a story of one of the last times he was arrested. They had buses lined up for the people arrested, both male and female. The officers used cattle prods on them to get them on the bus. They took them to a remote makeshift jail. There was nothing in the large room but a bucket and a sink. They were held there for days until one night they were let out at midnight while the KKK was having a meeting on Highway 80. They decided not to walk home and stayed at the prison until someone came to pick them up. Smiley was warned when he returned to his foster home that if he kept marching, he'd risk being put out of his house. He felt the woman was looking out for him and for years, Smiley would visit her when he returned to Selma.[3]

The youngest marcher on that Sunday in March was 9-year-old Sheyann Webb-Christburg. I spoke to Mrs. Christburg on the phone in May 2024 and her story is truly incredible to believe, especially knowing how young she was at the time. She was present for the tragic events on the Edmund Pettus Bridge that day and she embarked on the Selma to Montgomery march as well. Again, all of this and she hadn't even reached double digits in age. She, like Richard Smiley, is one of the few people who were at the march and are still alive to talk about it.

Webb-Christburg was born and raised in Selma. She was your typical precocious child, wide-eyed, with a great smile and dark eyes that were alive with energy. She grew up poor in the George Washington Carver Homes public housing project and was the baby girl in her family. Webb-Christburg was an active child, always into something, intelligent and curious about the world. She was always one who wanted to participate in everything. Her life revolved around school, church and family. That would change on January 2, 1965.

Webb-Christburg was playing with her friend Rachel West on that same day in front of the famous Browns Chapel. The church was adjacent to the apartment where she lived in. She noticed a bunch of cars pull up in front of the church as she and her friend moved closer to the commotion. It was then that she saw a man surrounded by others taking care of him. One man asked the girls if they knew who the man was. They did not. He introduced the man to the girls.

That man was Dr. Martin Luther King, Jr.

King saw the girls and went over to talk to them.

Webb-Christburg explained how the conversation went, "He asked us the usual questions one would ask a child. Where did we live? Where did we go to school? How old were we? We answered as they walked him to the back entrance of the church for a strategy meeting. We got to the back door and the other man told us we needed to go home and play."[4]

Bloody Sunday 79

King heard this exchange and jumped in and asked the man to let the girls come into the church meeting with them. He took them by the hand and got two chairs for them. King got one for himself and sat down with them.

Webb-Christburg still remembers the conversation. "He told us what was about to happen in Selma and he asked, what do you little girls want? We didn't know what to say. He said, when I ask that you need to say freedom. He then said, when do you all want freedom? Again, we didn't know what to say. He said, when I ask you when do you want your freedom, you need to say that you want it now."[5]

It was a moment that changed Webb-Christburg's life forever. She ran home and told her parents who she had met. She still remembers that her father said one thing and that was it, "The only thing my father said was: stay away from that church and that mess."[6]

She didn't understand why her father said that and why he was not as excited as she was about meeting Dr. King. However, she had made up her mind that she would see Dr. King again, despite what her father had said to her. It was all very exciting for her.

"After meeting Dr. King, my life began to take a different turn. He struck a chord with me and I still remember vividly the first day I met him," Webb-Christburg recalled.[7]

Webb-Christburg's life changed forever after meeting Dr. King and seeing the special attention that he gave her and her friend. She would never forget that. She didn't know the impact it would have on her for years to come. However, with the little girl attending those meetings and Dr. King taking her under his wing, the movement had truly begun for her.

Webb-Christburg was determined to make a change, especially for her parents, even though at first they had discouraged her. The more they were around the Civil Rights workers that she would bring home to stay, the more they understood and saw she was being taken care of.

"I saw and heard and learned more as to what was happening because of the civil rights movement people I was around. I knew my parents weren't registered voters and I wanted that for them. As a little girl, I wanted to fight for them because it was risky for them in terms of losing their jobs," Webb-Christburg remembered.[8]

When March 7 arrived, despite her parents understanding her drive, they begged her to stay away from the Edmund Pettus Bridge march.

She cried and they agreed to let her go.

The results would change her and the country forever.

***

80   GOOD TROUBLE

The images that not only stunned Americans but also the world saw on Sunday, March 7, 1965, put the Black Civil Rights movement in prime time. Images that people would never forget. The images that showed the White population defiantly suppressing the voter registration goals of the Black population. The only witness that had nothing at stake was the blue sky on that Sunday morning in March.

The decision to march didn't happen until right at the last moment. The marchers knew what faced them, including Sheriff Jim Clark, a man who could be volatile and dangerous.

Clark was the stone-faced sheriff of Dallas County, Alabama, and cut a striking figure. He'd been the sheriff there since 1955. He was the face of segregation in that area and the marchers knew that. A face that had a double chin because of his heavy weight and his sheriff's hat routinely cocked to the left side of his massive head. He was a large man who stood over six foot two and weighed well over 220 pounds. On his lapel he wore a button that read simply: "Never." All civil rights people knew what that defiant message meant. His attire included a billy club, pistol and cattle prod.

Clark was born in Alabama in 1922. He was a WWII veteran and worked in the war as an engineer and gunner with the Air Force in the Aleutian Islands. After leaving the war, he came to Dallas County to raise cattle and work on a farm. In 1955, he was appointed sheriff after the current sheriff at the time passed away.

He was known for his widespread violence against civil rights demonstrators, especially those who were trying to register to vote. On Clark's watch, protesters had been beaten and tear-gassed in the past. He'd also been helped in the past by what people called "the sheriff's posse." This posse was comprised of horse riding volunteers armed with whips and clubs to terrorize Black demonstrators.

In early 1965, during a voting rights demonstration by young Black citizens, Clark accosted the demonstrators with a cattle prod from behind. The cattle prod made the demonstrators run fast, and they later became physically ill from the exhaustion of running from Clark's cattle prod.

On another occasion on February 5, 1965, which was caught on television, Clark confronted Reverend CT Vivian of the SCLC on the steps of the courthouse in Selma on a rainy day.

Rev. Vivian was raised in Illinois and participated in many sit-ins over the years, even in his home state. He went on to attend seminary school in Nashville, Tennessee. It was there where he met other civil rights leaders such as John Lewis and others and learned how to work the nonviolent approach

Bloody Sunday 81

against hostile people. Later, he became a member of King's SCLC. When Rev. Vivian was asked to visit Selma, he commented, "Selma was home to a virulent, racist sheriff, Jim Clark [...] (who) was almost certain to respond less than peacefully to our peaceful initiatives. We needed a conflict that would demonstrate our plight [...] Such a response, we hoped, would sicken Northerners."[9]

Rev. Vivian had a line of people behind him on the sidewalk beside the courthouse and was attempting to get them inside so they could register to vote. He was not a man who would be easily intimidated, being tall and skinny. Clark, dressed in his suit, tie and hat was armed with a club and blocked Rev. Vivian's entrance.

Rev. Vivian said, "You are breaking the injunction by not allowing these people to come inside the courthouse and wait. This courthouse does not belong to Sheriff Clark but the people of Dallas County and they have come to register. What you're really trying to do is to intimidate these people. This is a violation of the constitution and the court order."[10]

Clark simply stood there and listened. He then turned his back to Rev. Vivian in a dismissive, disrespectful way.

Rev. Vivian continued, "You can turn your back on me but you cannot turn your back on the idea of justice. You can keep the club in your hand but you cannot beat down justice. And we will register to vote because these are citizens of the United States and we have the right to do it."[11]

Clark turned back around to face Rev. Vivian with a mocking grin on his face as he looked down the sidewalk and pointed to the Black citizens lined up to register, some with umbrellas in hand protecting them from the light rain. He said, "I'm looking down the line and see all the people that have been in jail for felonies."[12]

Clark and his uniformed deputies laughed at those comments.

Rev. Vivian disputed that and explained that the felonies those people may have on their records were trumped-up charges from Sheriff Clark and his men.

Rev. Vivian continued to bait Clark when, finally, Clark turned around and ordered the cameras to be turned off as his deputies began to push the crowd back off the sidewalk. Clark then suddenly punched Rev. Vivian in the face. The force of the punch caused him to fall down on the courthouse steps.

Clark stood there above him, club in hand, looking at his victim. The look was one of hatred and disgust.

However, Clark didn't realize that one cameraman hadn't turned off his camera and got the entire incident on film.

82   GOOD TROUBLE

Rev. Vivian continued to talk to him as he was arrested, "Arrest us, you don't have to beat us."[13]

"Clear outta here!" one of Clark's deputies yelled at the crowd.

"People have the privilege to vote," Rev. Vivian responded.

Clark and his men continued to shoo away the cameramen and reporters, forcing them across the street from the courthouse.

Rev. Vivian said, "You beat us but refuse to register us. What kind of people are you?"[14]

The whole world got to see what kind of people Clark and his bully men were because of that one cameraman who kept filming. The incident made national news. It was the first time that Selma was on the map in terms of the Civil Rights movement.

During another protest, Clark punched a Civil Rights leader so hard that he broke his hand from the impact. A bully description of Clark was a kind one, he came off as a racist tyrant who ruthlessly enforced segregation, even with his fists.

Clark despised the civil rights demonstrators. He said the following about them: "What they want is Black supremacy."[15]

J. L. Chestnut Jr. was one of the people at the march and said the following, "I walked over to the Montgomery side of the Edmund Pettus bridge before everybody else and stationed myself at the side of the highway. State troopers and Clark's posse were standing in the road and along the side in front of several stores. We were about two blocks beyond the foot of the bridge."[16]

The marchers knew what was ahead of them. Lewis and the other leaders knew there would be some type of confrontation. They also knew that a number of arrests and the prospect of spending time in jail were strong possibilities. Lewis and the leaders also knew there was a chance they would be stopped and perhaps roughed up a bit by the officers. Clark had made an announcement the night before that he needed more deputies for the march. Lewis and the leaders didn't think they would make it all the way to Montgomery.

Early that morning, around 500 plus Black marchers left Browns Chapel and walked six blocks to Broad Street. They then continued across the Pettus Bridge which ran across the Alabama River. The weather was your typical March weather—a mixture of a bit of winter and spring with a chilly wind that went through the marchers' overcoats and bones.

Smiley talked about the preparation, "We all met at Browns Chapel and organized there early in the morning, it was a cold, overcast day and we all had coats and caps on. Since I'd been to jail I had two pairs of pants on with

Bloody Sunday 83

pajamas underneath so I put in a lot of candy just in case we were jailed and I needed food."[17]

The crowd of marchers was a mixture of young people and older citizens and they all carried a variety of things in their hands, such as lunch bags and bedrolls. There were men, women and children from all strata of society, from teachers to preachers to manual laborers. Many of them had just come from church and were still dressed in their Sunday finery. Many of the women had high heels on and even Lewis and some of the other leaders wore a suit and tie and dress shoes. They all had dreams of better lives that could come from this march, be it voting rights or housing rights. Lewis admitted that they had no real plan; they would march and see where the day would take them. He said, "None of us had thought much further ahead than that afternoon. Anything that happened beyond that- if we were allowed to go on, if this march did indeed go all the way to Montgomery-we figured we would take care of as we went along. The main thing was that we do it, that we march."[18]

J. L. Chestnut was an attorney in Selma at the time and was active in the Civil Rights movement during the 1950s and '60s. He'd been born in 1930 to a father who owned a grocery store and a mother who was a teacher. He was born and raised in Selma and graduated from Dillard University and received his law degree from Howard University in 1953. Chestnut reluctantly returned to his home in Selma and opened his law practice. He was the first-ever Black lawyer in the city and then started to represent civil rights cases throughout Alabama. In 1963, he worked with SNCC to organize nonviolent demonstrations in Selma. Chestnut was known for his humor and charm. His way in the courtroom was described as having a clever and mesmerizing way with words. Equally important, he always remained cool and collected under any type of stress.

John Lewis said the following about Chestnut, "I don't know what would have happened to us in Selma if it wasn't for Chestnut. Selma was a vicious place, vicious. I don't know how he survived there, I really don't. He used the law to help liberate the black folk of Alabama."[19]

Now, Lewis was at what would become one of the most famous marches in the era of the Civil Rights movement. On that Sunday morning, he felt a meaning for his life beginning to crystallize; his purpose was right in front of him.

It was almost 4 p.m. as Lewis, Williams, and the other leaders gathered the marchers around them. Lewis read a short statement with the press there as well, so everyone knew why they were marching. Reverend Andrew Young of the SCLC also spoke, reminding the marchers of what they should and shouldn't do: "The march intends to keep off the highway. We will be marching on the shoulder of the road. And will not in any way be interfering in the route of traffic. And we urge you to be careful and make sure you don't get on the highway."[20]

Dr. Shannah Gilliam explained why her grandfather didn't go on the Bloody Sunday march. "They planned it at Reverend Reese's house. They knew there would be some recourse from the public safety officers and that's the reason my grandfather wasn't there on Bloody Sunday. But, it had to be done. They knew it would be dangerous."[21]

Lewis gave a short prayer, and then they began to lead the marchers out. Over six hundred of them.

Reverend Reese was there on that fateful Sunday. Marvin Reese, Jr. said, "My grandfather was in the front, near the middle of the marchers. He was in charge of keeping all of the marchers three feet apart because in Selma, if you marched and you weren't three feet apart, you could be arrested."[22]

At 17 years old, Carolyn Doyle King was there. She told me that she was about to graduate from high school and was with her mother at the time of the march. Doyle King still remembers going from Browns Chapel to the bridge. Her father stayed back at the church, part of the Courageous Eight, and didn't want to lose anyone on the front line. Doyle King told of why she and her mother were there that fateful day, "We didn't want fame or publicity. We just wanted the right to vote and we wanted to be treated like first class citizens."[23]

Linda Gildersleeve-Blackwell, as a child, remembers her family packed into the stationwagon, following the marchers from behind. Her father had helped organize the local people for the Bloody Sunday march and the Selma to Montgomery march. "On the day of the march we were behind the marchers, me, my sister, my parents and my cousin and aunt."[24]

The Alabama state troopers were dressed in their crisp blue uniforms and white helmets and at the time numbered about 50. They were waiting approximately 300 yards beyond the end of the Pettus Bridge. Behind and on each side of the troops were more than a dozen men on horseback and about 100 white citizens, there as spectators. The men on horseback were dressed in khaki uniforms. They also carried nightsticks that looked like baseball bats. About 50 Black citizens stood watching the activity beside a bright yellow school bus. They were as far as possible from the troops. The marchers went past about 40 more men on horseback at the other end of the Pettus Bridge.

The troops stood shoulder to shoulder beside each other in a straight line across both sides of the divided four-lane highway. They put on their gas masks and raised their nightsticks, slowly using them to hit their hands in a motion

Bloody Sunday 85

that was preparing them to use the nightsticks on the marchers. The sound of the nightsticks was ominous, almost like a preparation for battle.

The marchers saw the danger that was in front of them as it sent shudders throughout the group. They began to slowly march as the wind buffeted them, two at a time. People from all walks of life, Selma citizens who included teenagers, teachers, preachers and hairdressers.

The marchers made their way down Sylvan Street. This was the Black part of Selma. They then headed down Water Street. Now, they were out of the Black neighborhood and it got eerily quiet. Nobody said a word; you just heard feet on pavement. Down Water Street, the marchers turned right and walked along the brown, still river until they arrived at the base of the Edmund Pettus Bridge.

They didn't say a word as many of them no doubt had the chill of fear going down their spines. They edged closer, hearing unnerving sounds from the troopers in front of them. They knew the inescapable belief that the marchers were now depending on each other for confidence and protection. The armed White men were in front of the newspaper building, the Selma-Times Journal. Some of them had glib smirks on their faces but they said nothing.

As the marchers turned onto the bridge, they stayed on the narrow sidewalk. The road had been closed to any traffic, so there were no cars there. The only sounds on the bridge were the noises of the horses.

Smiley talked about what they saw, "When we almost got downtown we saw a bunch of guys on horses. We got a little nervous and started questioning our plan. We wondered what they were going to do. But we kept marching, then we saw the state troopers lined up across Highway 80."[25]

When the marchers were about 50 feet away, a voice called out on the speaker system that had been set up there.

That voice was one of the troops.

His name was Major John Cloud. He began to speak to the marchers in a firm, direct tone. "It will be detrimental to your safety to continue this march and this is an unlawful assembly. Your march is not conducive to the public safety. You are ordered to disperse and go back to your church or to your homes."[26]

Hosea Williams took a deep breath and answered from the head of where the marchers were. He asked, "May we have a word with the major?"[27]

Major Cloud shook his head and answered, "There is no word to be had."[28]

The marchers were in awe of the bravery of Williams. It was risky, but what other option did they have at this point?

86   GOOD TROUBLE

Williams asked the same question again. He was readying himself for a potential attack.

Major Cloud seemed evasive. He gave the same answer and his patience was running thin.

Smiley said, "When we got there the police told us that this march was illegal and you cannot march any further."[29]

Finally, Major Cloud gave a chilling response. "You have two minutes to turn around and go back to your church."[30]

Stone silence on both sides.

Sheyann Webb-Christburg's young eyes couldn't believe what they were seeing.

"I could see the police with the billy clubs, the horses, the dogs and my heart began to race quickly. I knew something was going to happen."[31]

The marchers were determined not to turn back. Honestly, even if they wanted to go back, there were too many people to do so.

Cloud frightened the marchers as much as Sheriff Clark did. They both seemed to simmer with rage about the current events. The marchers could not yet know for sure the true meaning of Cloud's words.

Nobody said a word as the Black marchers stood nervously, seeing the troops hitting the nightsticks in their hands, preparing for a showdown.

A few more seconds went by.

The marchers stood together with their fate unknown, and they stood together proudly and defiantly. The silence was as still as the clouds above them in the sky.

Lewis knew there were few options as he said, "We could have gone forward, marching right into the teeth of those troopers. But that would have been too aggressive, I thought, too provocative. God knew what might have happened if we had done that. These people were ready to be arrested, but I didn't want anyone to get hurt. We couldn't go forward. We couldn't go back. There was only one option left that I could see."[32]

Lewis said to Williams that they should kneel down and pray. Williams nodded in agreement. They turned around toward the marchers and asked everyone to begin to kneel down and pray. However, they didn't have time to do anything.

The next sound was Major Cloud's booming voice after a few seconds.

"Troopers, advance and see that they disperse!" he ordered.

Those were the petrifying words that the marchers did not want to hear. Their hands trembled at what was to come next.

Bloody Sunday 87

The troopers and possemen moved forward as one formidable machine past the Haisten's Mattress and Awning Company in the background on the side of the highway. It appeared as if they were one big blue ocean wave with their uniforms. The only sounds were the stamp of their thick boots, the howls of the white crowd cheering them on, and the clicks of the horses on the pavement heading toward the marchers.

The marchers had nowhere to go. They couldn't even turn and retreat off the bridge. There were hundreds of people behind Lewis and the other leaders, bridge railings on both sides and nothing but the river below them.

Alabama state troopers and volunteer officers of the Dallas County Sheriff's office slammed into a row of Black marchers with tear gas, nightsticks and whips. A cacophony of screams and shrieks filled the air, and the noise was deafening. They went after men, women and children. This was the response by Governor Wallace to enforce the order against the protest march from Selma to Montgomery.

Smiley explained what he saw, "Once we kneeled to pray, they attacked us with billy clubs and tear gas. They beat us all the way back across the bridge. Some of the horses came across the bridge and some of the men had cattle prods. I didn't get hit but I got tear gassed."[33]

The troopers moved briskly into the crowd as the first twenty or so Black marchers were pushed to the ground. The marchers screamed, arms and legs flailing in the air. The bags and other items they had been carrying were scattered across the grass dividing strip and onto the pavement on both sides of the strip. The ones who were still on their feet quickly retreated with horror on their faces.

Lewis was one of the first ones to be hit as he remembered, "The first of the troopers came over me, a large, husky man. Without a word, he swung his club against the left side of my head. I didn't feel any pain, just the thud of the blow, and my legs giving way, I raised an arm- a reflex motion- as I curled up in the prayer for protection position. And then the same trooper hit me again. And everything started to spin."[34]

The troopers continued to use force, swinging their nightsticks with no fear of hitting any of the marchers. You could hear that awful, sickening sound of nightsticks coming down on limbs and heads. White spectators who'd lined the area on the south side of the highway to watch the show, with their Confederate flags waving in the air, cheered loudly to show their support of the troopers knocking down the Black marchers. They continued to cheer as if they were at a football game as the troopers on horseback knocked down marchers, and the

Black citizens screamed in terror and tried to get together in a protective shield from the advancing troopers.

The Black marchers tried not to suck in the tear-gassed air and huddled together in an effort to lessen the impact of the men on horseback who rode through them. They continued to scream and shiver with fear. Then, there was a loud sound, almost like a blast that went through the air on the bridge. One of the marchers glimpsed in the direction of the troopers and terrifyingly yelled out, "Tear gas!"

The dark cloud of tear gas swallowed up the air above the marchers. Everything slowed down like a moment in time that was frozen. They tried to cover their mouths with their hands just to get some breaths out and not choke on the air around them. The tear gas stung their eyes and their skin like tiny rocks. It was almost impossible for them to see anything through the choking smoke. It would later be revealed that this particular tear gas was a highly toxic one, called C-4. It was used specifically to create a wave of nausea for the intended victims.

Lewis described what it was like when the tear gas exploded: "I began choking, coughing. I couldn't get air into my lungs. I felt as if I was taking my last breath. If there was ever a time in my life for me to panic, it should have been then. But I didn't. I remember how strangely calm I felt as I thought, this is it. People are going to die here. I'm going to die here."[35]

What would be known forever to the world as Bloody Sunday in the United States had begun.

FIGURE 1: Livingstone College students Richard Stewart, Vaughn Eason, Charles Keyes and James Boger are led to the patrol car after attempting to enter the main floor and integrate the movie theater in Downtown Salisbury, North Carolina, in fall 1962. Source: The Livingstonian 1962, Livingstone College, Salisbury, North Carolina.

FIGURE 2: Two-minute warning by Selma police to marchers with John Lewis in brown trench coat—Bloody Sunday. March 7, 1965. Source: 1965 Spider Martin/Briscoe Center for American History.

FIGURE 3: One of the troopers takes off his gas mask after the Bloody Sunday attack near the Edmund Pettus Bridge, standing over a victim of the beatings, with a billy club in his hand. Source: 1965 Spider Martin/Briscoe Center for American History.

FIGURE 4: The four-day march from Selma to Montgomery begins with the Edmund Pettus Bridge in the background—March 21, 1965. Source: 1965 Spider Martin/Briscoe Center for American History.

FIGURE 5 : Sheyann Webb- Christburg and Dr. Martin Luther King Jr. at a break during the Selma marches—March 1965. Source: Sheyann Webb-Christburg.

FIGURE 6: Marchers on their way to Montgomery, escorted by the Alabama National Guard—March 22, 1965. Source: 1965 Spider Martin/Briscoe Center for American History.

FIGURE 7: Forest Grant Jones and Betty Coates Jones on their wedding day—August 21, 1965. Source: Forest Grant Jones and Betty Coates Jones.

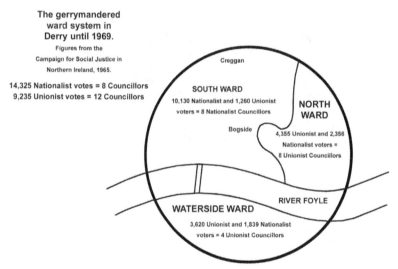

FIGURE 8: Derry's gerrymandered wards until 1969. Source: Unknown, Julieann Campbell.

FIGURE 9: Old Derry poster—late 1960s. Source: Unknown, Julieann Campbell.

FIGURE 10: Derry Civil Rights Association banner—late 1960s. Source: Courtesy of Museum of Free Derry.

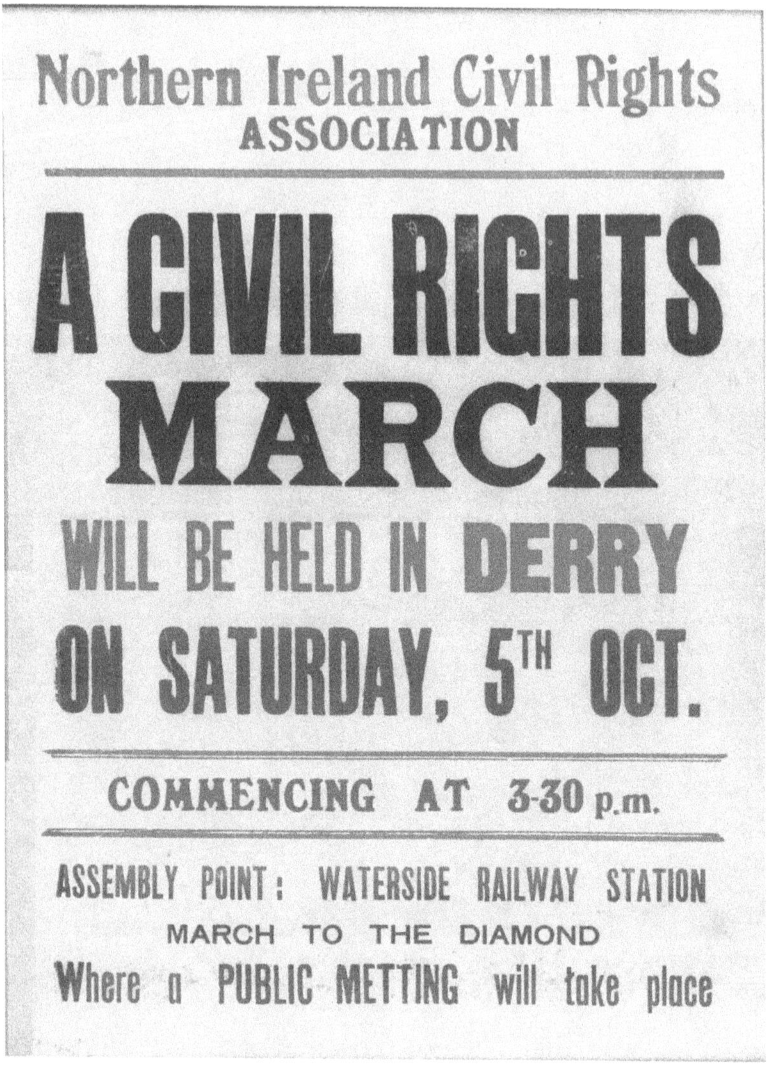

FIGURE 11: Northern Ireland Civil Rights Association poster for Civil Rights march on October 5, 1968, in Derry. Source: Courtesy of Museum of Free Derry.

FIGURE 12: October 5, 1968, Duke Street Clash in Derry during Civil Rights march. Source: Unknown, Julieann Campbell.

FIGURE 13: Scenes at Burntollet during the People's Democracy March—January 1969. Source: Pacemaker Press.

FIGURE 14: Bloodied protester after the attack on Burntollet Bridge—January 4, 1969. Source: Pacemaker Press.

FIGURE 15: Scene from People's Democracy March—January 4, 1969. Source: Pacemaker Press.

FIGURE 16: Vinny McCormick, one of the 1969 marchers who took refuge in the nearby river. Source: The *Irish Times*.

FIGURE 17: John Hume arrested by a British soldier during a peaceful Civil Rights protest in Derry, 1971. Source: Alan Lewis Photopress Belfast.

FIGURE 18: A mass demonstration against internment in the Bogside, 1971. Source: The *Derry Journal*.

FIGURE 19: British soldiers move in to try to displace a sit-down protest at Elmwood Terrace and Laburnum, Derry, 1971. Source: The *Derry Journal*.

FIGURE 20: A protest at the Martello Tower near Magilligan Beach near the British Army camp where local internees were held—photo taken through a loophole in a nearby fortification. Source: The *Derry Journal*.

FIGURE 21: Young men throw stones at the RUC Barracks at Rosemount after 60 men were snatched from their beds on August 9, 1971. Source: The *Derry Journal*.

FIGURE 22: John Hume remonstrates with a British soldier at the top of Westland Street, Derry, 1971. Source: The *Derry Journal*.

FIGURE 23: Billy McVeigh facing down an Army truck during internment protests in Derry, 1971. Source: Billy McVeigh/Clive Lumpkin.

FIGURE 24: Bernadette Devin, 1980s. Source: Pacemaker Press.

FIGURE 25: Eamonn McCann, 1980s. Source: Pacemaker Press.

CHAPTER 14

BLOODY SUNDAY—THE IMPACT

The conflict that March morning on the Pettus Bridge was the result of the newfound impetus in the Black community that they would not be denied their rights anymore. It stemmed from World War II when Black soldiers fought so valiantly for freedom and democracy, then came back home to the South and were treated as second-class citizens. In the following 20 years, there were attempts to suppress voting throughout the South, and whites in the South claimed that they would not integrate under any circumstances.

The troopers rushed toward the marchers in a wave as some fell down to protect themselves and others ran as they were chased by the troopers and men on horseback. The tear gas continued to settle on the marchers as nightsticks swung indiscriminately on women and children. J. L. Chestnut Jr. described what he saw as the nightsticks flew, "Through the haze of tear gas, I saw a posse man raise his club and smash it down on a woman's head as if he were splitting a watermelon."[1]

The scene was pure chaos.

The marchers gleamed with sweat as they dragged themselves onto the grassy area, hunched over, enduring the beatings.

Lewis described what he saw, "I really felt that I saw death at that moment, that I looked it right in its face. And it felt strangely soothing. I had a feeling that it would be so easy to just lie down there, just lie down and let it take me away."[2]

Some of the marchers were so weak from the nightstick blows that they could not even move or stand up. Many of them thought they were about to die. Some fell to their knees, praying for their lives and attempting to protect their bodies. But as the marchers' situation deteriorated, the event descended into a Darwinian state of survival of the fittest.

GOOD TROUBLE

Roy Reed, a reporter who was there on the scene from the *NY Times*, described what he saw after the troopers and possemen went after the marchers:

The troopers rushed forward, their blue uniforms and white helmets blurring into a flying wedge as they moved. The wedge moved with such force that it seemed almost to pass over the waiting column instead of through it. The first 10 or 20 Negroes were swept to the ground screaming, arms and legs flying, and packs and bags went skittering across the grassy divider strip and on to the pavement on both sides. Those still on their feet retreated. The troopers continued pushing, using both the force of their bodies and the prodding of their nightsticks. A cheer went up from the White spectators lining the south side of the highway. The mounted possemen spurred their horses and rode at the run into the retreating mass. The Negroes cried out as they crowded together for protection, and the Whites on the sidelines whooped and cheered. The Negroes paused in their retreat for perhaps a minute, still screaming and huddling together. Suddenly there was a report like a gunshot and a grey cloud spewed over the troopers and Negroes. Tear gas, someone yelled. The cloud began covering the highway. Newsmen, who were confined by four troopers to a corner 100 yards away, began to lose sight of the action. But before the cloud finally hid it all, there were several seconds of unobstructed view. Fifteen or twenty nightsticks could be seen through the gas, flailing at the heads of the marchers. The Negroes broke and ran. Scores of them streamed across the parking lot of the Selma Tractor Company. Troopers and possemen, mounted and unmounted, went after them.[3]

More tear gas bombs went off in the sky above the marchers. One witness to the event thought they heard a gun go off and said, "It was a shotgun blast [...] the pellets tore a hole in the brick wall of a hamburger stand five feet from him."[4]

Minutes seemed like hours for the marchers as time went by. After fifteen minutes, a good number of the Black marchers had been detained. Other marchers started to walk in the direction of the Selma city center through the haze of tear gas. They were coughing, sobbing and struggling through what they had just encountered and seen. A few women were simply lying on the grassy area on the bridge where the troopers had knocked them down savagely. Troopers walked toward them and ordered the women to get up and vacate the area. The women did not move, stunned by what had occurred.

Lewis was bleeding from his injuries to his head and the pain was almost unbearable. He was still on the ground, looking around at the carnage. He said, "I could see a young kid- a teenaged boy-sitting on the ground with a

Bloody Sunday—the Impact 91

gaping cut in his head, the blood just gushing out. [...] People were weeping. Some were vomiting from the tear gas. Men on horses were moving in all directions, purposely riding over the top of fallen people, bringing their animals' hooves down on shoulders, stomachs and legs."[5]

The scene was incredible for many observers from the press. A mob of White citizens began to join in and attack both cameramen and reporters. People started to unspool details about what had occurred on Pettus Bridge. Witnesses said they saw possemen using whips on the marchers who were trying to run as they crossed the bridge again. Lloyd Russell, a photographer on the scene, said the following about what he'd seen from the other side of Pettus Bridge: "At least four carloads of possemen overtake the marchers as they re-entered Broad Street [...] the possemen jumped from the cars and began beating the Negroes with nightsticks."[6]

Some of the Black marchers did not go down without a fight. Ron Gibson, a reporter from the Birmingham News, said the following: "Sheriff Clark led a charge with about half a dozen possemen to try to force the Negroes from Sylvan Street into the church [...] the Negroes fell back momentarily, then surged forward and began throwing bricks and bottles [...] the officers had to retreat until reinforcements arrived. One posseman was cut under the eye with a brick."[7]

There were well over 200 troops and men on horseback with riot guns and pistols that chased down the Black citizens of the Browns Chapel Methodist Church into their apartments and houses. On the front page of the New York Times the next day was the following: "Alabama Police Use Gas and Clubs to Rout Negroes."[8]

Lewis finally was able to get up and move back across the bridge. The possemen continued to chase the marchers back toward Browns Chapel. Lewis and the other leaders tried to get as many marchers inside the church as possible for their own safety.

Sheyann Webb-Christburg remembered the scene as she followed the adults' lead and ran for her life. All she wanted to do was to get back home.

"I'll never forget it. It was the most traumatic experience of my life as a child and I'll never forget what happened on that march. People were falling, bleeding and crying. I was running like many others off of that bridge, my eyes were burning real bad from the tear gas. I was really in a frantic state of mind, trying to run and make my way home because the dogs and horses were still running behind people. I was running and Hosea Williams picked me up and my little legs were still galloping in his arms and I turned to him and said in my childish voice, "Put me down because you're not running fast enough," Webb-Christburg recalled.[9]

92   GOOD TROUBLE

Richard Smiley said about the horrific scene, "Once we got back across the bridge, they beat us all the way back to Browns Chapel."[10]

There were at least 17 Black marchers who were hospitalized with injuries and about 40 more who were given emergency treatment for minor injuries and to help with the effects of the tear gas. Dr. King was supposed to be the leader of the march, but he ended up not going because he learned that the Alabama troopers would block the protest march. Mrs. Doyle King and her mother were among the first ones to be arrested in the first wave of marchers in the group that was on the bridge.

The ground floor of a two-story building next to the Browns Chapel was turned into a makeshift hospital to help the injured. Marchers were on the floors and chairs, a number of them crying openly and screaming in pain. Little girls were moaning with injuries and some were unconscious on tables. Doctors and nurses worked frantically to help the injured and aid tear-gassed marchers with baking soda and water to ease the burning in their eyes. A number of marchers reported many injuries. There were marchers who suffered broken ribs, broken arms, broken legs and many bruises and cuts to their bodies. Others had broken jaws and teeth.

A United Press International reporter gave his account of the possemen chasing the marchers: "The troopers and possemen, under Gov. George C. Wallace's orders to stop the Negroes' Walk for Freedom from Selma to Montgomery, chased the screaming, bleeding marchers nearly a mile back to their church, clubbing them as they ran. Ambulances screamed in relays between Good Samaritan Hospital and Browns Chapel Church, carrying hysterical men, women and children suffering head wounds and tear gas burns."[11]

Lewis was among the number of people who were injured in the march. Before Lewis went to the hospital for treatment, he and Hosea Williams led the marchers back to the church after their run-in with the troops. He made a speech to the marchers who had gathered inside the church; all of them were angry and crying because of what they'd just been through on the streets.

Lewis said, "I don't see how President Johnson can send troops to Vietnam- I don't see how he can send troops to the Congo- I don't see how he can send troops to Africa and can't send troops to Selma, Alabama."[12] The crowd erupted in agreement with those words from him. He continued, "Next time we march, we may have to keep going when we get to Montgomery. We may have to go on to Washington."[13]

He had been admitted to the Good Samaritan Hospital with a possible skull fracture. Lewis said the waiting room was packed with others who had

Bloody Sunday—the Impact 93

suffered injuries from the officers and possemen on the street. Everything smelled like tear gas; that bitter smell permeated the area.

After Lewis's speech was printed in the NY Times, in Washington DC, the Justice Department announced that agents for the FBI (Federal Bureau of Investigation) in Selma had been directed to, "make a full and prompt investigation and to gather evidence whether unnecessary force was used by law officers and others to halt the march."[14]

The troopers and possemen, more than 150 of them, had continued to beat anyone still on the streets. They finally left the location later that night. The marchers and other Black civic leaders headed to Browns Chapel to meet and strategize about what to do next. There were well over 700 present at the meeting. They pondered the situation in front of them. The plan was to march two days later to Montgomery.

After the marchers were beaten back to the church, some of the marchers talked about going back to their houses and getting their guns. They were frustrated and angry. Reverend Reese and others persuaded them not to. He implored that they needed to stay the course with the nonviolent way of thinking.[15]

Christburg knew she was lucky. "Hosea Williams comforted me and the others all the way back to my home at the GW Carver projects."[16]

From the outset, Hosea Williams, John Lewis and the other leaders had been dealt a difficult hand. It was a well-organized march facing huge odds with one of the most dangerous sheriffs in the South, but Lewis and Williams had done all they could to preserve the spirit and goals of the march and to lift the marchers' psyches. The marchers were showing signs of physical and mental exhaustion. The leaders knew that if they did not quell the disillusionment of the marchers, it would destroy any goals they had.

Hosea Williams stood in front of the solemn-looking group and surveyed the scene as it looked like survivors from a war battle. He knew that unity was crucial to their mentality. He said the following to the group that evening, "I fought in World War II and I once was captured by the German army, and I want to tell you that the Germans never were as inhuman as the state troopers of Alabama."[17]

When the news of the bloody march was broadcast all over the world, it was greeted with disgust and disbelief. People in other countries wondered how your own people in a country built on liberty could be so cruel. The news showed fifteen minutes of the march and the attacks on the marchers. Lewis explained the impact that the scenes had on the country and the public in general, "[...] something about that day in Selma touched a nerve deeper than anything that had come before [...] the mass movement of those troopers on foot and riders on horseback rolling into and over two long lines of stoic, silent, unarmed people. [...] The sight of them rolling over us like human tanks was something that had never been seen before."[18]

The world couldn't believe what they'd seen. Women and children were being attacked by armed men on horseback. President Johnson knew he would have to act on what had been on the television for the world to see. Dr. King agreed that there would be a march and he would lead it.

Mrs. Gildersleve-Blackwell said, "The video of Bloody Sunday brought everything to light. People knew about segregation but when you see it in your face and the hatred that was associated with it, it takes on a whole new meaning."[19]

For the Black Civil Rights movement, there would be no more looking back in fear.

CHAPTER 15

THE AFTERMATH—THE SELMA TO MONTGOMERY MARCH

Twenty-four hours later, Martin Luther King Jr. woke up and was confronted with the grim reality of what had occurred on Bloody Sunday. He decided that he and the others would finish the march to Montgomery. King and the other leaders were determined not to turn back. King heard from the Selma marchers about their harrowing experiences with Sheriff Clark and his possemen and called their determination to finish the march an unfinished goal. Despite the disappointment and heavy injuries on Bloody Sunday, King was determined to keep the march afloat and going and to fulfill the end result of making it to Montgomery. Despite the agony that marchers had endured on Pettus Bridge, they had remained incredibly loyal to King and his belief in what they were trying to do. Looking at the marchers, King saw their spirit was still alive, struggling but alive and he hoped that would be enough for them to prevail with the march.

Dr. King went to see John Lewis in the hospital. When visiting Lewis, Dr. King explained the public and media furor happening on the national and international stages. King assured Lewis that the march would move forward. The federal government and Justice Department representatives had arrived at the hospital to interview Lewis. King saw what they were doing as something bigger, something that would resonate for years to come as seen by these words: "I want young men and young women who are not alive today but will come into this world with new privileges and new opportunities. I want them to know and see that these new privileges and opportunities did not come without somebody suffering and sacrificing for them."[1]

The march would not take place on Tuesday since there was a judicial injunction by the judge. King and other leaders tried to find a compromise.

96 GOOD TROUBLE

Incredibly, Governor Wallace had the brazenness to proclaim that what Clark and the deputies did the day before actually saved lives. The country was on fire and demanded action. Two days after Bloody Sunday, there were demonstrations and marches in over eighty cities to protest the brutality seen in Selma and to speak about passing the Voting Rights Act. Congress also proclaimed the Selma attack a tragedy and that voting rights had to be passed as soon as possible.

Feelings for voting rights legislation gained momentum. Lewis had been in the hospital for three days at that point and was excited by what he was seeing and hearing throughout the country.

Two days later, King addressed supporters in Brown Chapel and said, "We have a right to walk the highway. We have the right to walk to Montgomery if our feet can get us there. We must let the nation know and we must let the world know that it is necessary to protest this threefold evil—the problem of the denial of the right to vote to police brutality that we continue to face and faced in its most vicious form last Sunday, and then the attempt to block first amendment privileges."[2]

Richard Smiley, one of the marchers on Bloody Sunday, said about the King speech at Brown's Chapel, "Dr. King said your soul is in Montgomery but your body is here." He tried to encourage us about moving forward because we were confused about what had happened on Bloody Sunday. [3]

King decided to march on Tuesday, March 9th, and nobody knew what was going to happen with another confrontation on the Edmund Pettus Bridge. Over two thousand marchers, led by King left Brown's Chapel early Tuesday afternoon. They headed the same route that John Lewis and others had taken close to forty-eight hours ago. All of the marchers thought they would try to make their way to Montgomery as well.

The marchers in unison sang the song, "Turn Me Round," as Dr. King led them in front of the Texaco gas station on the right side of the road, with the iconic red letters shining in the sky.

King and the marchers were stopped at the bridge by a U.S. marshal who read an order from Judge Johnson. The order stated that the march was against the original injunction.

King continued with the marchers and led them over the crest of the bridge. When they got to the bottom of the other side, there were armed troopers waiting for them again, a sight that was eerily similar to Sunday when the marchers were beaten severely. The marchers nervously waited for the worst to happen.

Rev. Ralph Abernathy, one of Dr. King's top leaders, was with King when they were faced with the troopers and said, "Let us bow in prayer." The

The Aftermath 97

marchers all got on one knee as the troopers armed in riot gear simply stood and watched. Abernathy continued, "Pray that Black and White people will live together right here in Alabama, and in the black belt of brothers. And the lions will lie down with the lambs, the calf and the tiger together. Until that day comes, keep us restless and dissatisfied. Keep us working and working and fighting for freedom."[4]

When the prayer ended, surprisingly the troopers stood aside and made a path for the marchers to make their way to Montgomery. Dr. King and the marchers said nothing. What they did was simply turn around and head back to Brown's Chapel. This was known as Turnaround Tuesday.

Smiley was there for that march as well and said, "They let us kneel and pray and we turned around and went back to Browns Chapel."[5]

Many of the marchers were both angry and confused. They didn't have any idea what was going on. What the marchers didn't know was that King had made a deal the night before with the federal authorities. He agreed that he'd only march to the bridge, turn around, and wait to hear what happens with the hearing about the march. The march on Tuesday was a symbolic move for King. It was something he thought he had to do after what had occurred on Sunday.

John Lewis had agreed with King's actions when many others didn't. He said about King's decision, "I had no problem with what Dr. King did. I thought it was in keeping with the philosophy of the movement, that there comes a time when you must retreat [...] there is nothing wrong with coming back to fight another day. Dr. King knew that Judge Johnson was going to give us what we were asking for if we simply followed procedure."[6]

The night of March 9, 1965, there were attacks on several clergymen in the city of Selma. King was at Browns Chapel that night and said the following to the audience about the attacks: "You know things happened here today... concerning the three Unitarian ministers who were beaten about an hour or so ago. I understand one was so brutally beaten that he had to be rushed to the hospital in Birmingham with a possible brain concussion. I wish that we now bow our heads in silent prayer for these brothers who came here to be with us today and who marched with us across the Alabama River, who marched to witness for our freedom and who marched to witness their own personal dedication to the cause of justice."[7]

Reverend James Reeb died from injuries sustained that night, two days later on March 11, 1965.

After Reeb's death, the violence got worse in Alabama, especially in Birmingham and Montgomery. Word was also getting around that Judge

98 GOOD TROUBLE

Johnson was close to agreeing to lift the injunction that the marchers wanted. Due to the tense atmosphere in Selma and all around the nation, President Johnson decided to address Congress on March 19, 1965. The address was televised that same evening. It was probably the most important speech of his presidency and definitely the strongest words any President had ever made about the civil rights movement.

President Johnson said, "At times history and fate meet at a single time in a single place to shape a turning point in man's unending search for freedom. So it was at Lexington and Concord. So it was a century ago at Appomattox. So it was last week in Selma, Alabama. [...] What happened in Selma is part of a far larger movement which reaches into every section and state of America. It is the effort of American Negroes to secure for themselves the full blessings of American life. Their cause must be our cause too. Because it is not just Negroes, but really it is all of us who must overcome the crippling legacy of bigotry and injustice. And we shall overcome."[8]

The speech was over forty-five minutes long. It was interrupted forty times by applause, and twice the President received standing ovations.

The following day, Judge Johnson announced that he had issued his ruling. The march from Selma to Montgomery would be allowed. President Johnson also stated that he would use federal troops along with police units to help the marchers walk peacefully and safely without injury or the loss of life to Montgomery.

The march would begin on Sunday, March 21, 1965. This time the leaders would have five days to prepare, and it wouldn't be the spontaneous march that Bloody Sunday was. Many groups would end up participating: SNCC, SCLC, NAACP, the Courageous Eight and other human rights and civil rights groups. They planned for everything, which included: air mattresses, blankets, tents, generators, and campsite materials.

Mrs. Gildersleeve-Blackwell said of the preparations, "Everybody saw what was going on in Selma and dropped what they were doing and came, and they converged on Selma. It was a beautiful thing to see. People of all races and faiths to bring light to the situation."[9]

Just like the originally planned march, it would be a protest march/mass demonstration to get the aid and assistance from Alabama Governor George Wallace to grant the Black citizens in the state of Alabama their constitutional voting rights. The demonstration march to Montgomery would also ask to end police brutality and to highlight that it was a serious problem for the Black community that needed to be dealt with and brought attention to. The march would be nonviolent and peaceful in nature.

The Aftermath 99

It was announced that the two westbound lanes of Highway 80 between Selma and Montgomery would be closed off for the march, which would last five days. The traffic during those days would be re-routed to the eastbound lanes. Helicopters and planes would patrol the air, and demolition teams would make sure the area before the marchers was clear of any hazards such as bombs.

On Sunday, March 21, 1965, the march began at Browns Chapel around 1 p.m. with over three thousand people ready to be led by Dr. King and the other leaders. King and the others wore Hawaiian leis. He led in front and was accompanied by John Lewis, Rosa Parks, and Reverend Reese from the Courageous Eight. People from all over the nation had joined the column of marchers. All types of people from all walks of life: ministers, nuns, teachers, Black and White. Following the procession were newsmen in their cars along with the procession of marchers.

As the marchers approached the Edmund Pettus Bridge, the same troopers were there just like they were when they beat the protestors on Bloody Sunday two weeks ago. However, this time, the National Guard was present. Minutes later, they were out of the city and on the hard pavement of Highway 80.

Sheriff Clark was on the side of the road watching the marchers in his signature dark glasses and fedora. He had his usual "NEVER" button on his left lapel with a white background and dark letters. A reporter approached him to get his view of the new march.

"Sheriff Clark, are you heaving a sigh of relief that all of this is moving out of your county?"[10]

Clark gave a smirk and said, "I think Martin Luther King will do as much as he wants to and he'll move out [...] It's all been due to outsiders [...] It's made up of one fourth communists and one half pro communist."[11]

The first day of the march, the group covered over seven miles. When evening came, the campsites were set up to help with the temperatures that had dropped quite a bit. A family named the Halls owned a farm where the marchers camped for the night. There were well over two thousand marchers who slept in the large tents they had brought with them. Dinner that night consisted of spaghetti, baked beans, and coffee. Everyone enjoyed the evening together, building fires, singing songs, and soaking in the camaraderie.

Webb-Christburg was there as well. "When the march took place, I was still that disobedient child. Instead of going to school, I would march miles, and then I would get transported back with the cars taking the food and supplies back and forth. But I'd still get up and join them again the next day."[12]

Richard Smiley said this about the march to Montgomery, "It wasn't easy on the way to Montgomery. The National Guard was there to protect us, but

100 GOOD TROUBLE

even they didn't like us. You could tell that. Some would make comments to us. We marched several miles a day, and we would camp out on the property of Black owners. And they would feed us everywhere we went. We would march in the rain; it didn't matter to any of us."[13]

Reverend Reese was on the first leg of the march as well. Marvin Reese Jr. said about his grandfather's involvement with the long march, "He did the first leg and then stopped to take a pastor's job. He ended up catching back up with the group later on in the march."[14]

The second day of the march, the stride of the marchers was better than on the first day. The temperature was about thirty degrees when they left first thing in the morning. The marchers arrived in Lowndes County around noon. This was a county where the population was overwhelmingly Black. However, because of voter disenfranchisement, this was a county with fewer than 60 registered Black voters. Along the trek through the county, Black residents were on the side of the road, smiling and cheering the marchers on. They ended up covering close to sixteen miles before it became dark. That night, the marchers stayed on the land of Rosie Steele, a 78-year-old Black woman. That evening, the cool temperatures were also were accompanied by a cold rain.

Dr. King returned to the march on the third day, Tuesday, around noon after a speaking engagement in Cleveland, Ohio. He was dressed in a brown trapper hat, almost as if he was a hunter looking for a raccoon, and a black jacket. The weather was horrible as the marchers, now numbered three thousand, walked on a road widening to four lanes without a limitation on the number of participants. The rain lasted most of the day. John Lewis said about the atmosphere, "The weather was miserable, but no one complained. No one got tired. No one fell back. To me, there was never a march like this one before, and there hasn't been one since. The incredible sense of community [...] was overwhelming. We felt bonded with one another, with the people we passed, with the entire nation."[15]

A reporter walked with King as they marched and interviewed him.

"How do you feel about the protection that's been given to you on this march?"

King continued to march and said, "I think this is a real demonstration of the commitment of the federal government to protect the constitutional rights of Negro citizens. The protection has been very thorough, and they are working under the guidance, power, and influence of the federal government to see that things are carried out in an orderly manner. So, I think that everybody has to recognize that this symbolizes a new commitment and a new determination

The Aftermath 101

on the part of the federal government to take the kind of vigorous line that will assure the rights of Negro citizens in this nation."[16]

The marchers covered close to eleven miles on the third day. They were just miles outside of Montgomery, Alabama.

Dr. King was dressed in a blue short-sleeve shirt with a funny-looking sailor hat on his head and dark pants on the fourth day. A reporter walked with him again, trying to get a few words from him. As they marched, King and his wife were flanked by men carrying the American flag.

The reporter asked, "Dr. King, how are things shaping up for tomorrow?"[17]

"Things are shaping up beautifully [...] We have people coming in from all over the country. I expect we'll have representatives from almost every state in the Union and naturally a large number from the state of Alabama. And we hope to see the greatest witness for freedom that has ever taken place on the steps of the capital of any state in the South, and this whole march adds drama to this total thrust."[18]

That evening at the campsite outside of the city of St. Jude, a number of international celebrities had arrived there to join in with the marchers before the last miles to Montgomery. They included Harry Belafonte (who performed for the marchers that evening), Nina Simone (who did a blistering rendition of Mississippi Goddamn for the marchers), Sammy Davis Jr., Tony Bennett (who sang for the marchers), Shelley Winters, Ossie Davis, Leonard Bernstein, Johnny Mathis, Peter, Paul and Mary (who sang for the marchers), and Joan Baez. Interestingly enough, they all got on the stage which was made from stacks of coffins that were loaned by a funeral home. You read that right, a stack of coffins!

As night came over the marchers, the march had turned into a festive occasion for well over four hours. The crowd had grown by the hour by hundreds, only adding to the already thousands of people there, close to 20,000.

That night, Dr. King took the stage to speak to the crowd, "I just want to say to you how much we are indebted to all of the famous artists and entertainers who have taken time to be with us in Montgomery, Alabama, as we march on the state capital tomorrow morning."[19]

That statement brought rapturous applause from the crowd as they knew what lay ahead of them the next day.

Sheyann Webb Christburg had made her way to St. Jude as well, but trouble was brewing for her, being a young child on the march and with no parents around to accompany her. She was there the night before, but not for long.

"I was on the last leg of the march to St. Jude, and during this time, I was under the umbrella of Dr. King's entourage. His secretary found out my

102   GOOD TROUBLE

parents didn't know I was there, and they were contacted. My dad came to pick me up from St. Jude the night of the rally. I cried all the way back home because I wanted to march."[20]

It was an absolutely gorgeous, sunny fifth day for the last leg of the march on Thursday, March 25, 1965. Over 50,000 people were now were in the group of marchers that headed for the state capital building, the home of Governor George Wallace. However, there was a tension felt among the people as they prepared for the last leg. Orange vests were handed out to the 300 who had marched all the way and would walk behind Dr. King. The marchers had six miles to go, and they would be at the front steps. At the same time, there had been a death threat against Dr. King, one of the many at the time on the leader. Because of the threat, the ministers on the march all wore blue suit. They hoped that with them all dressed alike, a possible sniper wouldn't have a sure shot since they wouldn't be able to tell from that far who was who.

Richard Smiley talked about finally reaching Montgomery, "We got into Montgomery with all of the dignitaries such as Sammy Davis Jr. One guy that we called Jim had walked all the way on his crutch to Montgomery. When we got there, that's where Dr. King prepared us for his speech 'How Long, Not Long'."[21]

In one of the famous pictures as the group neared the capitol building, Reverend Reese was there, walking beside Coretta Scott King. Marvin Reese Jr. said, "You can see my grandfather with his hat on next to Dr. King's wife. In his hand, he was holding Dr. King's speech 'How Long, Not Long,' that he would give at the steps of the capitol."[22]

There was another surprise attendee at the state capitol that day.

It was Sheyann Webb Christburg.

"The next day, my father got up early in the morning. He didn't punish me, and he took me back to the march and joined me marching from St. Jude to the capital."[23]

Marching was in her heart, and she had made it to the finish line.

The 50,000-strong group walked past the Whitley Hotel with onlookers peeking through the windows for a glimpse of the spectacle. The marchers made their way around the fountain on Court Square and up Dexter Avenue. Black and White citizens lined the street to watch. The marchers ended up in the middle of the square in front of the shiny white state capitol building, with the Confederate flag swaying back and forth in the March air. Helicopters were up in the sky keeping an eye on the events. Word was Governor Wallace was inside, but no one ever did see him that day of the march. The scene in front of the capitol appeared like a military zone with hundreds of National

The Aftermath   103

Guard and Army troops who patrolled along the expanse of Dexter Avenue. You could also see soldiers on top of buildings who kept an eye from above.

A podium was set up on the trailer of a flatbed truck. There were loud-speakers and a microphone for whoever got on the stage. There were a few different speakers and a performance from Peter, Paul, and Mary. The last part was Dr. King on the stage. John Lewis said it was, "one of the most important speeches of his life."[24]

Officers in green helmets were aligned to guard the Capitol and were positioned on the steps.

Dr. King got to the microphone and took a deep breath. As he began to speak, he knew his words would resonate with all Americans, not just Black and White.

He started:

Last Sunday more than 8,000 of us started a mighty walk from Selma, Alabama. They told us we wouldn't get here. There were those who said we'd get here only over their dead bodies. All the world today knows that we are here and we are standing before the forces of power in the state of Alabama saying we ain't gonna let anybody turn us around. Today I want to tell the city of Selma. Today I want to say to the state of Alabama. Today I want to say to the people of America and the nations of the world that we are not about to turn around. We are on the move now. Yes, we're on the move and no wave of racism can stop us. The burning of our churches will not deter us. The bombing of our homes will not dissuade us. The beating and killing of our clergymen and young people will not divert us. The wanton release of their known murderers will not discourage us. We're on the move now. Like an idea whose time has come. Not even the marching of mighty armies can halt us. We're moving to the land of freedom. I know you're asking today how long will it take? Somebody is asking how long will prejudice blind the visions of man. I come to say to you this afternoon how ever difficult the moment, however frustrating the hour, it will not be long. Because truth crushed to earth will rise again. How long? Not long. Because no lie can live forever. How long? Not long [...] our God is marching on. Glory, hallelujah [...] his truth is marching on.[25]

King's voice had never sounded so powerful. It was no doubt one of his best, if not the best, speech he'd ever made. Even better than the "I Have A Dream" speech.

The nonviolent protest in Selma won many supporters through the violent images on television. It had swung public opinion toward the marchers more than anything else could come close to. As President Johnson said afterward,

104   GOOD TROUBLE

"There is no Negro problem. There is no Southern problem. There is only an American problem."[26] These words were part of his movement to finally do something about voting rights.

Sadly, there were some negative impacts from the Selma to Montgomery march. One was that Mrs. Doyle King's family was one of many families that were blacklisted in the state of Alabama. Ernest Doyle suffered financially, and the family had to have help to pay their mortgage. Mrs. Doyle King's mother (Ruth Doyle) was a teacher at the time, and she ended up losing her job because she had attended meetings for civil rights. Ruth Doyle ended up taking a teaching job in Georgia and would drive round trip to Selma. Unfortunately, she was killed in a car accident during one of those round trip drives from Georgia.

Mrs. Doyle King said the following about how her family was treated, "We were blacklisted in the state of Alabama. Even when I left the South to teach in the North it had an impact on me. We were penalized so much because of the movement, I was reluctant to talk about the civil rights movement anywhere because we could lose financially. In Alabama, we couldn't get jobs, we couldn't get loans from the banks. I blame it indirectly for my mother's fatal car crash in Georgia. Even our home on Franklin, we had to get help for our mortgage."[27]

It was a difficult return for Richard Smiley as well. On his way back to Selma in the back of a flatbed truck, he noticed a car that had run off the road but thought nothing about it until later when he had found out why that car was off the road. Smiley learned that a White woman, Viola Liuzzo, had been transporting marchers back to Selma from Montgomery when they were ambushed by the Klan. Leroy Moton, a classmate of Smiley's, was in the car with Liuzzo, and he miraculously survived.

Smiley got to his foster home and saw that all of his possessions were on the front porch. His social worker told him that he had to leave. Smiley became homeless for some time after that and ended up staying at the offices of the SCLC. He also ended up dropping out of high school. The story ended on a good note for Richard Smiley as he ended up living in Tampa, Florida after completing high school and acquiring his Bachelors and Masters degrees. He is still involved with civil rights and goes to Selma each year for the anniversary of the march. As a foot soldier, he has met Presidents Obama and Biden, both of whom celebrated his historical accomplishments.[28]

Smiley looked back on what he did in 1965 and said, "We laid the foundation. We were committed to the right to vote. We didn't care if we died or whatever. We didn't know it would be historical. It was that important for us. That's why we got beat on the bridge."[29]

The Aftermath

Bloody Sunday and the Selma to Montgomery march were two events that spearheaded what happened four and a half months later on August 6, 1965. President Johnson signed the Voting Rights Act on this date.

President Johnson made the speech for the signing of the bill which included, "Wherever by clear and objective standards states and counties are using regulations of laws and tests to deny the right to vote then they will be struck down. The 89th Congress acted swiftly in passing this act and I intend to act with equal dispatch in enforcing this act."[30]

The speech was called the "We Shall Overcome" speech. No doubt it was one of the most important speeches any American president had given about the question of civil rights.

The law was signed in the President's room of the Capitol. It was of great historical significance since it was the same room in which President Lincoln signed the Emancipation Proclamation. The law was a huge moment; it was strong and included the suspension of literacy tests as a barrier for voting and the appointment of federal examiners to replace local officials as voter registrars. Interestingly enough, the United States is currently having issues with right-wing conspiracy theorists believing that the last point is under threat by 'corrupt' voter registrars.

That day was the climax of a long road for many Black Americans. It ushered in a day for a new America, with equal rights for all. For Civil Rights, it was the apex for the nation. One observer said, "[...] a brilliant climax which brought to a close the nonviolent struggle that had reshaped the South."[31]

Dr. King said later about the Selma march and the Voting Rights Act, "The real victory was what this period did for the psyche of the Black man. The greatness of this period is that we armed ourselves with dignity and self-respect."[32]

Mrs. Gildersleeve-Blackwell said about the events surrounding the Selma march, "The people of Selma took a stand and people hold Selma up as the start of the civil rights movement. Other places were a part of it but people point to Selma. Without Dr. King, the Courageous Eight and others, we wouldn't have gotten the traction for the movement and the voter registration process. Lots of people came to Selma for the marches and left. The people who lived there in the situation don't get enough credit for orchestrating and facilitating things to get the Voter Rights Act."[33]

Carolyn Doyle King was awarded the Voting Rights Congressional Gold Medal for being a part of the Selma to Montgomery march. This is the highest award given to civilians. She was honored as one of the 'foot soldiers' who was there at the marches. I was struck that she did not mention this to me during her interview. Her daughter, Dr. Shannah Gilliam, actually was the one who brought it to my attention. I think that shows the humility that Mrs. Doyle King has to this day, even though what she did was extremely heroic and brave.

The march changed the trajectory of Sheyann Webb Christburg's life as well. She reflected on that with me.

"Me growing up in the movement, I am truly grateful for having the opportunity to meet Dr. King, John Lewis and so many others that have passed on. I was not only a child participant but I was being mentored in a unique way. If I hadn't been in the midst of the civil rights movement in Selma, my life would have been different, including my thoughts and decisions."[34]

The Selma to Montgomery march had solved many issues. But just like Northern Ireland, the road forward would lead to many twists and turns, some good and some bad.

CHAPTER 16

THE BEGINNING OF THE CATHOLIC CIVIL RIGHTS MOVEMENT

When Ireland was partitioned in 1921, the impact was devastating for the Catholic population. The Protestant leadership's goal was to push out the Catholics and continue their stronghold on power in Northern Ireland. The events were reminiscent of the Reconstruction years after 1865 in the United States when the Black population received limited power and the pushback from White supremacists was immediate, with eventually years of terror, with Blacks being killed, burned out of their homes, pushed out of politics and left with little or nothing. For the Catholics in Northern Ireland, many of them migrated south across the border permanently. Similar to the pushback that the Blacks saw in the late 1880s—threats, violence, fired from their jobs. Stormont (the government for Northern Ireland run from London) formed the RUC and the B Specials, the latter of which terrorized the Catholic population. Comparing the B Specials to the Ku Klux Klan would not be a huge stretch.

Sadly, the Catholic population, like the Blacks under Jim Crow, had a little protection under the law. With the Special Powers Act in 1922, anyone could be arrested without a warrant or could be held for long periods of time without a charge or any type of trial. The police could search anyone without cause, introduce curfews indiscriminately and ban meetings. Torture was also not out of the ordinary, committed by the B Specials. This was similar to the whippings that the Ku Klux Klan would administer to Blacks or Whites who helped Blacks in the late 1800s.

Northern Ireland had been living under these laws, even in 1968.

Up to that point, nothing had changed for the Catholic citizens in Northern Ireland. However, the winds of change were surely blowing in the country.

108   GOOD TROUBLE

On August 24, 1968, the Northern Ireland Civil Rights Association, which had been around for a couple of years, decided the time was ripe to emerge and march and talk with the populace. The organization had been formed in early 1967 by a group of Catholics who had been influenced by the progress made by the Black population through their own civil rights movement in the United States. They organized a march from Coalisland to Dungannon. The route would conclude with a rally in the marketplace of Dungannon. The distance of the march was a relatively short one, only three miles. Bernadette Devlin was one of the people at the march, along with her brother and another friend.

She was still a student at the time and said she saw it as, "[...] an opportunity to go and catch up with all your friends and not to work that Saturday. That was my noble motive for going on the Coalisland march."[1]

One of the organizers, Michael McLoughlin, had visited the local RUC office a few weeks earlier to put in his application for the march. It mentioned there would be over 5,000 marchers and 20 bands, and civil rights placards and banners would be carried by the marchers. He said about the situation years later, "It was a bit ambitious, but we did expect 2,000-3,000. We had prepared the civil rights ground very well over a period of years, from 1963, so people were ready for it. They were going to come out, and they did come out."[2]

The march was supposed to begin at 6 p.m., and it was a beautiful, sunny evening for the procession. Crowds started to gather together in the main square of Coalisland.

When the group began to march, it was almost seven and they were led by a group of children playing accordions. Even though people had said this was not a political march or a religious one, people showed up with all types of banners saying: The Young Liberals, The Young Socialists. Men, women and children were carrying all types of signs, others saying: "End Discrimination," "Justice for All" and "Civil Rights." But they were not allowed to carry them during the march. Devlin mentioned that stewards were with them, shouting at the marchers like they were in the Army: Pick up your feet, one, two, one, two.[3]

The first Civil Rights march in the history of Northern Ireland had officially begun.

Devlin described the scene of the march, "It was an event. It was the first civil rights demonstration Northern Ireland had ever seen, and we all jogged happily, eating oranges and smoking cigarettes, and people came out of their houses to join the fun. Marchers were dropping off at every pub on the way,

The Beginning of the Catholic Civil Rights Movement   109

and the whole thing had a sort of good-natured, holiday atmosphere, with the drunk men lolloping in and out of this supposedly serious demonstration."[4]

Another group that helped with the march was the Homeless Citizen League. They were a group of young mothers. The mothers had been remembered from their protest in 1963 when they walked around the streets of the town with their baby carriages (called prams in Northern Ireland) because they were unable to secure a house for their families. This is another good example of how housing discrimination was rampant throughout the country.

The town of Dungannon was split into three different wards, but the housing had been constructed so that two of the wards would always produce Unionist candidates because of the voting rules. This would easily give the Dungannon Urban Council a majority Protestant leadership. The majority of the Catholic population were jammed into one ward. That meant poor housing and horrible conditions for the families living in those quarters.

Austin Currie, a local Nationalist Member of Parliament, was inspired by the US Civil Rights campaign and believed the march was needed. He and others had been told by the police that there had been opposition to the march and that trouble was a strong possibility. They recommended that it be rerouted. Currie and the other leaders refused and they proceeded with the march.

Francie Malloy was a 17 year old at the time and worked the march as a steward. He is now a member of the Sinn Fein political party. He said about the march, "It was magnificent. The crowds were out, they were two and three on the footpath, and they were singing We Shall Overcome. You felt we'd actually started off something new."[5]

But, as they approached Dungannon, the marchers were stopped in their path. There was a rope barricade in front of them and a huge police presence. A Loyalist crowd of protestors were behind the rows of police. As would become the norm, the Loyalist crowd were there because of Rev. Paisley; they would always schedule some sort of counterdemonstration to the Catholic march. The civil rights marchers were not going to be allowed to march.

One of the officers came over to the group and explained that, for safety reasons, the marchers needed to change their route and go into the Catholic part of Dungannon.

After those comments, the whole mood of the marchers changed.

Devlin said of that moment, "I do believe that then for the first time it dawned on people that Northern Ireland was a series of Catholic and Protestant ghettos."[6]

The stewards simply lined up, joined arms, and the speeches started. They started right there in front of the barricade, an impromptu meeting with speeches and the whole nine yards. Some people were yelling out to others that they should carry on and force their way through.

A truck was brought in as a platform for the civil rights leaders to speak. They added chairs for the speakers and a microphone. The speakers announced that they would not carry on into the town of Dugannon since this was a non-violent, peaceful march.

The marchers were getting frustrated with the realization that they would not go forward. One of the Civil Rights leaders said, "This is a non-political, peaceful demonstration. Anyone who wants to fight should get out and join the IRA."[7]

The leaders decided it would be best to wrap up the march and meeting since there was nothing else that could be done at that time. They did sing "We Shall Overcome" to finish it off. At that time, nobody really knew anything about civil rights or the civil rights anthem that had used for years in the US South.

By the time the song had ended, the NICRA (Northern Ireland Civil Rights Association) had driven off, and many of the marchers started to walk away, going on their way. A few Catholic marchers who had ventured on their own into Dungannon were beaten up by Unionist supporters, but overall it was not a bad day. Additionally, the police after it was all done, were not that bad toward the Catholics.

Devlin and others, however, were not so happy with the politicians' role in the march, "We knew something was wrong with a society where the rate of unemployment rarely fell below ten per cent; where half the houses lacked at least one basic amenity. The politicians tried to tell us it was a non-political demonstration [...] The crowd at that first ever civil rights march was interested in people's needs."[8]

Some people believe to this day that the civil rights marchers should have continued on. Others say they did the right thing because that could have caused a huge confrontation that would have turned ugly with the police and the loyalist crowd.

Currie was happy with the end result of the first civil rights march as they all sang "We Shall Overcome," which was reminiscent of the early ones in the Black civil rights movement in the States. He said, "That made a good ending. I think it was the first time there really was the civil rights anthem in Northern Ireland."[9]

The Beginning of the Catholic Civil Rights Movement   111

Another marcher that day commented, "You were at the beginning of something. You were developing something, you were growing something, and you felt you were going to achieve civil rights. The very fact that people had come together and stood up for their rights, I felt things had moved in a great way."[10]

One more thing to remember about that first march in October 1968: it wasn't just a new Civil Rights march. It was also a new thing for Catholics to be marching, full stop. There had been times in the late fifties and early sixties when the Protestant Orangemen marched. The Protestants did it on purpose to show that they could march in any area in Northern Ireland, even a Nationalist one. This march showed that Catholics were no longer going to stand by and do nothing; they would march as well, whenever they wanted to. Permit, no permit.

That first march made a huge impact on Bernadette Devlin. Since the riots in 1968, Devlin worked with the student group called People's Democracy. The group was closely related to groups in the Black Civil Rights Movement such as SNCC and others. People's Democracy had organized sit-ins and created the seventy-three mile protest march from Belfast to Derry. When thinking about the first march she said, "When you go to something like that, all the pieces click into place and you know why you're there. Some people know they've made the wrong decision and they know they shouldn't be there because you can feel where it's going, you can sense it, there's power in it. But for me I thought, yep, it all makes sense to me. This is where I should be, and this is what we need."[11]

Devlin was a folk hero for the Catholic minority in Northern Ireland, just like John Lewis was for Blacks in America. Both Devlin and Lewis demanded equal rights when it came to jobs, housing and local voting rights. They both constantly fought for people who were both poor and oppressed. Tom Foley, who wrote an article about her autobiography in 1970 said, "The book might have well been written by a black Bernadette Devlin in Harlem or Mississippi."[12]

Bernadette Devlin sympathized with Americans who were in slums and who were hated because they were Black and poor. She said, "To all these people, to whom this city and this country belong, I return what is rightfully theirs, this symbol of freedom of New York."[13] It was a golden key that was given to Devlin during a visit there, but given back to Robert Bray of the Black Panthers by Chairman of the Derry Labor Party, Eamonn McCann.

McCann told the story about the return of the key, which he still laughs about to this day.

112 GOOD TROUBLE

"Bernadette came back with this key on Wellington Street in Derry. This was after Fred Hampton had been killed in the States, one of the Black Panthers. And we asked her, 'What the hell are you doing with that key with the Blacks being killed over there?'"[14]

McCann headed to the States with the key to give it back. He said it wasn't tough to find the Black Panthers as he used that famous item from this time period, a phone book.

When he went to the headquarters of the Black Panthers, McCann was nervous. He explained that people like Stokely Carmichael were idolized by people in the Irish Civil Rights movement. McCann said, "There was something romantic about them. Their style, their self-confidence. If you were young like us, all of that was very attractive."[15]

McCann still remembers the first thing he was asked by the Black Panthers when he arrived at the headquarters.

"Do you want a jelly doughnut?" one of the ladies in the Black Panthers asked him.

That immediately relaxed McCann after hearing that introduction. Once the key was returned to the Panthers, word got around, and all of the meetings that McCann had scheduled in the States were canceled over the next few days. One of the people that he was going to meet with in Boston told him the reason for the cancellations in clear words with a racial slur, "You are associating us with those n....."[16]

McCann said he was basically thrown out of America because of his returning that key to the Black Panthers.

***

As abolitionists in Britain, we often see America—specifically the Black radical tradition in America—as the home of abolition. This is for good reason; with revolutionaries such as W. E. B. Du Bois, George Jackson and Angela Davis, Black Americans have been pioneering abolition for centuries. However, an abolitionist tradition is much closer than many of us realize. If we were only to look to the North of Ireland—or the occupied six counties—we would find a long, popular struggle against the oppressive forces of prisons and policing. Policing in Ireland was a colonial invention to suppress anti-British dissent, and it had functioned that way for centuries. After the partition of Ireland in 1920, Irish Catholics in the North of Ireland faced brutal state violence for their very existence. Gerrymandered into squalid ghettos, terrorized by police, and segregated from society, any attempt to argue or demand basic civil

The Beginning of the Catholic Civil Rights Movement

rights was ruthlessly suppressed by the state. During the early months of 1969, further acts of police brutality and loyalist vigilantism moved the Derry and Belfast movements away from nonviolence and toward self-defense. Catholics in Northern Ireland occupied a position that was comparable to Blacks in the United States.

Another leading figure in the Civil Rights Movement for the Catholics was Fionnbarra O'Dochartaigh. He passed away in 2021, and as Father Patrick Lagan said at his funeral, "O'Dochartaigh had done so much in his life from housing to employment."[17] Father Lagan said O'Dochartaigh would forever be associated with the civil rights movement in the 1960s.

O'Dochartaigh came from Derry and grew up in a republican family. He joined the Civil Rights movement after his older brother was arrested and jailed for speaking Irish. O'Dochartaigh studied in Manchester and later attended Cork University, where he studied law. He was a member of the Derry Housing Action Committee and was a popular leader in the housing protests, which started before the civil rights movement in Derry in the late 1960s. He was also a co-founder of the Northern Ireland Civil Rights Association (NICRA). Additionally, O'Dochartaigh was one of the leading organizers of the first civil rights marches on Duke Street in Derry on October 5, 1968. This was the same march that withstood an attack by the RUC.

Before the march on October 5, Derry was known as a place of despair, poverty and the realization that if you were Catholic, you could be stuck in a continuous wheel where nothing would ever change for your population. At that time, twenty-five percent of the population was unemployed and male unemployment was more than a third of the population. The sad fact was that since Northern Ireland was created, the total unemployment rate had never been lower than twelve percent for Catholics. The city was starting to be known as a flashpoint for the frustration that Catholics all around the country felt. The history of the city is poignant with the Siege of Londonderry in 1689, when the citizens inside the walls held out against the Catholics for over one hundred days before help arrived. For Protestants, it is still a place of pride because of that standoff. Many Protestants see Derry as a symbol of courage against all odds.

In 1968, Derry was truly the powder keg of Northern Ireland.

Bernadette Devlin was at the first march and it was her first time ever in the city of Derry. She had been determined to be at the march, "My only reason for making the journey on that day was to join in the civil rights march. For many years, all my visits to that city would be in connection with the struggle for civil and human rights, social and economic equality, self-determination and freedom."[18]

The posters that were put out for the march explained it all:

"Northern Ireland Civil Rights Association-

A Civil Rights March will be held in Derry on Saturday, 5th Oct. Commencing at 3:30pm.

Assembly Point: Waterside Railway Station, March to the Diamond, Where a Public Meeting will take place"

The march had been organized to draw attention to the issues faced by the Catholic citizens in Derry. Those included the usual: housing, employment and politics. The group behind the idea for the march was the NICRA (Northern Ireland Civil Rights Association). The group didn't know Derry that well and their route would be from Duke Street in the Waterside area, across Craigavon Bridge and through the city walls.

When the march was announced, the Loyalists announced that they would hold a parade on the same day, at the same time and on the same marching route as the civil rights group.

The Stormont authorities came out and announced a ban on all marches and parades. Neither side listened to the ban. It is fair to point out how the footprint of Northern Ireland after that could have been different if the march had been allowed to proceed. Sadly, we'll never know what could have been.

On a gray October 5 day, the activists decided to go ahead with the march. The ban had the opposite effect with the desire to have a huge turnout, with only 400 people gathering at the start point. On the sidewalks, there were hundreds of onlookers, curious about what was happening. Eamonn McCann said, "It was a very disappointing crowd."[19] There was a large gathering in an area in the city center called the Diamond. Interest and intrigue surrounded the march.

That being said, Devlin was impressed with the energy of the crowd. "It was electric that day. You could see it on people's faces- excitement, or alarm, or anger. Derry was alive."[20]

Signs in the crowd read: "One man, One vote" and "Smash Sectarianism."

There were speeches by several Civil Rights leaders; all three speeches lasted a combined five minutes or so.

There were hundreds of RUC officers at the march. They surrounded the narrow Duke Street. The marchers could also see that the attitude of the RUC was different than it had been before. They were armed with black batons and their steel helmets. This would later be known as a police tactic called 'kettling', where the police basically surrounded the group.

The Beginning of the Catholic Civil Rights Movement   115

Billy McVeigh was there on Duke Street at the young age of 16, from a family of nine sisters and five brothers. I was honored to meet Billy in March 2024 near the Bloody Sunday Museum in the Bogside. Billy is now 71 years old, a former boxer and still fit as a fiddle. He's got a great smile, not much hair, full of jokes and a twinkle in his eye. One of the first things he showed me was a scar that healed to look like a cross on his right shoulder blade, ironic for he has cheated death many times since his teenage years. There is a mural of him in front of the Bloody Sunday Museum, depicting him facing down the British Army tanks armed with only a brick in his young hands during the Battle of the Bogside in 1969. We shared stories, a cup of tea and exchanged numbers. He's now a friend and I love his WhatsApp messages. He's a character, in a good way. McVeigh was also featured in the BAFTA-nominated "Once Upon A Time in Northern Ireland."

The reality behind the fascinating mural is that nobody in the area knew anything about the photograph. This tank was coming at full speed toward Billy. After he launched the brick, they fired four or five rubber bullets at him. As Billy fell to the ground, the tank was still coming at him. A guy rolled a nail bomb toward the tank. Billy knew he would either get killed by the tank or jump over the nail bomb. He quickly made the decision to jump over the nail bomb and he got away—one of many bullets dodged by Billy during his life, literally.

Billy described what he saw that day on Duke Street: "I remember being fascinated by the amount of people that turned up which galvanized the movement. You didn't have to knock on doors to say we need support. People came out automatically because there was a clear injustice going on. We needed housing, we needed jobs. We needed One man, One vote. Without votes, you weren't going anywhere. The amount of people meant it was a necessity at that time."[21]

Billy talked from experience as he and his family lived in a three-bedroom house in the Bogside. He didn't know until years later that each bedroom had a family in it. He had to sleep in a drawer as a young kid. All the families shared a kitchen and an outdoor toilet. He had already dropped out of school before the Duke Street march a couple of years earlier, at the age of 14 to help support his family. He talked about how religion permeated everything there at the time, "When you went into a job and they asked you what school did you go to and you said St. Joseph's, you were out."[22]

Tension could be felt in the air. Stewards were in the crowd and could be heard saying, "Please everyone stay calm. Stay calm." In the meantime, the police confiscated some of the banners from the marchers. Word was spreading that some marchers had already been injured, but nobody had witnessed it.

116 GOOD TROUBLE

One leader of the NICRA got up on a chair in the middle of the marchers and asked them to go home since this was a peaceful march, and they didn't want any trouble.

The marchers would have none of that. People were shouting all sorts of things about "nobody is going anywhere."

Delia McDermott remembered the October 5th march in Derry. She was only 15 at the time and lived in Derry. I interviewed Delia on the phone in December of 2023, and she still remembers the march. "It was the first one I remember. The civil rights march in 1968. It had John Hume and Ivan Cooper. I wasn't actually at the march. I heard the march because I lived about four minutes from the bridge."[23]

The mood of everyone there was starting to turn ugly.

Devlin noticed this, "These were men who had no work, these were real men of no property. Their grievances were genuine, and the more the police stopped them from marching, the more bitter they became."[24]

The marchers were peaceful. There was no act of physical or verbal violence, but unfortunately, that didn't stop what was about to happen.

Then, suddenly, everything exploded.

Even to this day, the video footage of what happened is shocking. The next few minutes would change the direction of Irish history and the Catholic protest against perceived Protestant hostilities and actions. The pictures went around the world, which would show the world how the Catholics were being suppressed of their civil rights and free speech in a supposedly democratic society.

The RUC officers rushed forward, wielding their batons from both ends of Duke Street. The sound of batons slamming into skulls was sickening. They swung them from side to side without any true justification. As the batons swung back and forth, the officers kicked and punched anything and anyone that was in front of them.

Old and young were attacked, women screamed and children ran for their lives. One elderly man didn't even see it coming when he was struck from the side across his face with the baton. It sounded like wood on bone. There was complete confusion as the marchers ran into each other while fleeing in panic from both ends of the street.

Bernadette Devlin described the scene, "I stood there like a statue, watching people being clubbed all around me. The thing I remember most clearly to this very day is the expression on the faces of the police- [...] they were enjoying it. It was if they had waited 50 years for this."[25]

The Beginning of the Catholic Civil Rights Movement   117

The officers then brought out water cannons against the marchers to break up the march. It was like the scene out of Birmingham, Alabama, with the officers there using water cannons against Black marchers. Unionist officers sprayed water all over the crowd, including the shops and anything else they could spray, even going across Craigavon Bridge. The cannons were put on full speed, with enough power to throw people off their feet or push them along in a forceful manner. The marchers who ran to the bridge were forced back across it. John Hume was one of the people who had been hosed. Hume later said about the march, "All hell broke loose [...] I'll never forget the hate I saw in the faces of the police."[26]

Devlin saw the carnage around her and said later, "You could feel the hatred. That's my recollection of that day. It was my first realization that the police hated us."[27]

Hundreds of people, including women, children and older individuals, were sprayed. People reported that the water had a strange brown color to it with an off smell. The number of people injured was close to one hundred. One MP, Anne Kerr, explained that she had been able to seek shelter in a café after being soaked by a cannon and said other girls weren't so lucky and ended up both drenched and injured.[28] Some marchers found escape routes through alleyways and other areas, but many didn't escape the mayhem.

Delia McDermott said the following about what she saw when she ventured out. "I was 15 at the time and I came down to see it at the end of John Street and the police were there. I ran into a house because the police started to lay into them. That was my first experience of the Troubles and my first experience of civil rights."[29]

The government and police of Northern Ireland treated the civil rights movement like it was an organization bent on the destruction of the way of life there, similar to when the state of Alabama branded the NAACP as a terrorist organization.

Derry was now becoming the Selma of Northern Ireland.

Bernadette Devlin saw the comparisons with Selma clearly, "I think the impact on public opinion was something like what happened after Dr. King's people were beaten up by Bull Connor's policemen on that bridge in Alabama. Suddenly, fair-minded people everywhere could see us being treated like animals."[30]

Later that evening at the City Hotel, the 'Derry Citizens Action Committee' was formed by a group of people that included John Hume, Ivan Cooper and other Catholic leaders.

The Duke Street march had brought the civil rights movement into the view of both national and international audiences. Millions of people saw it on the Irish channel, RTE. One of the most striking photographs of the march was Gerry Fitt, who had blood gushing from his head wound. Devlin was sure that Fitt knew what he was doing, "Gerry Fitt made a very astute political decision that if the press were to be interested in it, there would have to be an interesting head, so Gerry stuck his in the way and got sliced—proceeded to bandage it very ostentatiously and gave interviews outside the City Hotel. In between interviews he would come into the bar and take the bandage off and have a few drinks and go out again when he was called upon."[31]

The headlines the next day of the Belfast Telegraph said the following: "DERRY SHOUTS and the world hears"

Reactions in Britain were not surprising. Public opinion was on shaky ground but it didn't change the response. McCann summed it up well, "[...] a howl of elemental rage was unleashed across Northern Ireland, and it was clear that things were not going to be the same again. We had indeed set out to make the police overreact. But we hadn't expected the animal brutality of the RUC."[32]

Devlin was also at the march and said the following about the protest demonstration, "What horrified me was the evil delight the police were showing as they beat people down, then beat them again to prevent them from getting up, then trailed them off and threw them on for somebody else to give them a thrashing."[33]

During the October 5th Duke Street march which could be seen as the first civil rights march, people lined up outside the railway station, and on the opposite side, the RUC lined up. This prevented the marchers from accessing the route into the old walled city of Derry. When there was no movement from either side to vacate the area, the RUC head ordered his men to draw their batons and clear out the numbers of people from the area. Afterward, the city of Derry experienced two days of rioting.

This march was one of the starting points of the Troubles. The demonstration created the People's Democracy. It also made an impact on O'Dochartaigh's future endeavors. His twin sister Deirdre marched with him on that day. During the RUC attack on the marchers, the two of them had to hide in a café. In an interview with the Irish Times, his sister said of that incident, "We took off our coats which were covered in blood but they came in looking for us. I remember an RUC man with his baton, I remember the look of hatred on his face, I'll never forget it."[34]

The Beginning of the Catholic Civil Rights Movement 119

The Duke Street march also forced the prime minster of Northern Ireland, Terence O'Neill, to introduce a program of reforms which would include the allocation of housing on the basis of need and changes to the voting legislation.

Currie said of O'Neill's changes, "In such a very short time most of the abuses were rid of. It was a remarkable victory."[35]

During this time, the Catholics looked closely at what the Blacks were doing in the States with their own movement. The movement in Derry adopted the civil rights song "We Shall Overcome" as their anthem and used SNCC's slogan "One Man, One Vote." This was one of the main goals of the NICRA, to make sure that the poorest in society, who did not own property, should still be able to vote. The people in Derry even started calling themselves "the White Negroes of Derry." The marchers in Derry saw themselves slowly changing from protestors to people who would resist the government and the powers that still ran Northern Ireland from London.

The way the police handled the situation in Derry on October 5th was inept and unnecessary, very similar to some of the marches that had occurred in the US South in the mid-60s. The attack was vicious and unforgiving. It changed life for the Catholic population in Northern Ireland. The press, television and radio coverage helped show the nation and the international world how heavy-handed the police were toward the marchers.

It shook people to the core, seeing skulls bashed in, blood pouring from people and the police seemingly enjoying what they were doing. Devlin mentioned afterward that she went straight for the closest pub to calm her nerves. "I walked into a pub, literally shaking, and swallowed my one double whisky neat without tasting it."[36]

Because the events had so much media coverage, it also brought a global focus to the events in Northern Ireland at that time. Devlin said of the impact of the October 5 march, "At some time in a country's history there are enough people who feel the same way, the same time to create a force and change the pattern of events. That's what happened in Northern Ireland in the autumn of 1969."[37]

The Duke Street march also helped create the People's Democracy group. This group formed when students from Queen's University staged a sit-in protest. Leaders of the group saw this as an opportunity for something bigger. It was a group of students, both Catholic and Protestant. They were all upset about the police brutality that they had seen in Derry on October 5. The People's Democracy was dedicatedly nonsectarian, so they would appeal to both religious sides.

Devlin said about the October 5 event at Duke Street, "[...] the Unionist Government did the Civil Rights movement a favor. They gave it life in one day. Without the police (reaction) it would have taken much longer to get off the ground."[38] Now the Civil Rights movement organizers planned to make bolder statements such as the idea of the Belfast to Derry march. The leaders took the SNCC's Selma to Montgomery march in 1965 in which the marchers had been beaten savagely by law enforcement, as their inspiration for their own march in early 1969.

1968 was a year that could be seen as a success for the Civil Rights movement in Northern Ireland, with the new schemes for housing. The good thing was that it was accomplished through nonviolent mass protests.

However, there were still issues such as voting rights and the situation with poverty that concerned many people in the country.

As the memory of the success of the Dungannon march faded, Derry started to be seen as a powder keg for frustration and tension within the Catholic community.

More had to be done in the eyes of many across Northern Ireland. Civil rights groups were popping up all over the country, mostly in the main towns, but Derry was the city where the numbers were huge and organization was focused on both goals and results.

Looking back at the Duke Street incident, the police had helped swing public opinion toward Civil Rights. They had put the spotlight on the Catholic struggle for the world to see. The Civil Rights movement had originally begun as a group of middle-class Catholics putting pressure on the local authorities. But after the October 5, 1968 events, that one day had created a huge national civil rights movement.

The planned march would be near Burntollet Bridge, an area that was in the heart of a unionist/Protestant stronghold.

That would prove to be a pivotal part of the Belfast to Derry march.

CHAPTER 17

BELFAST TO DERRY MARCH—THE BEGINNING

The feeling throughout the people who made up the People's Democracy was one of defeat, despair and guilt for what happened at the march on October 5, 1968. There was also anger that was festering among the group about the treatment of the marchers at the hands of the RUC in the streets of Derry on that day. One PD member said, "I knew the police were going to stop the march and that there was going to be trouble [...] I didn't conceive of the Unionists as being as thoroughly bad as they were. I didn't foresee things like police perjury for example."[1] After those events of October 5th, the People's Democracy held numerous smaller marches around the cities of Belfast and Derry. There were some in the group who leaned toward a more militant view, who wanted to push the envelope but were persuaded not to, those militants had been watching and learning from the militant Black Panther group in the United States.

The People's Democracy had factions that were to the left of the Northern Ireland Civil Rights Association (NICRA). Bernadette Devlin admitted at that time, "We didn't want to clean up the system; we wanted to destroy it, uniting Catholic and Protestant workers against the system in both Belfast and Dublin [...] that was the basic contradiction within the civil rights movement: Did we want political equality for Catholics or social and economic justice for all?"[2]

Michael Farrell was one of the leaders of the People's Democracy at that time and brought everyone together for a meeting. The meeting was a boisterous one with accusations flying at each other and toward the police.

Farrell was born in 1944 in Magherafelt in County Derry and was a founding member of the People's Democracy from its inception. Farrell's parents were born and raised in the South, so he didn't have the ingrained knowledge

121

122   GOOD TROUBLE

of the Northern Ireland situation that others he was around him had. He was educated at Queen's University in Belfast and Strathclyde University in Scotland. Farrell returned to Northern Ireland at a time when the civil rights movement had exploded into national view. He had the fashionable lamb chop sideburns and was sometimes bearded with brown hair. Over the years, Farrell had a good grasp of what was happening in the North and said, "The two things that came across very clearly were, one, the almost apartheid nature of society. Though people, Protestant and Catholic, lived side by side literally, there was very little contact between them. Secondly, you learned very quickly from the other children at school that Catholics couldn't get jobs in a whole range of occupations. There was no point in applying for jobs under the local authorities or within the Northern Ireland civil service for instance [...] they didn't bother applying for these jobs, they were just closed to them."[3]

However, Farrell did a good job to calm the emotions and have everyone focus on moving forward and continuing with the Civil Rights movement. This was when the group was truly transformed into a formidable organization in the country. They made the important decision about what their demands would be when they created leaflets, carrying the slogans below that would be handed out to the public:

One man, One vote
Fair boundaries
Houses on need
Jobs on Merit
Free Speech
Repeal of the Special Powers Act

This was a huge first step for the group. A committee of ten people was elected, including Bernadette Devlin and others. Devlin was still commuting back and forth from Cookstown to Belfast.

The People's Democracy was officially started on October 9, 1968.

Devlin knew what they needed: "I came to believe, by thinking about the futility of the violence we had seen (March 5), that we needed more than anything else to build up a disciplined, non-violent force. If we hadn't panicked and run in Derry, the police couldn't have done the amount of damage they did."[4]

Many in the community were excited to support the People's Democracy and what they stood for. The citizens saw the student group as one for a hope for a better future for all in Northern Ireland. The Liberal Party at the time

Belfast to Derry—the Beginning   123

praised the group, saying that they were "an example of effective, responsible and non-violent protest" (PD 1968–73, 1974).[5] This was very similar to how the different communities saw SNCC in the United States.

Another connection between the Catholic Civil Rights movement and the Black Civil Rights movement was the support of the church that both groups wanted and needed. The PD demonstrated this by a statement they made on October 15, 1968: "At this most crucial time in our community, if we are to avoid the forces of violence which surround us and if we are to achieve our ideals of peaceful change then more than anything else we need the heartening support of the religious bodies of this province."[6] Both groups in the States and in Northern Ireland had loyal supporters from the church who marched with them and tried to protect them when events got ugly in the streets on many occasions.

Devlin was working in her uncle's bar at the time and remembers people complaining while drinking, "I'd hear people complaining over drinks, but nobody was doing anything. One day I heard that the civil rights movement was planning a march to protest public discrimination. I said to myself, By God, I'll be there. And I went. It was a great success."[7]

Not everything went according to plan for the People's Democracy. Just like the Black Civil Rights movement in America, there were different factions that wanted different things. Some thought the PD weren't forceful enough, while others would get upset if violence did erupt and blame the marchers. John Hume was skeptical of the factions that wanted more than a nonviolent approach, and he said, "Their tactic was that wherever there was a confrontation with the police a spontaneous meeting should be held and votes taken. They wanted the right of anyone in the crowd to get up and speak. I wondered did they in fact want the crowd to get out of control."[8]

In America, the Black Panthers wanted more action from Dr. King, John Lewis, and others. In Northern Ireland, there was a Marxist side that continuously wanted to push things to the limit with the government. Particular irritations for some people in Belfast would be the pickets at a site where government officials would visit or a sit-down in the middle of a busy street that would halt traffic. Just like SNCC and other civil rights organizations such as the NAACP, the People's Democracy was not the only group fighting for civil rights. There was the Londonderry Citizens' Action Committee, which was very effective in Derry and had held several demonstrations. In the months after the October 5 march, the People's Democracy experienced some moments where they had to contain members from going after the police.

124   GOOD TROUBLE

As the marchers prepared for the trek from Belfast to Derry in January 1969, their demands were simply were "jobs and houses for everyone." This was almost the completely same demand for the Blacks in the United States at the time. Devlin in particular knew she had to create her own student group which became known as "The People's Democracy." She had researched how Irish Catholics before her had made mistakes and she was determined not to make the same ones. On New Year's Day 1969, the People's Democracy began a four-day civil rights march. Some called it "The Long March of January" from Belfast to Derry. This historic march was inspired by Martin Luther King Jr.'s "March on Selma." The march from Belfast to Derry would take the protestors through known Loyalist strongholds, where the threat of violence would be heightened.

The Unionist Party was opposed to the Belfast to Derry march, but the government was not prepared to completely ban the long march. The Orange Order was another group that was opposed to the march as well. The Orange Order, also known as the Loyal Orange Institution, is an international Protestant fraternal order based in Northern Ireland and primarily associated with the Ulster Protestants. Interestingly enough, the Irish Times and the Belfast Telegraph (the two major newspapers on the island) both ran editorials on December 30, 1968, stating that they recommended caution and care with the upcoming march.

Bernadette Devlin did not like the reforms about the march that had been proposed and knew that the march had to happen, and she needed to be a part of it, as well as the People's Democracy. Devlin was watching the development closely as the People's Democracy, united on some topics, now split into a middle-of-the-road faction and a far-left Marxist one. Until then, Devlin had maintained that they could ride the wave of belief in the process, but that was becoming more and more difficult. Similar to what had happened in the United States with their Black civil rights movement, the dispute centered on the simple matter of which way to go; it raised serious questions about the leadership and followers. But it is clear that she felt a duty to be at the long march. Devlin said, "Our function in marching from Belfast to Derry was to break the truce, to relaunch the civil rights movement as a mass movement and to show people that O'Neill was [...] offering them nothing. What we really wanted to do was to pull the carpet off the floor to show the dirt that was under it so that we could sweep it up."[9] As seen with Devlin's statements, this march was seen as action to signal nothing would suffice for the Catholics but full equal rights.

This was Devlin's time to shine. She seemed composed and prepared to deal with the dueling personalities for the upcoming march. Unrelenting, brave and determined, she had emerged as a leader who would not take no for an answer.

Belfast to Derry—the Beginning   125

Tensions were high on the eve of the march. The comparisons to the Selma to Montgomery march in 1965 in the US South were valid because the Catholic Civil Rights movement saw that as a template for them to follow. They compared their own long march to the famous one led by Dr. Martin Luther King. The People's Democracy put out a statement before the march that said, "We are marching because nothing has really changed since the Government's package of reforms in November which was condemned as inadequate by the entire Civil Rights movement and even the British Prime Minister, Mr. Wilson. It is, perhaps, as well to repeat that we are demanding not privileges but rights and that in marching to Derry we are merely exercising another fundamental democratic liberty."[10] Those words show that the march to Derry, just like the Selma march, was one to show the country the Catholics wanted their democratic freedom and full equal rights. The decision to use the Selma to Montgomery march template and do the long march from Belfast to Derry was the moment that the students separated from the left wing. The timing was very important because the prime minister at the time, Harold Wilson, saw that there had to be some flexibility with the demands of the civil rights movement. His concern was seen in his comments in late 1968, "Political leadership has a responsibility and a motive to assess the informal power behind the conflicting demands of social groups and to find a basis of accommodation in terms of cost and risk. In doing this they must adjust their own and their followers' values to make the accommodation feasible or face the dangers of direct action and escalated violence and counter-violence. Where a community drifts towards alienation and violence, leaders of the establishment cannot evade the responsibility of adjusting majority values to moderate minority needs."[11] Wilson was spot on with this recommendation. In November of 1968, there was talk of housing improvements, repeal of the Special Powers Act, and other items that would focus on the Catholic community. However, this was received as conciliatory by groups like the PD who felt insignificant by the left wing. Michael Farrell and others decided to pause the marches to see how the proposal for change would play out.

However, pressure from within the People's Democracy fueled the decision to continue with the long march from Belfast to Derry. People within the group saw the chance that they were taking. Another group called the Derry Citizens Action Committee said about the decision to march, "[...] long conversations with Bernadette Devlin [...] expressed the view that the march would lead to sectarian violence."[12] Devlin explained that they almost had to do the march so the existing political groups wouldn't take over, including the ultra-socialist ones. She wasn't happy about how it all played out but decided that she would

126 GOOD TROUBLE

participate. Despite the rising tensions within the group, on the eve of the march there was generally a new, reinvigorated sense of purpose for many of them. The feuding factions were now united by a common enemy.

In a personal, secret message from Prime Minister Harold Wilson to Northern Ireland's Prime Minister Terence O'Neill on December 23, 1968, he expressed concern about the voting reforms in Northern Ireland. Wilson said:

SECRET December 23, 1968.

Thank you for your letter of December 6 following our discussions on November 4 and my letter of November 19.

I have studied what you say and have read your Government's announcement of the measures you propose to take. I welcome these whole-heartedly. It must be the hope of all of us that they will be speedily brought into effect in an atmosphere of peace and tranquillity.

It will not, however, come as any surprise to you that my colleagues and I are disappointed that you have not so far felt able to announce a policy of early introduction of universal adult suffrage in local government elections. To us this seems to stand at the very heart of citizens' rights, and I believe we must discuss this again. I think it would in any case be valuable for us to meet again some time in the New Year, but I recognise that the timing of this must depend to some extent on developments in Northern Ireland. I shall be in touch with you again in the New Year.

I am grateful for what you say about the support of successive Governments here, and in turn my colleagues and I fully recognise, as I have said on a number of occasions in Parliament, the improvements which your administration is helping to bring about in the quality of life in the part of the United Kingdom in which the Northern Ireland Government has responsibility. That represents indeed a contribution to the life of the nation as a whole.[13]

I have, as with our previous exchanges, marked this letter 'secret', but I would naturally expect you to feel free to show it to your colleagues.

Yours sincerely,
(SGD H.W.)

Captain The Rt. Hon Terence O'Neill, D.L., M.P.[14]
(National Archives UK, Northern Irish politicians respond)

On January 1, 1969, approximately eighty people started out on the long march from Belfast under the banners of "Civil Rights" and "Anti-Poverty."

The Catholic Civil Rights Movement would never be the same.

CHAPTER 18

DAY ONE—JANUARY 1, 1969, BELFAST TO DERRY LONG MARCH

Inspired by the United States civil rights march from Selma to Montgomery, approximately 25 members of the People's Democracy started their march from Belfast to Derry, which would take four days and cover over 73 miles. NICRA (The Northern Ireland Civil Rights Association) and a group of Catholic nationalists in Derry had tried to persuade the marchers not to make the four-day journey, given the tense atmosphere in the region. The march was modeled on the Selma to Montgomery march in Alabama in 1965, led by Martin Luther King, Hosea Williams, John Lewis and other Black leaders at the time. In the eyes of the People's Democracy, this would be a test for the Stormont government.

Eamonn McCann was in his early 20s at the time and said about the connection to the Selma to Montgomery march, "We absolutely looked at what was going on in the States and said we want to copy that template. The Selma to Montgomery march was the model for Belfast to Derry. In our own naïve way, we wanted to be associated with them."[1]

Michael Farrell, one of the leaders of People's Democracy, said at the time, "Either the government would face up to the extreme right of its own Unionist Party and protect the march from harassing and hindering immediately threatened by Major Bunting, or it would be exposed as impotent in the face of sectarian thuggery, and Westminster would be forced to intervene, re-opening the whole Irish question for the first time in 50 years."[2]

Derry, at this time, was the last stop of the long march, which was appropriate. Gerrymandering and housing discrimination were rife there. Hardly any Catholics were employed by the local council. The Protestants had the majority of the housing. Derry would also be the eventual place where the

128   GOOD TROUBLE

Troubles would begin. In January 1969, the population of Derry was two-thirds Catholic and one-third Protestant. Just like in the US South, the White population did everything they could to suppress the Black vote, knowing the power they could wield if they did. Because of that, the White population continued to control the politics there, as did the Protestants in Northern Ireland, in particular Derry, as the politicians often redrew the electoral boundaries. Also, unemployment continued to be a huge issue, as Farrell said at the time, "[…] appalling slum conditions in Derry and yet people just couldn't get houses. They had to live in converted army huts. They had to live a couple of families to a house and so on."[3]

The first day involved a walk from Belfast to Antrim.

The event started on a cool, wet morning outside of Belfast City Hall around 9 a.m. The true goal of the People's Democracy long march was to protest for equal voting rights and improved public housing; all of it inspired by the new form of peaceful protest, from the US South that had attracted attention from around the world. The People's Democracy carried placards and banners with a variety of messages:

'Civil Rights 1969'
'Civil Rights March'
'Anti-Poverty March'
'Houses for all, Jobs for all'
'One house, One family'

The housing question with the vote was such an important issue, not only Derry but also in cities like Armagh, Dungannon and Enniskillen. It came down to two votes. If you lived with your parents, your mother and father had the two votes. It didn't matter if you had five others in the house; the house got those two votes and no more. The vote was limited to those who owned the property and their spouses only.

The Loyal Citizens of Ulster (LCU), led by Major Ronald Bunting, issued a statement calling on, "all those who value their heritage (to take every possible action within the law to hinder and harass the) so-called civil rights marchers."[4] Bunting sounded very similar to Alabama Governor George Wallace and his response to the march to Montgomery in 1965. The LCU that Bunting led was basically a front for the East Belfast section of the Ulster Protestant Volunteers, known as a Loyalist and reformed fundamentalist paramilitary group between 1966 and 1969, and many of its members also belonged to the UVF (Ulster Volunteer Force), another paramilitary group.

Day One—Belfast to Derry March   129

Bunting had a large face with wide brown eyes and thick eyebrows. He was slightly balding with his dark hair parted on the right-hand side. Bunting was commissioned into the Armagh and Down Army Cadet Force in 1946. He resigned in 1950 when he transferred to the Royal Electrical and Mechanical Engineers as a lieutenant. He retired with the honorary rank of Major in 1960. After leaving the army, he worked as a college professor at the Belfast College of Technology. He broke into politics when he became close with Reverend Ian Paisley and started to lead in Paisley's campaign against the NICA (Northern Ireland Civil Rights Association). At the time of the long march from Belfast to Derry, Bunting was preparing to run in the general election later in 1969. Ironically, Bunting's son, Ronnie, at the time was dipping his toes across the lines with Irish nationalists and playing both sides.

Documents that were released in 2010 to the University of Ulster's Conflict Archive confirm that Protestant loyalists targeted the marchers as soon as they set out on the march from Belfast City Hall. By this time in the morning, the numbers had gone up. One document said, "At 8:50 am on Wednesday, 1st January 1969, about 50 members of the People's Democracy assembled at the front of the City Hall, Donegall Square, north Belfast."[5] Opponent watched the marchers from the beginning as Major Bunting and his group, including Rev. Paisley, stood holding Union Jack and Ulster flags.

McCann told a humorous story about the Loyalists who surrounded City Hall. "Before we left Belfast, we had a meeting at City Hall. The Loyalists were standing at the edges of the crowd with baseball bats and sticks. The chair of the People's Democracy said anyone could be a member, you just had to show up. So, the chair told the Loyalists that they were now members of the People's Democracy and that they could vote. You can imagine how that went down."[6]

When the members of the People's Democracy started to slowly make their way off of Dongeall Place around 9:15 am, they were met with resistance. There were also latecomers to the march and the number of marchers was close to 70 now. There were groups of people for both sides now in the street. Some shouted abuse and others cheered the marchers on, depending on which side of the issue they were on.

"When we left City Hall there were now about 70 people with us. Students and few hangers on," McCann said.[7]

Major Bunting's supporters were lined up and some of them attempted to pull down one of the civil rights banners that marchers were holding. However, in a surprising move, the uniformed RUC police stepped in and prevented Bunting's supporters from taking the banner.

130 GOOD TROUBLE

Many of the marchers were taken aback, seeing the rage in the eyes of Bunting's supporters.

After the potential of an ugly confrontation was avoided, Major Bunting's supporters continued to wave their Ulster and Union flags as they walked through the center of Belfast near Donegall Place.

The marchers continued buoyed by that one kernel they had to believe in—hope for a better Northern Ireland and their families. The risks were large, but they still believed in what they were doing. Farrell, Devlin and others had shared their visions with the others; they were all tired of the rights of the Catholics being ignored. They had little time to relish their triumph in the first leg of the long march to Derry.

Major Bunting's brown eyes were blazing like fire when he left the march as the protestors had reached the outskirts of Belfast near the Bellevue Zoo. New people who continued to join the march as the protestors walked. Drivers who passed the march offered cheers and words of praise for what the marchers were doing. Some even gave cigarettes to passing walkers.

By lunchtime, the marchers had arrived in Templepatrick. They stopped there for an impromptu meeting. Mostly, the meeting was about the signs that the marchers were carrying.

They continued on as the marchers were in fine form, singing all types of songs—anything they could think of: Irish songs, rugby songs and drinking songs. Everyone was happy to be together, singing and marching in the relatively calm weather for a January day.

The marchers went on forward and every now and then would be yelled at by passers-by in their cars, shouting that they would get the marchers once they arrived in a city called Knockloughrim. The city was well known for being a bastion of right-wing, anti-Catholic groups. However, the marchers never made it to Knockloughrim since the RUC prevented the group from walking through.

Later that day, the marchers did meet another group of Loyalist followers. The anti-Catholic group was waiting for the marchers at Antrim. The RUC officers kept the groups separated on Antrim bridge. The sounds of the Loyalist drums filled the cool January air and Major Bunting could be seen with the Loyalist group.

The group from the People's Democracy met with County Inspector Cramsie. He was the one who was in charge of the officers at the Antrim bridge. He saw that there was only one thing that could be done and that was

Day One—Belfast to Derry March 131

that the marchers needed to turn around and head back home. That was not going to satisfy the marchers, so the standoff began. The marchers explained that they needed to go through Antrim to a hall where they would spend the night.

The officer conferred with Major Bunting and the Loyalist crowd that blocked the way. When Inspector Cramsie returned, he explained that the group couldn't go through Antrim. The People's Democracy group and the Loyalists went back and forth, meanwhile traffic was being held up by the commotion. The marchers decided that they'd take a page out of the Black Civil Rights movement in America and simply sat down in the road. All the while, the incessant drums never stopped.

The marchers told the police that they would leave the road area so the traffic could get through. However, they said they would march afterward through the area where they needed to. At that time, more and more officers showed up to help with the standoff on the bridge. When the extra officers showed up, they violently forced the marchers off the road and literally into the hedges on the side of the road.

Devlin talked about this as she basically got trampled on, "Do you call yourself an officer or are you a Paiselyite in disguise? You, sir, are a very incompetent old man. If you can't control this force or so-called police, why don't you retire and let somebody who's fit to do the job take over?"[8]

McCann explained, "We were attacked on that first day of the march. People knew we were coming and we said we would not be stopped. We shall not be moved."[9]

After some tense moments in the standoff, the marchers agreed to be lifted by the police to the hall and began to move back down the road. Funny that the Loyalist group began to hoot and holler as they saw the marchers going back; they probably thought they were heading back home but they ended up at the hall.

Once the group arrived at the hall, they stayed there for the night as Devlin and other leaders fixed soup and coffee for the over 120 marchers who were now in the group.

During the night, the police entered the community hall as the marchers slept and claimed there was a bomb scare. They told the students that they needed to leave immediately. The students didn't believe the police and refused to leave. The police couldn't believe it, shook their heads and left the students to their own devices, never to mention the bomb scare again.

132   GOOD TROUBLE

McCann talked about that first day of the march and the lack of support they felt. "When we left Belfast for Derry, nobody supported us. Nobody. The Civil Rights Association had disowned us. But they weren't going to stop us from marching."[10]

What happened in the following days drove a heavy divide between the already polarized communities in Northern Ireland.

CHAPTER 19

DAY TWO: BELFAST TO DERRY—TOOME

The one person who would become a problem for the Catholic Civil Rights movement for years would be Reverend Ian Paisley.

Paisley was born in Armagh in 1926. Loyalism was pushed into his psyche by his father who was a true Unionist and Loyalist. Paisley was a strong believer in the Bible, and he went on to become a Baptist minister after preaching even in his teenage years. Paisley was very reminiscent of the US Southern Baptist preachers who extolled the separation of the races, loving God, doing the right thing and in the night would be supporters of the Ku Klux Klan and would terrorize Black families. He formed his own church at age twenty-five. A church called the Free Presbyterian Church of Ulster, a violently anti-Catholic church. Paisley was also was horrific in his words and actions towards the Pope.

The second day of the long march continued as the route took the People's Democracy into Toome, Antrim. Toome was a majority Nationalist village, and the marchers knew it would be a tense situation all day. It was a cloudy day as the marchers entered to a large contingency of support from the people who lived there. The group started out early that morning, around 6 a.m. The goal was to get through the city of Randalstown early on the way to Toome, before the Loyalist group got organized. Word was spreading that the Loyalists were gaining more and more followers.

However, 6 a.m. wasn't early enough as the marchers were stopped by another group of officers. Behind the officers was a large number of Loyalist followers, shouting abuse. And this time the Loyalist followers were armed. In their hands were pick-axes, saw-blades and scythes. Bunting and his supporters followed the marchers by car. A marcher from the People's Democracy threw a flowerpot at Bunting's car and ended up being the first person convicted for violence on the long march. This, despite the fact there had been two days of Loyalist attacks on the marchers almost constantly.

Devlin explained what the scene looked like in front of her: "The general impression was that any marcher who got into Randalstown wouldn't leave it with his head in place."[1]

In the ever-present tenseness of the situation, Devlin decided that she and another leader of the People's Democracy would go and try to reach Prime Minister Harold Wilson on the phone. They never did reach Wilson and nothing came from the obligatory phone call from MP Devlin.

So far, there had been little antagonism from the majority of people simply living in the towns that the marchers were going through. However, it could be seen by what happened with Major Bunting and Reverend Paisley in Belfast that there were organized groups that wanted to harass the marchers every step of the way in their four-day march to Derry.

Even on the second day, the RUC was offering no support or protection for the marchers. The RUC officers were even seen chatting and joking with the groups that were there to harass the marchers. My parents said the same thing of the Salisbury, North Carolina police when they chatted up the Klan members as my parents marched by themselves, with no protection on the other side in 1963.

When Devlin returned to the scene of the standoff, the police had agreed to escort the marchers around Randalstown. The police would lead them around in a surprising change. However, this did not happen right away, as the marchers had to wait for a couple of hours for the cars to arrive to escort them around the town.

The police cars finally arrived, and the officers led the marchers around Randalstown so they could avoid potential trouble. But the police played games at first by simply driving around in circles and not really leading the marchers anywhere. Only when the marchers threatened to stop and go their own way did the police finally start to lead them to Toome.

Once the marchers arrived in Toome, the People's Democracy began to march into the town. When they arrived in Toome, most of the people in the city were marching with the People's Democracy. Again, they were faced with police in front of them. Behind the police were the usual Loyalist followers; some of them were government Unionist leaders.

The marchers knew what was in front of them again and were prepared to be re-routed by the police yet another time. However, when the police did offer another route for the march, the protestors walked it but were faced with

Day Two: Belfast to Derry—Toome 135

another group of police and Loyalist followers. This time the marchers didn't relent. Devlin said, "(the police) had twenty minutes to clear the Paisleyites, after that we were walking forward."[2]

This was something Devlin and the leaders were comfortable saying since, at the time they were outnumbering both the police and the Loyalist followers in Toome.

The rest of the second day, the plan was to march through the village of Gulladuff and the town of Maghera to Brackaherielly. The group would spend the night in Brackaherielly. The second day's march would be close to 20 miles and with the morning's shenanigans, they were already behind schedule for the day.

Things had calmed down since the morning and the marchers maintained a good, quick pace along the route. There were about six hundred in the marching group by now. However, the students from the People's Democracy were now outnumbered by the supporters who had joined them on the first two days of the march. Nighttime was already approaching when the group reached Gulladuff. Upon arrival, there was a great reception for the marchers. The supporters came out to greet the group and escorted them into the great hall. The townspeople had prepared soup and sandwiches for them. They advised the marchers to stop for the evening and not go anywhere since it was dark. Additionally, word had gotten to the town that Paisley and his group were waiting secretly a few miles ahead on the route, ready to attack them if they approached the area.

There were a number of marchers who were not swayed by the townspeople's plea for them not to march anymore that night. There was a group among the marchers that was tired of the nonviolent approach and wanted a fight with the Loyalist supporters. The marchers went back and forth debating the topic, and in the end the townspeople of Gulladuff agreed to transport the marchers by car to Brackahereilly.

The marchers were able to avoid the town of Maghera, where the Loyalist supporters were waiting to attack.

The 600-strong group of marchers were now 40 miles outside Belfast. They had completed half of their march and still had two days to get to Derry. Devlin, the leaders and the rest of the group were still nervous about spending the night there, thinking the Loyalists would still find a way to attack them.

As with many marches in the United States, the police refused to protect them. However, one of the townspeople told the group of marchers that evening, "You make your beds. Bed down for the night. And let none of you walk outside the hall. We will guarantee you perfect safety."[3]

McCann talked about the connection again with the Selma march, "Every night we stayed in local houses or buildings. Again, it was just like the Selma march. And the knowledge that others had marched like this in the States in Selma, singing and marching. It was a good feeling."[4]

The night was quiet, and there were no issues with the marchers spending the night at the hall. It looked as if there was nobody watching the hall, but the townspeople had their backs. The group rested and prepared for day three of their march.

They had to continue to march for their husbands, sons, wives and daughters and their mothers and fathers who'd lived through difficult years under Unionist rule.

CHAPTER 20

DAY THREE OF THE BELFAST TO DERRY MARCH

The events that occurred on days three and four of the long march from Belfast to Derry would polarize communities across Northern Ireland.

The third day was a long and tiring one, but for the marchers it would end up being the best out of the four by far.

They headed for the Glenshane Pass. The view of the mountains was stunning for the marchers, and the air was crisp and clean. The feeling was jubilant as they forgot how tired they were and focused on the wide-open march.

The radio gave reports on the progress of the marchers which cheered them on with: "The students have reached Glenshane Pass [...] they should be over it this afternoon [...] My God, the students have reached the top of the pass! They seem to be running up it! Hardship really makes these young people all the more determined."[1]

There was a welcome sight at the top of the pass. A pub called "The Ponderosa" (I actually saw the sign promoting this pub back in 2022, on my way to Derry—it is still there and known as the "highest pub in Ireland"). It was a sight to be seen in the middle of the mountains. The owner of the pub greeted the marchers and made sure there was plenty of room inside for the group. The marchers stopped and almost all of them had something to drink before they headed off down the pass into the town of Dungiven.

The town of Dungiven was prepared for the marchers and knew they were on their way. Citizens there had made sandwiches, found cigarettes and there was even a doctor who offered assistance with the marchers' worn-out feet and trouble with blisters. The castle was opened up for the marchers so they would be able to wash up after the long march.

137

138   GOOD TROUBLE

Townspeople lined the street and whooped and cheered as the marchers came through. There was a Catholic school on the route and all of the students had come out to greet the marchers as the teachers followed them out and attempted to corral them back in. This was not a get-out-of-school-for-free day, as the teachers shouted at them.

A few miles outside of Dungiven, there was a fork. Both choices of roads led to the city of Derry. The marchers had planned to take the left fork which would lead them through the towns of Feeny and Claudy. However, the police asked the marchers to take the right fork. This one was a more direct path and would detour them around Feeny. The officers claimed that they would not be welcome in Feeny and there would be a chance for trouble there. The marchers were getting tired of being rerouted by the police, so they decided to ignore the cordon of the police.

They agreed on how they would march into the cordon as Devlin said, "[...] Arms linked, heads down, keep a steady pace, one-two-one-two; no matter what happened you were to keep walking. If the person beside you fell, you were to hang on to him and trail him along till he could regain his balance. If a person was knocked unconscious, you were not to let go but use him simply as body weight."[2]

The marchers began their way to the cordon and followed the procedures that the leaders had laid out. However, the police had also linked their arms and began to push back against the marchers.

One reporter gave their story of what was happening for the radio listeners; it sounded like they were giving play-by-play commentary on some sort of sporting event: "And the marchers are now approaching the police cordon. The police have forced them back. No! The marchers are forcing themselves forward! Yes, yes! The police are moving back! No, the cordon is holding tight! Yes! The marchers are back! Forward! Back! Forward! Back! My God! The marchers are through! They're all through! There are policemen in the ditch! The marchers are pouring through, they're just running up the road. They've gone through!"[3]

Luckily, there were not many officers there at the point. Approximately two hundred of them faced off with the marchers. The officers confronted the marchers at the front, some of whom were women, including Bernadette Devlin. They continued to push back and forth; nobody got hurt, but some officers did end up in a nearby ditch because of the pushing.

The marchers got through the cordon and headed down the road toward Feeny. Interestingly enough, more police showed up but only to escort the marchers as they lined the streets and followed behind them.

Day Three—Belfast to Derry March 139

McCann told a story about how he accidentally became friends with two notorious Northern Irish women from the Troubles during the march to Derry.

"I remember two young women marching behind me. They were talking about music, politics, and talking about other women in the march. In the middle of the march, I finally turned around and said, 'Will you shut the f.... up.' The two women turned out to be Dolorus and Marian Price."[4]

These were the notorious Price sisters who were chronicled in Patrick Radden Keefe's incredible book, *Say Nothing.*

Dolorus and Marian Price were both born into a staunch Irish Republican family in Belfast. They both eventually joined the IRA in 1971. Both Price sisters participated in the infamous March 1973 Old Bailey courthouse bombing in London, as they detonated car bombs at the Old Bailey and three other locations. Both were arrested when they returned to Ireland and were given life imprisonment for that. Dolorus and Marian carried out a long, famous hunger strike while being imprisoned; they only survived because they were force-fed by prison guards. They were released in 1980 on humanitarian grounds. Dolorus died in 2013 at age sixty-two. Marian is still alive and living in Belfast, in her seventies.

McCann said about both of them, "We ended up being friends. I visited both of them when they were in jail. I still go to see Marian when I'm in Belfast. The last ten years of Dolorus's life, I was probably closest to her because so many people were not speaking to her at the time."[5] This was because of her involvement with the IRA, specifically transporting accused traitors across the border into the Republic. The accused traitors were never seen again, called "The Disappeared."

***

Derry was now only ten miles away. The end was near for the marchers. Once the marchers got past Feeny, they arrived in the town of Claudy. A number of them got drinks at the hall in town and afterward participated in a meeting.

Meanwhile, things were brewing in Derry in a bad way. Later on that fateful night of January 3rd, Derry faced a horrible night of rioting after the Loyalist meeting at the Guildhall city hall building. Many Catholics had gathered outside, knowing the Loyalists were meeting inside. However, they disassembled when the police started wielding their batons. Reverend Paisley led the meeting with his supporters, including Major Bunting. Bunting told Paisley's supporters to be near Burntollet tomorrow morning to, "see the marchers on their way."[6]

This would foreshadow what would face the marchers the next morning.

CHAPTER 21

LAST DAY OF THE BELFAST TO DERRY MARCH

It was a late start for the marchers on January 4. The events in Derry had been an indication of the simmering violence that was underneath the surface of the population there. The students were trepidatious that it would be difficult for them to control the nonstudents who were participating in the march. The marchers and supporters had planned to complete the final leg of the march from Claudy to Derry. During the night, a bus and other vehicles had been delivering bottles and stones to a field outside the village. Interestingly enough, the emergency telephone service in the area had suffered some type of "breakdown of service," so no outside communication was available.

Farrell held a meeting and explained that anyone who didn't think they could fall in with the nonviolent way of protesting should leave the march now. He explained to them, "No retaliation should be offered except where danger to life or limb is likely to be occasioned in the immediate instance."[1]

McCann sometimes found a bit of humor in these morning meetings that the People's Democracy would have. "Every morning we met and had to agree to march the next day. If not, we would probably have to split up in the typical Irish tradition."[2]

Eamon McCann added before they left, "In the last three days we have come more than sixty miles. I will not remind you why we embarked on this activity. We knew from the beginning that this was a protest of a most serious sort. We decided to march as a gesture of solidarity with the deprived. [...] For three days we have been harassed and abused without any retaliation on our part. Today we may face provocation beyond anything yet seen [...] We must agree that not one single person will retaliate even to save himself from injury.

142 GOOD TROUBLE

[…] And any trust you still have in the RUC is, in my opinion, quite misplaced. We are on our own and our only weapons are the principles we have adopted."[3]

A few minutes after the meeting had ended, they were on a road around 10 a.m. with the numbers in their group around 300. They were about seven miles from Burntollet Bridge. The road was eerily quiet and serene.

As the marchers arrived on the main Dungiven-Derry road and approaching Burntollet Bridge, six miles outside of Derry, they were stopped for close to thirty minutes by approximately one hundred RUC police officers. The marchers were about a mile from the bridge. At the same time, hundreds of Catholic sympathizers were at the scene. Farrell said he was told by the police the following, "it was only going to be a very minor type of skirmish."[4] It seemed to Farrell and the others that the RUC were trying to protect the marchers from anything bigger. The People's Democracy leaders reluctantly assented. This time the police didn't redirect the marchers but said they could lead them past the protestors. The police took the lead for them.

Farrell, Devlin and the marchers found it hard to know what to believe since the RUC hadn't tried to protect the march at all up to this point. There had been rumors that the RUC colluded with the anti-Catholic support, which created great confusion for the marchers. They didn't know who they could trust. Even among the RUC, the marchers could detect flickers of loyalty to Paisley and his supporters.

Farrell addressed the crowd of marchers and warned them all of a possible attack and that the officers were there to protect them and get them through.

The marchers were becoming uneasy. They had no idea that they were walking into a trap. Some of the marchers were so anxious about what was ahead that their stomachs cramped. There was a Loyalist group up ahead, nothing out of the ordinary for the marchers since they had left Belfast days ago. Thinking the RUC were there to escort the marchers, they walked towards the Loyalist group. The RUC officers were kitted out in helmets, riot gear with shields, and got their batons. They walked alongside the marchers.

The marchers linked arms like their Black counterparts did in the Selma to Montgomery march, stayed on the right side of the road and kept their heads down. They were prepared for any stone-throwing from the crowd as they kept a good stride. As Devlin told the ones around her, "Look, it's not a matter of pride, it's a matter of efficiency. If you walk with your head down, you'll walk further. Walk with your head up and you mightn't have an eye when the stone lands."[5]

Last Day of the Belfast to Derry March 143

They kept walking with a hedge on the side of them, the officers and the Loyalist group in front of them. Nothing happened as they marched. No stones, nothing.

The interesting thing was that the marchers could see, lined up on the side of the road through the hedges, stones and bottles. They were almost lined up in a very orderly fashion.

The officers that were escorting the marchers looked completely different from the officers who were outside the hedges, off the road. Those officers seemed to be having friendly conversations with the Loyalist groups. The Loyalists sang their songs loud and clear for everyone to hear.

In front of the marchers were hundreds of B Specials who were there on the route. They wore armbands to distinguish themselves from the marchers when they used their clubs, iron bars, stones and bicycle chains with which they armed themselves. They were determined to block the marchers' entry into the historic city.

Burntollet Bridge was ahead of the marchers, an area that was picturesque, tucked into the hilly countryside of the Derry area. A high hedge hid the view from the marchers of the hill above them. The police did nothing about the men gathered on the hills above.

From both sides of the road came a flurry of bricks and bottles that immediately stopped the march.

Devlin explained the scene, "From the lanes burst hordes of screaming people wielding planks of wood, bottles, laths, iron bars, crowbars, cudgels studded with nails, and they waded into the march beating the hell out of everybody."[6]

As the marchers reached the bridge, they were attacked by a well-organized Loyalist mob which included many members of the B Specials. There were well over three hundred of them. The attackers' eyes blazed with anger, weapons in their hands. They had acquired stones that had been transported in bulk from a nearby quarry, the same ones that the marchers had seen on the side of the road earlier.

Farrell said of the scene in front of them, "There was a police jeep in front of us, and a group of 5 or 6 RUC men who stopped the jeep and took out shields and helmets and put them on, and that's when I realized something more serious was happening."[7]

The attackers on the marchers had gathered stones and other missiles, including sticks that were studded with stones. They used these to brutally beat both male and female students.

144 GOOD TROUBLE

McCann said he was lucky that he had not been attacked. "I was with Bernadette and Michael Farrell up front but luckily I wasn't attacked. We were three in a row. It was our strategy to keep together in line and I was a lucky one. And we weren't up front because we were brave or had planned it. It just so happened that way. We didn't know any better."[8]

The marchers who had pledged for nonviolent protest ran for their lives in a panic. Stones began flying all over the marchers. Some jumped into the river and hid below the bridge. Others were chased by Loyalists who were brandishing staves and waving Union Jack flags at the same time.

Devlin explained when she was attacked and injured: "As I stood there I could see a great big lump of flatwood, like a plank out of an orange-box, getting nearer and nearer my face, and there were two great nails sticking out of it. By a quick reflex action, my hand reached my face before the wood did, and immediately two nails went into the back of my hand [...] I rolled up in a ball on the road, tucked my knees in, tucked my elbows in, and covered my face with one hand and the crown of my head with the other. Through my fingers, I could see legs standing round me [...] about six people were busily involved in trying to beat me into the ground, and I could feel dull thuds landing on my back and head. Finally, these men muttered something incoherent about leaving that one, and tore off across the field after somebody else."[9]

It was a horrific scene, straight out of Bloody Sunday in Selma with the march in tatters. The Loyalist group were beating marchers everywhere that could be seen, into the fields and in the river. Marchers were being chased into the woods like members of the Black population in the States were by the Klan across the country. Some were trapped on the road and being beaten within an inch of their lives. It was a riot, if one had ever been seen.

The police stood, watched and did not intervene in the beatings the marchers were receiving.

However, in some cases, there were marchers who were bleeding from the head, and people knew they needed to get to the hospital quickly. Some officers did help them into a truck to get them out of harm's way. A few of the officers obviously did not want to see anyone killed at least.

Vinny McCormack was a marcher there and said, "The police moved back from the side of the road, leaving the march open to attack. It was almost like a military operation, and that's what startled us. The rocks came first of all, and then the attackers."[10]

News reporters who were there, attempting to film the march, were also attacked. One news photographer reported that he had been thrown over a hedge and beaten with sticks. The photographer said, "I went across the field

Last Day of the Belfast to Derry March   145

and they cornered us. We had to jump into the river […] and I got under a small bridge. A woman who came under the bridge with us got hysterical and started screaming. We had to get from under the bridge and they stoned us as we came out."[11]

Marchers continued to be shocked by what had happened as victims lay before them with horrible injuries. One man who was following the march explained that a Molotov cocktail had exploded in the road directly in front of his car. He drove past the march because he was fearful of being caught and attacked.

McCormack was one of those who jumped into the cold Faughan River. "I was very frightened. So long as we were in the river we seemed to be fairly safe, but I was very, very frightened."[12]

Farrell and others frantically helped the marchers at the front of the procession to safety when the stoning started. However, those at the back, mostly women, were singled out to be beaten by the attackers. Many of them were beaten severely with cudgels that had nails driven into them, and some were pushed into the frigid water of the River Fahan.[13]

Farrell said, "I could see people with blood pouring out of their heads and people were saying to me that so many had been taken to the hospital. I saw several police vehicles there with police sitting in them. And there was a crowd of guys with white armbands on, with their clubs, smoking, and having a rest and some of them were chatting to the police."[14]

Bernadette Devlin described the scene of what they walked into, "[…] from lanes at each side of the road a curtain of bricks and boulders and bottles brought the march to a halt. From the lanes burst hordes of screaming people wielding planks of wood, bottles, laths, iron bars, crowbars, cudgels studded with nails and they waded into the march beating the hell out of everybody."[15]

The attack lasted for just over thirty minutes, which seemed like an eternity for the marchers who had been beaten. The marchers were finally able to regroup along the road.

After things had calmed down a bit from the attack, Farrell surveyed the group to see if there were any other injuries. He said he saw the following: "[…] the ambushers, who were wearing little armbands, and the police were standing around chatting and smoking quite happily. There was no attempt by the police to disperse them, arrest them or anything like that. […] I sort of observed this for a minute or two until some policeman said to me, (For God's sake get out of here, they'll kill you.) I got out of it as fast as I could […] the collusion was complete."[16]

146 GOOD TROUBLE

Not only had young students, both men and women, been sent to the bridge to be beaten relentlessly, but the pause in the march by the RUC had been rooted at least partly in a covert plot.

One journalist described the RUC's action that further sullied their reputation among the Catholic population: "Members of the B Specials [...] watched passively by our (escort) or more than a hundred police, attacked with nailed clubs, stones and bicycle chains. Of the eighty who had set out fewer than thirty arrived in Derry uninjured."[17]

Devlin and Eamonn McCann both decided that they had to get to Derry to finish the march. They both hoped that they wouldn't find anyone dead on their way there. They had been attacked even though there had been over 100 constables in riot gear to "protect them."

The march continued.

The protestors who were able to walk continued on as petrol bombs were thrown at them from ditches along the road. They were met by supporters on the outskirts of Derry who joined in with them on the march and warned of trouble ahead of them.

Just like when the marchers returned to Selma after Bloody Sunday, they sang as loudly as they could. They sang "We Shall Overcome." They followed that with "The Internationale."

As Devlin said about the singing, "[...] it was never sung with more fervour than coming away from Burntollet Bridge. That was our strong point: we had faced the attack without fighting back, and we had come out of singing."[18]

The attacks continued on the marchers as they made their way into Derry through the predominantly Protestant Waterside area. This was on Irish Street and Spencer Road. There was a storm of bricks, stones, bottles and petrol bombs. Farrell ended up being knocked unconscious by a stone that had been hurled at him. He still remembers what a nurse said to him afterwards, "You people deserve this, bringing trouble into our town."[19]

Paul O'Connor was 13 at the time of the march and remembers walking with friends, still in his school uniform, to greet the marchers. He said, "A lot of people were bleeding, a lot of people were injured, and they'd clearly just gone through something pretty awful. My vivid memory is of us all bolting down that road, everybody shouting, run, run."[20]

The police recommended that the remaining marchers be alert as they stood against houses to avoid the missiles. When there was a brief respite, the marchers would make a run for it to get out of harm's way.

The marchers eventually made it to Craigavon Bridge and over to the city side.

Last Day of the Belfast to Derry March   147

Eamonn McCann loved what he saw. "Thousands were all along the road on our way from Burntollet. There was this moment after the attack, three miles outside of Derry, we went past a Loyalist estate and people were on a ridge stoning us. And we expected that, but there were no injuries. When word of this got back into Derry, we came over the crest of the hill at the Waterside at Irish Street and there were thousands of people there. All of them had come from the Bogside. They joined the march side by side and that was wonderful."[21]

Finally, they had arrived in the city center of Derry as over 3,000 people huddled together in the streets to greet them. They whooped and cheered for the marchers. A platform that had been put up at Guildhall Square near the city hall building. The people wanted to hear from the marchers.

McCann couldn't believe what he saw in front of him in Derry. "It was a great feeling to march down into the Bogside. By the time we reached Derry, after Burntollet, there were thousands there waiting for us. We were marching and singing- two, four, six, eight, smash the state."[22]

Billy McVeigh was one of those who greeted the marchers. "I was here that day they returned from Burntollet. I remember everybody coming across the bridge with blood on them. The police just let them get attacked. The police in Northern Ireland and America were always good at leading you into a trap. The police didn't help them."[23]

Gerry Duddy said, "Burntollet was wide open on the road, they got the marchers down in the valley. They had trouble running. It was all orchestrated. And when you learn about that, no wonder people took up arms and stood up against the system that wasn't working for them."[24]

Bernadette Devlin got on stage to speak to the marchers and the crowd that had gathered that day, "We have marched from the capital city of Northern Ireland to the capital city of injustice."[25] The crowd became jubilant with those words from her. Those words from her were published all over the world about the city of Derry.

McCann said, "There's a lesson in what we saw in Derry. The Civil Rights movement was now seen as something incredible. The people who had disowned us were now welcoming us. Honestly, I think they sensed us becoming popular and changed their minds about us and that they better get on board with what was happening around us."[26]

Around 500 Loyalists came down Shipquay Street and even though they were separated from the civil rights supporters by police, there was a short flashpoint of stone-throwing between the two groups. When the main crowd left the scene, the police brought in a water cannon and a clash broke out between the police and civil rights marchers. The police ended up pushing into the crowd, forcing them back into the Bogside neighborhood.

Later that evening, the RUC did something they would regret later on, going into the Bogside and kicking off counter-riots. They ended up smashing windows, hurling slurs at the Catholic population, and beating anyone who dared to stand up to them. The rioting continued into the early morning hours and well over 150 people ended up in the hospital.

The next day, a group had gathered at the intersection of Lucky Road and St. Columb's Street. They decided to do some graffiti in a particular area. Eamon McCann was there and recommended the slogan, "You Are Now Entering Free Derry." The slogan was handwritten at the time on the wall but later was replaced with the iconic black block lettering on a white background in August of 1969 after the Battle of the Bogside. The place remains a center for public meetings in the Bogside and is the place I met Billy McVeigh and Julieann Campbell for my interviews in Spring 2024.

The Free Derry wall continues to be a worldwide symbol for civil rights supporters throughout the world.

***

Looking back at the bloody event at Burntollet Bridge, Farrell admittedly said, "I've always wondered since then whether the hold-up [...] was so that the attackers could get better organized before we arrived because we were definitely led into an ambush by the police."[27] This sounds similar to what the marchers walked into on the Pettus Bridge when confronted by the police and the possemen. Some would say after events at Burntollet that the march was doomed from the start, just like the Selma march.

O'Connor agreed that Burntollet was a turning point like Selma, "Not because the march had been attacked, because in some ways that was to be expected, but because the forces of law and order colluded entirely in that attack from beginning to end, and there were no consequences, no accountability."[28]

Devlin and the other leaders of the People's Democracy were surprised and horrified by the collusion that the RUC and Loyalist supporters were involved the ambush at Burntollet Bridge. The Sunday Observer in London compared the plight of the Nationalist working class in Northern Ireland to the population of America's Black ghettos.

It is truly amazing that nobody was killed at Burntollet Bridge and at the Selma march. However, over 85 marchers needed medical attention after the

Last Day of the Belfast to Derry March   149

ambush at Burntollet. Nobody was ever brought to justice for what happened that day, nor is it likely that they ever will be.

Eamonn McCann agreed with the surprise that nobody had been killed there. "I'm absolutely amazed nobody was killed there. It was naivety. It wasn't courage, it just didn't occur to me the danger we were in."[29]

On January 5, 1969, the day after the long march from Belfast to Derry ended, the Sunday Press ran this headline: "TERROR OF DERRY- 200 injured as march ends in riot." The report went on to say:

> Riots escalated again in Derry after the end of the four-day, 80 mile, civil rights march from Belfast. The casualty total was quoted as high as 200, with at least 89 people treated in Altnagelvin Hospital just outside Derry. Others had their injuries attended to elsewhere. Two armoured water cannons were in action in the city just before nightfall and there were repeated baton charges in Strand Road and around Butcher's Gate. People fled in all directions as the water cannon, with their klaxon horns blaring, roared through the centre of the city. After the civil rights demonstration broke up in Guildhall Square, and despite appeals by stewards to disperse and go home, sections of the crowd tried to reach the Diamond, which is within the ancient city walls. Major Ronald Bunting, leader of the Loyal Citizens of Ulster, had announced that he had planned to stage a trooping of the colours-the red, white and blue Union Jack. Hundreds of people of all ages tried to storm their way through several approacheds to the Diamond, but police tenders blocked the archways around the city walls. Rumour was rife, and when it was reported that one of the water cannons had knocked down a young person without stopping, the crowd became incensed and four baton charges by the RUC were made in the area of Strand Road and William Street.[30]

The long march from Belfast to Derry was followed up by months of protests, demonstrations, violence and tensions among the Unionist Party and Rev. Paisley.

Major Bunting and Reverend Paisley were both sentenced to prison starting in March 1969 for their part in the confrontations at different civil rights demonstrations. They were found guilty of unlawful assembly at a march in Armagh in November 1968.

The pair served only two months and were freed under a general amnesty in May 1969.

150 GOOD TROUBLE

Terence O'Neill, Prime Minister of Northern Ireland at the time, made a statement the day after the Burntollet Bridge incident on January 5, 1969. Here is his statement in full:

> I want the people of Ulster to understand in plain terms events which have taken place since January 1. The march to Londonderry planned by the People's Democracy was, from the outset, a foolhardy and irresponsible undertaking. At best, those who planned it were careless of the effects it would have, at worst, they embraced with enthusiasm the prospect of adverse publicity causing further damage to the interests of Northern Ireland as a whole. [...] Clearly Ulster has had enough. We are all sick of marchers and counter-marchers. Unless these warring minorities rapidly return to their senses we will have to consider a further reinforcement of the regular police by greater use of the Special constabulary for normal police duties. [...] Enough is enough. We have heard sufficient for now about Civil rights, let us hear a little about civic responsibility. For it is a short step from the throwing of paving stones to the laying of tombstones and I for one can think of no cause in Ulster today which will be advanced by the death of a single Ulsterman.[31]

This quote is quite reminiscent of what some White leaders thought of the 'agitators' coming South and putting things in the minds of their 'good' Blacks.

The hope had come true for organizers like McCann, Farrell and Devlin. The Belfast to Derry march, often marred by violence along the way, seemed to solidify public support for Catholic demands much like the 1965 Selma to Montgomery march focused the attention of the United States on the plight of Black people in the US South. Each of the days of the Belfast to Derry march, Loyalist groups confronted, hassled and attacked the marchers who took part. At no time during those days did the RUC, who were there, ever try to stop any of the attacks. The ugliness of the incident at Burntollet exposed the violence that peaceful protestors had endured to television viewers and news readers across the world. This only made support for the Catholic civil rights movement stronger, just like the public relations victory after the Selma march. Also, the B Specials were disbanded a year later.

Billy McVeigh explained the changing feelings in Derry, "They started off as peaceful marches and the RUC and police started to battle us because they announced that they were illegal marches. Some of us threw stones and bottles to protect ourselves. In 1968 and 1969 we never had problems with people coming out of their houses and supporting us and the civil rights movement."[32]

Last Day of the Belfast to Derry March   151

Farrell later wrote, "The march was modelled on the Selma-Montgomery march in Alabama in 1965, which had exposed the racial thuggery of America's deep South and forced the US government into major reforms."[33]

Devlin was amazed by what they had done with the Belfast to Derry march, "It is impossible to describe the atmosphere, but it must have been like that on V-Day; the war was over and we had won; we hadn't lifted a finger, but we'd won."[34]

The end result of the four-day march may not have been achieved by Farrell, Devlin and the other leaders with the Belfast to Derry march. However, it did put a spotlight on the organized discrimination that the Catholic population had endured for years, similar to Bloody Sunday in Selma. It showed how far the police, government and Loyalists would go to derail any move forward to Civil Rights support.

The ambush of the People's Democracy at Burntollet became a defining moment for the Troubles; it was also the time when the public's view of the Civil Rights movement turned in favor of the students and the marchers.

CHAPTER 22

BATTLE OF THE BOGSIDE

There had already been struggles for the soul of Northern Ireland. One was Derry's Duke Street confrontation in October 1968. The second was taken from the Selma to Montgomery template, the Belfast to Derry march. Now, was the third one. With tensions had been heightened in the predominantly nationalist city of Derry,because of the continued gerrymandering and discrimination, the Unionist Party still held power in local government even though it only had a third of the vote. The city was in a state of chaos with disillusionment bubbling up everywhere you looked. The young Catholics used their pent up frustrations and aggressive behavior towards the RUC and Loyalist groups. This set up the Bogside battle, where the potential for trouble was huge.

Another controversial event was the beating death of 42-year-old Sam Devenny on April 12, 1969. Devenny, an undertaker and father of nine, had been watching clashes between the police and rock-throwing youths in his Bogside neighborhood when some of the kids ran into his house as the police charged. Devenny locked his door, but the police knocked it down with a plank and began clubbing him and other family members. Devenny was hospitalized with a fractured skull which needed twenty-two stitches, wounds to his eyes and mouth, a heart attack and internal injuries. A number of his daughters and sons were pummeled around their backs and legs with batons and beaten on the head. He was released the next month but died after he collapsed in July 1969. An investigation later showed in 1970 that Devenny and his family were law-abiding citizens with no ties to the IRA.

Sam Devenny's death had escalated tensions in the city of Derry, especially within the population in the Bogside area.

154 GOOD TROUBLE

Interesting story, during my visit to Derry in June 2024. I was in the bar ordering drinks for me and Julieann Campbell. I had a man on one side of me and a woman on the other. The tall man had a beret on and started to speak to me.

"Are you friends with Julieann?"

"Yes, sir."

"I heard you're writing a book."

"Yes, sir."

"What's it about?"

I proceeded to talk to him about the premise of the book, and he said that it sounded like a great idea.

The blonde woman beside me, nursing a drink, spoke up and said, "That sounds like a great book. You'll get a lot of good information here in Derry with our people."

I thanked both of them and took the drinks to our table.

Julieann looked past me and said, "Do you know who that woman is that you were talking to?"

I did not.

"She is one of the daughters of Sam Devenney."

I turned back and said, "Jesus. I had no idea."

"Only in Derry," I said to Julieann.

One of the daughters who saw her father beaten to death in their own living room.

***

On April 22, 1969, the following suggestions were made to remedy the situation in Northern Ireland by Bernadette Devlin and other leaders during the debate in the House of Commons. She and the others came up with this list:

1. Repeal of the Special Powers Act
2. Extension of the Race Relations Act to cover religious discrimination in Northern Ireland
3. An end to religious discrimination in employment (especially legal profession, top civil service) and against Labour and Catholic members and trade union representatives in Government bodies.
4. An end to religious discrimination in housing allocation
5. Stricter supervision of local authorities methods and allocating houses
6. An end to gerrymandering

Battle of the Bogside 155

7. One man, one vote
8. Crash programme of economic development especially- west of the Bann- reversal of policies which led to Mr. Copcutt's resignation (one of the planners of the town) over the siting of the new town of Craigavon and denial of university to Londonderry
9. Some application of Trade Disputes Act 1965 (United Kingdom) to Northern Ireland
10. Disbandment of B Specials?
11. If necessary, strip Unionist government of power, while simultaneously granting elementary demands for Human Rights
12. Improvements generally in housing and job opportunities

More general points- which received varying emphasis were:

1. The British government has ignored warnings in the past and it is too late to do anything now
2. The Unionist party represents too many vested interests to make sure that reforms are genuine
3. The Unionist party will in any case split before it can carry out thorough reforms[1]

There is no doubt that tensions were high in 1969 as a secret report came out on July 14, 1969. It was labeled: Northern Ireland: Political Summary for the Period 10th to 14th July, 1969. Memorandum by the Home Office. At the top, it read "This document is the property of her Brittanic majesty's government". It contained the following:

2. Rioting in Dungiven, Londonderry and elsewhere

There has been intermittent rioting and violence in Northern Ireland throughout the weekend. Incidents took place in Belfast, Lurgan and Limavady but the main centres of violence were Dungiven and Londonderry.

Dungiven

2. Supporters of the Civil Rights Movement staged a "sit-down" to obstruct an Orange Procession on Saturday morning; they rejected requests from the police to move and some stone throwing took place when police removed them bodily. Later in the day Nationalist youths broke into the Orange Hall but

156   GOOD TROUBLE

dispersed when the parish priest intervened. During the night, however, and again on Sunday night, the mob attacked the Orange Hall with stones and petrol bombs and the Orange Hall was virtually sacked. Police reinforcements were diverted from Londonderry, including some members of the Special Constabulary although the latter were unarmed.

Londonderry

3. Crowds gathered during Saturday afternoon and stones were thrown as Orangemen returned from their service during the afternoon. The evening was comparatively quiet although there were large crowds in the streets; violence started about midnight and continued throughout the night. Roman Catholics from the Bogside district attempted to enter Fountain Street in the Protestant area and the main task of the police was to keep the two mobs apart. Stones were thrown, looting took place, fires were started and petrol bombs were exploded.

4. An uneasy calm returned during Sunday but similar violence was resumed during Sunday afternoon and again that night. During the night a party of seven policemen were trapped by a hostile crowd in a cul-de-sac. The Sergeant in charge ordered the crowd to disperse and fired a single warning shot in the air when they refused. The crowd still refused to disperse and the party then fired a volley of warning shots in the air whereupon the crowd dispersed slowly. Shots were fired at the police in another area of Londonderry at about the same time. Two men have been taken to hospital with gunshot wounds and the Northern Ireland government is investigating the circumstances in which they were received.

Casualties and Arrests

5. On Saturday night a total of 38 people were injured in Northern Ireland, including 16 policemen. On Sunday night 20 civilians were injured of whom four were taken to hospital and 29 policemen were injured of whom three were taken to hospital. There were 21 arrests on Saturday and 16 on Sunday.

Use of Troops

6. The Northern Ireland Government did not ask for troops to intervene. An infantry company was, however, moved from Hollywood, near Belfast, to H.M.S. Sea Eagle in Londonderry as a precaution on Saturday afternoon.

Battle of the Bogside

7. The Ministry of Defence have agreed to transfer three Wessex helicopters from Great Britain to Northern Ireland, again as a precautionary measure. The helicopters are amongst those which have already been allocated for use in Northern Ireland if required.

8. One complete infantry battalion is due to move into the Londonderry area during the course of 14th July. Each of the other two infantry battalions in Northern Ireland has one company at one hour's notice to move. Responsibility for guarding eleven key points is to be handed over to the Royal Ulster Constabulary during 14th July, leaving only four for whose protection troops will be responsible.

[...]

Responsibility of the Civil Rights Association and Other Bodies

11. The violence appears to have arisen as a result of tension caused by the processions associated with Orange Day, and there is no evidence that any of the civil rights organisations was in any way responsible. It is noteworthy that the processions themselves passed without incident except at Dungiven (see paragraph 2 above). The violence has been unequivocally denounced both by the Derry Citizens' Action Committee and by priests of the Roman Catholic Church. There were however some signs of organisation, for example in constructing barricades to prevent the police from entering the Bogside, and it is possible that some extremists may have been responsible – perhaps associated with People's Democracy or with the Irish Republican Army. There is however no definite evidence at this stage. In general the incidents seem to have represented simply hooliganism and the old-fashioned conflict between the Nationalists and Unionists in the Province.[2]

***

This set the stage for what would happen in the Bogside later that summer.

Historically, August was a month of pride for the Protestant population in Derry. This dated back to 1688 when Derry City was saved by thirteen Apprentice Boys (at that time a Protestant fraternal society founded in 1841 based in Derry) who closed its gates when the Catholic armies were first seen from miles away (I've seen these gates and I have to say they are impressive).

The siege started because of 'fake news' that had spread from a letter that convinced the Protestant population that the Earl of Antrim's Catholic troops were coming to murder them. However, the city walls were never breached despite being besieged several times in the 16th century, which gave Derry the nickname: 'The Maiden City'. This was a siege that created death for thousands of people which started because of lies and betrayals. The slogan of the siege that followed was and continues to be, 'No Surrender' for the Ulster Protestants. Visitors all throughout Northern Ireland will see these words scrawled on walls, sidewalks, everywhere you can imagine. Even today, the words provoke pride and a sense of defensiveness. By August 1969, the march by the Apprentice Boys was seen as a pointed way to show their Protestant supremacy, quite similar to the groups of people holding Confederate flags and shouting slurs at the marchers in Selma.

The lifting of the siege is celebrated on August 12 in Derry. The Apprentice Boys (they are not apprentices but Protestants from all over Northern Ireland) come into the town to march while the Catholics shut up shop. You will also see bonfires set by Catholics throughout the area, and in most cases before 1969, things had passed on without any major events for the most part. In most years in the past, nobody really paid attention to the march of the Boys; it was just the yearly march that passed without much notice. But 1969 was a different time. It was after Duke Street and the Burntollet incident. New people arrived in Derry to watch the festivities: reporters and cameramen from all over.

One Irish Times correspondent admitted why he was there, "I was here because I knew there was a fair chance that a riot would erupt in the city on the twelfth."[3]

The timing of this could be called nothing but provocative. Leaders from both sides pleaded for a complete ban on marches because of the tension across the country at the time. Government leaders refused to put their foot down. There was severe tension across the city of Derry, and many feared that there would be serious trouble if any marching took place.

August 12, 1969, was a gorgeous, warm and sunny morning when thousands of Apprentice Boys prepared to march through the city of Derry.

The three-day battle was televised around the world. People from all over saw the breakdown of law and order on the streets of Derry.

There were repeated calls by many for the protest march to be canceled by the Apprentice Boys because of the violence that could break out because of it, knowingdue to the tensions in the area. The thing that angered the Catholic community the most was the fact that several of their civil rights marches were not permitted, but the Protestant march was allowed to happen.

Battle of the Bogside

On the afternoon of August 12, Protestant marchers were assembling and planning to head down Shipquay Street, near the part of the city walls that looked down into the Bogside. Missiles were missiles thrown from both sides as the Protestants were curious about the Bogside, and the Catholic residents were prepared for a possible onslaught by the marchers.

The majority of the people in the Bogside had decided that they would ignore the march and, for their own protection, they would stay in the Catholic area outside the city walls. They would wait out the march until everything was finished. However, they would be prepared to fight if the all-day marchers dared to enter the Bogside.

There was an area in the city center called Waterloo Street. This area was a large intersection of two streets in the Bogside, William Street and Waterloo Street. Where these areas met was a main thoroughfare into the major commercial part of Derry. The area was where Bogside residents would enter the city center to shop or eat. This was the same area where there had been rioting over the past six months.

The RUC had placed barriers across both Williams and Waterloo to prevent anyone from entering or leaving the Bogside area. There were five Land Rovers parked in the center of the intersection. This formed almost another barrier between the Bogside and the marchers. This would force the marchers away from the Bogside and the residents there would never even see them.

On hand, prepared for the potential of trouble, were four RUC sergeants and twenty-four constables. They had brought full riot gear which remained in their vehicles at the time—helmets, shields and batons. There was also a huge number of press surrounding the area with television cameras ready to catch anything that sparked. There were even priests in the area, trying to calm the situation but receiving abuse from their own parishioners. John Hume described it as "justifiable anger" at Catholic watchers and priests trying to do what the RUC should have been doing. (CAIN, Battle of the Bogside, Russell Stetler, 1970)

The Catholic protestors could hear the drums banging and whistling flutes of the Orange Order. When the march approached the Bogside area of Derry, they were greeted by numbers of Catholics who jeered at them, shouted slurs, and threw stones at the Boys. The RUC officers who historically took the side of the Protestants, attempted to force the Catholic protestors back from the Boys march. The Catholic residents were also genuinely afraid of the Bogside being overtaken by the RUC officers. There were also a number of Loyalist militants who broke windows of houses on Rossville Street.

160 GOOD TROUBLE

At around 3:20 pm, more RUC officers had arrived at the scene after being alerted to heightened tensions in the area. At this point, the RUC had not arrested anyone or tried to break up the Bogside crowd. There was also no doubt that the officers were aware of the hordes of international press that were around them. Lieutenant Robbin of the RUC said about that, "the police were probably more self-conscious under the eye of television, as most people would be."[4]

As time went on, the stone throwing grew more and more frequent. The Catholic leaders attempted to calm the crowd to no avail. The Protestant marchers grew restless, and one of the MPs for Derry spoke to the crowd to ask them to get out of sight from the Catholic crowd. Some listened, some didn't. However, the Apprentice Boys parade did end without any major disruption, and those marchers left town soon afterward. But stones still flew in the area as the majority of the Protestant crowd went up Magazine Street. John Hume and other leaders ended up being hit by stones.[5]

Later the first evening, two flashpoints in the city began to get worse. The RUC believed that the Bogside population was growing frustrated and that there was a possibility they would come into the shopping and eating areas of Derry and have a full-scale riot on their hands. On the other hand, the Bogside residents saw themselves as trying to defend their homes from both the RUC and Loyalist groups.

Eamonn McCann was there and talked about the dealings with the RUC. "The cops were so hostile. They weren't there for peaceful conditions."[6]

On the evening of August 12, 1969, things escalated. The Bogside crowd began to throw petrol bombs. These petrol bombs were made mostly by women and children, kids as young as eight years old. A number of RUC officers retaliated that night and threw stones at the Catholic protestors. The officers were accompanied by a number of Protestant citizens who tried to help the RUC gain access to the Bogside. The RUC brought in extra Land Rovers and Humber armored vehicles to help. The officers went down William Street in front of the Rossville Street barricade, which was about ten yards from William Street and about five feet high, built from stones and planks. The barrier had well over two hundred people behind it. The RUC's goal was to calm tensions before nightfall. However, they came under a deluge of missiles and petrol bombs from people who lived in the high-rise, nine-story Rossville Flats.

Billy McVeigh told a humorous story about throwing a petrol bomb. "My grandma lived at number 9 down the road and my mother was there as well. I lit the petrol bomb, the fuse fell out, went down my back and lit me. I kept thinking I was going to either get arrested or blown up, all my friends ended

Battle of the Bogside 161

up dancing on my back, nearly crushing me to death. I had my good jacket on, dressed up like everyone else. You didn't leave the house in rags. I was more worried about my mother seeing the jacket messed up from the petrol bomb than getting arrested."[7]

Devlin, who never left the Bogside, said, "Kids of nine and ten carried (the petrol bombs) in crates to the front lines. The young girls collected stones and built the barricades, and the girls, the boys, and the men fought on the front line against the police."[8]

By 7:30 that evening, water cannons were being used to extinguish the effects of the petrol bombs in the area, and the RUC were very concerned about the situation. Many in the Bogside were on rooftops where they could easily throw petrol bombs down at the officers. As the night went on, the RUC debated what to do about the situation. A number of them had been hurt. At 11 pm, the decision was made by the Minister of Home Affairs to use CS gas. CS gas was commonly known as tear gas in the United States. It was the first time in the history of the United Kingdom that CS gas had been used.

Whoever was in charge of the use of CS gas was supposed to give a warning over a speaker. To this day, nobody is clear about what was said. Harold Jackson of The Guardian newspaper said the following of the CS gas use, "[...] heard absolutely nothing of the warning [...] was first aware that CS was in use when the first canister landed very near him, at about five minutes before midnight."[9]

During that summer, a leaflet that had been circulated throughout the Bogside area for its citizens that outlined what to do if CS gas was used and it included: 1. Take short even breaths, do not gulp or breathe deep as the as will only penentrate further into the stomach, 2. Do not rub the eyes, 3. If gassed do not drink for at least three hours, 4. Breathe through the following if available- an effective gas mask, a cotton surgicial mask carried in a polythene bag and soaked in water, lemon juice or vinegar, 5. A handkerchief soaked in water, 6. CS can kill in an enclosed space, therefore keep the flats closed against gas canisters. The last thing mentioned on the leaflet was "Defend the Bogside by Defending the barricades."

The CS gas came in standard cardboard canisters. The metal missile was inside the casing. It contained almost 13 grams of CS gas, dispersed through four holes. The CS gas was dispersed in a powder form in about thirty seconds. The CS gas was used in the Sackville Street area to move away the crowds. The effects on the crowd were immediate. The gas hung in the air, thick like fog in London, with a cloud of it covering the narrow streets. It seeped into the crowded houses in the area, suffocating the lungs of people and causing their

162 GOOD TROUBLE

eyes to burn like fire. Pictures circulated everywhere with the young and old struggling with the gas, and in some cases being overcome by it. Very few of the Bogside population had any gas masks to protect their faces. Instead, they used wet blankets or handkerchiefs that had been soaked in vinegar.

Devlin kept pushing people to not stop regardless of the gas, as she led them in the main area of the confrontation near Rossville Street, saying, "It's Ok once you get a taste of it."[10]

During the first day of the Battle of Bogside, the RUC had over one hundred injuries to their officers. There had been some minor damage to property but overall, the RUC believed their use of CS gas contained the situation. A makeshift hospital was even set up at a local candy shop; some people say that well over a thousand people had been treated there during the three-day battle. The worst injuries had been taken by ferry to Letterkenny Hospital.

John Hume issued a statement late that night, asking Westminster to intervene in the Derry situation. The Civil Rights Association put out a press statement that night saying:

A war of genocide is about to flare across the North. The CRA demands that all Irishmen recognize their common interdependence and calls upon the Government and people of the Twenty-Six Counties to act now to prevent a great national disaster. We urgently request that the Government take immediate action to have a United Nations peace-keeping force sent to Derry, and if necessary Ireland should recall her peace-keeping troops from Cyprus for service at home. Pending the arrival of a United Nations force we urge immediate suspension of the Six County Government and the partisan RUC and B-Specials and their temporary replacement by joint peacekeeping patrols of Irish and British forces. We urge immediate consultations between the Irish and British Governments to this end. Time has run out in the North.

Hume would later try to mediate between the marchers and a mob who wanted to stone or petrol bomb a local police station. As he walked up to the Rosemount police station, he was shot in the chest with a CS gas cartridge at point-blank range. It was a policeman at the door who shot him. He recovered from the gas quickly and continued to talk to the mob about refraining from using stones against the officers. The police finally stopped firing gas cartridges. Some say Hume saved the station; the officers disputed this by saying they were never in any true danger.

Battle of the Bogside 163

Bernadette Devlin and another leader also issued a statement: "The barricades in the Bogside of Derry must not be taken down until the Westminster Government states its clear commitment to the suspension of the constitution of Northern Ireland and calls immediately a constitutional conference representative of Westminster, the Unionist Government, the Government of the Republic of Ireland and all tendencies within the civil rights movement."[11]

Devlin was on the street, at the barricades with the people of the Bogside. In fact, she was out there helping the people build the barricades. She and the citizens were determined that they were not going to lose. The press put her picture everywhere, but it had the opposite reaction. The people of the Bogside were not going to let anything happen to her. One supporter said, "If they come in here to get Bernadette Devlin, we'll slaughter them all."[12]

McCann talked about his thoughts at the time and the barricades. "People barricaded the area because the cops were trying to get in. It turned out far more important than it seemed at the time. It seemed trivial at the time. The barricades were small, very small, they wouldn't have stopped anything. A truck would have knocked them down," he laughed.[13]

For the next two days, CS gas was continuously used by the RUC. The police still did not advance too much because of the petrol bomb throws that hadn't stopped since the first day. The officers never came closer than about fifty yards to the flats, so the Catholic groups on the rooftops had no issues with what they were doing or the effects of the gas. However, with the officers using CS gas, it raised the feelings of the Bogside citizens that they were under serious attack.

Billy McVeigh explained what happened to him during the battle. "I was shot with a rubber bullet, and I was 17 at the time of the Battle of the Bogside. Every year, the Orange marchers got closer and closer to the Bogside. And they had the police backing them up, like your parents faced with the Klan and the police in North Carolina."[14]

On Wednesday, August 13th, the RUC were asking for more supplies of CS gas around noon of that day. They were now facing into the Bogside near the right-hand side of Rossville Street.

The residents of the Bogside ended up creating barricades to prevent the RUC officers from entering the area. The barricades were being built on almost every street in the Bogside in an assembly-line style type of format. The barriers had been created from materials that had been stored in the Bogside area, hurriedly put together the night before and the morning of that second day, which consisted of pipes, paving stones, and anything else they could find

164 GOOD TROUBLE

to keep the police out. The newly formed DCDA (Derry Citizens Defence Association) stopped the officers from fighting back against the protestors.

Billy McVeigh said, "Enough was enough and the people began to fight back. When we put up the barricades just to keep them at bay, people came to the Free Derry Corner with crates of sugar and flour for petrol bombs and Molotov cocktails. People were passing them down the line to keep the guys out of the Bogside. We were fired up and the officers were fired up."[15]

Bernadette Devlin went into the Bogside and addressed the protestors. She talked about her time there, "There was an impression that I was everywhere, I suppose I was noticeable because it was me and maybe I shouldn't have been at it as a member of parliament. But looking back on it, my memory was I never slept for three days and three nights, I suppose. I was quite determined the police weren't coming in."[16]

By the end of the second day of the battle in the Bogside, injuries started to rise and the DCDA asked for every person available to come to Derry and help protect the Bogside. The Taoiseach of Ireland (comparable to President or Prime Minister) Jack Lynch threatened to send troops in and begged the UN to send troops to help. Taoiseach (another name for Irish head of government) Jack Lynch was denied by the UN, but the British government did eventually send troops into Northern Ireland.

One Derry resident said something about the troops that would haunt many years later, "I don't like British troops but they're better than the specials."[17]

On the third evening, the troops entered the city center a little after 5 p.m. This was right after the B Specials had arrived at 4 p.m. This made the Catholic population very nervous. Eammon McCann said of it, "Undoubtedly they would use guns. The possibility that there was going to be a massacre struck hundreds of people simultaneously. "Have we guns?" people shouted to one another, hoping that someone would know [...] suddenly fearful of what was about to happen."[18]

Delia McDermott remembered how scared she was when the B Specials arrived that afternoon as she talked about what was happening in the Bogside. "The area was closed because the B Specials came in. I hid with a friend under a stairway area and a woman and man found us and we hid with them until around five in the morning. We saw a bunch of people who'd been hurt."[19]

The relief from people on both sides was evident later as the troops made their way through the debris in the city. John Hume had spent most of the day trying to convince the Catholic crowds not to use violence against the officers. The Bogside residents were happy to see the troops rather than the B Specials.

Battle of the Bogside   165

The Army relieved the Specials and now there were over three hundred troops and Derry calmed down. The Army also agreed not to enter the Bogside.

The Bogside residents couldn't believe it. Their insurrection had been successful. The police had tried and tried to get into the Bogside, but they couldn't do it. They had driven them out of the Bogside. In a way, it was divine intervention because people still believe if the police had gotten into the Bogside, there would have been many casualties. Three days and three nights, and the citizens had won. The history of Northern Ireland would never be the same after the Battle of the Bogside.

Eamonn McCann was brutally honest about what happened over those three days in the Bogside, "I took the view in August 69, especially since what was happening was an attempt by the RUC, with Loyalist civilians mingling among them, to invade the Bogside and do violence to the people there. [...] A simple question was posed, was it right of the Bogside community to defend itself against physical attack? I had no problem doing that for the Bogside. [...] So, like everybody else, I joined in the defence of the Bogside and the rioting associated with it. Again, the consequences of it, which now appear to be obvious looking back, I don't think occurred to many of us at the time, even as late as the end of 1969 when British soldiers were already on the streets and there had been a number of deaths and so on. It was still only a tiny minority of people, who were disregarded at the time, who were forecasting that this was going to lead to the type of all-out horrendous struggle that we saw in subsequent years."[20]

Delia McDermott remembers her injuries from the Battle of the Bogside. "The next day I had five stitches in my head and we marched. It was three days and the B Specials finally moved out."[21]

Billy McVeigh felt like he and others knew the Bogside battle was inevitable. "Everybody knew this thing was coming- the Bogside in 1969. The song- Something's in the Air. Revolution was on the way. After three days and three nights, it was unbelievable that nobody was actually killed, even though it was hectic stuff."[22]

Billy also talked about the mural that was created after those violent nights. He explained, "The mural isn't about me. It's about civil rights. It's about equality. It's about housing, jobs. One man, one vote. Not only did they deprive us of our vote. If you were Protestant and owned a business and a house, you might have six votes. We struggled to get a vote."[23]

One of the odd things about the riots during these times in the Bogside was that most of the rioters wore suits, shirts and ties when they rioted. Billy

166 GOOD TROUBLE

McVeigh said that you rarely saw anyone out and about in tatters or raggedy clothes.

The remnants of the three-day battle in the Bogside were devastating. It was the worst violence that Northern Ireland had seen in over fifty years. The frustration and desperation were reminiscent of what the United States saw in the neighborhoods of Watts and Harlem when many Blacks destroyed the area. For more than fifty hours there had been day and night fighting, and when it was finished, the police were the ones who retreated. Pictures were even taken of Bernadette Devlin breaking bricks to throw at the RUC officers, which would later cause her to be charged and end up serving a six-month jail sentence. Luckily, nobody had died, but it did spark riots throughout the city of Belfast. It is also incredible that no guns were used during the three-day riot, probably the biggest reason that nobody had been killed. Troops were deployed to Derry for twenty-four hours, and they went to Belfast as well. The soldiers would remain in both cities for over thirty years and wouldn't leave until 2007, nearly ten years after the Good Friday Peace Agreement. Interestingly enough, the citizens would welcome the soldiers at first, but that would not be the case as time went on. It was also a sign that the British government was committing themselves to taking a more active role in the security and governance of Northern Ireland. The decision to send the troops into the streets of Northern Ireland would impact the country on many levels.

Julieann Campbell said about the Army, "They were supposed to be here for three months and they stayed for thirty to forty years. At the height of the Troubles in the 70s, there were well over 20,000 soldiers here."[24]

The other unfortunate result was the number of citizens who had lost their homes during the Bogside battle. The community that had lived for decades near the intersection of Rossville Street and William Street was destroyed. Records from the Derry Diocesan Archive show that almost twenty families lost their homes had to be rehoused.[25]

The Irish government actually stepped in and said they would provide aid to the citizens in the Bogside, but they ended up not sending anything close to military support for the people there. That would have caused a huge problem with the United Kingdom.

Riots had broken out across the six counties in Northern Ireland in places like Coalisland, Armagh, Dungannon and Belfast. Until the Battle of the Bogside, there were areas of Belfast that had still been mixed, with Catholics and Protestants living beside each other. As the violence increased across the city and nation, many families left their homes in fear of their lives. A number of houses had been burned to the ground in places like Conway and Bombay

Battle of the Bogside

Streets. A number of Catholic residents fled either south to the Republic of Ireland or across to England. The police and Loyalists went on a rampage, and the worst bloodshed was definitely in Belfast. In a scene reminiscent of the horrible riots that occurred in the early twentieth century in the United States, Loyalists went into Catholic neighborhoods and ended up shooting and beating any Catholics they saw. Just like the riots that occurred in Wilmington, Tulsa, St. Louis and Atlanta in the United States, the police joined the Loyalists with the B Specials as they began shooting unsuspecting Catholics throughout Belfast. Great Britain was forced to send in the army to get a hold on the situation. At that point, eight people had been murdered. Over 500 Catholic homes had been burned and 100 were injured.

Gerry Duddy said about the impact on Belfast, "Look at what happened in Belfast, streets burned down, families burnt out of their homes and families getting thrown out on the streets."[26]

Even to this day, nobody is one hundred percent sure about who started the Battle of the Bogside. Some will say it was started by the Protestant/Loyalist groups throwing down missiles which included all sorts of items, from the city walls on the Catholics who were looking up from the Bogside. Others will say that it started with the Catholic stone throwing at the Loyalists. Regardless, it set the wheels in motion for changes in Northern Ireland, both good and bad.

Up to that point, the protests had been based on nonviolent demonstrations against the injustices against the Catholic communities. Now, with the Bogside battle, it had taken on a feeling of a group of people who were more desperate and defiant, armed with stones and petrol bombs. Things in Derry and other areas in Northern Ireland had definitely escalated from the Battle of the Bogside.

Even today, the remants of the Battle of Bogside still linger. There are many who believe that the CS gas that was used caused many to suffer from different cancers today. Derry has one of the highest rates of cancer in that part of Europe. Julieann Campbell said, "Over 4,000 canisters of CS were used over that three night period."[27]

McCann had seen the evolution of the Civil Rights movement in Northern Ireland. "The first civil rights march was Duke Street in October 1968, where it was a few hundred people, very small numbers. After the baton attacks, Burntollet and the Battle of the Bogside, you had thousands. So at that moment you could see something historical happening, this was the start of something big. I'd love to say we stood back and knew what do to do next, we didn't. We had no plan. I'm still embarrassed when I look back on it. We had no clue what to do next."[28]

GOOD TROUBLE

Another result that was under the radar at the time was the split of the IRA. A new organization had formed, called the Provisional IRA. Not many people paid attention to this in the media, but the new, small group would be well known for the next thirty years.

The next months and the start of the 1970s would lead to more injustices against the Catholic community, with devastating consequences for the Catholic community across Northern Ireland.

CHAPTER 23

CONFLICT WITH THE POLICE, PARAMILITARIES, AND THE MARCHERS

There was a dramatic escalation over the summer of 1969 in the levels of violence that were seen in the streets of Northern Ireland. On August 12, 1969, the police pursued a gang of youthful rioters into the Irish nationalist district of Derry. Behind the barricades of 'Free Derry', marchers started to call for free bus rides, fair rents and equal pay for women. Like some Black protests in the United States, Northern Irish Catholics were hoping that an act of violence by the Protestants against them would have the potential to set off a revolution.

The leaders of Northern Ireland weren't the only ones keeping an eye on the Black civil rights fight in the United States. British intelligence kept a keen interest in the events as well. In 1967 the riots in Detroit, Michigan, were among the most violent and destructive riots in the history of the United States. There were six days of the worst rioting in American history which left 43 people dead, 467 injured and almost 2,500 buildings in ruins. To restore order, the state and federal authorities had flooded the city with paratroopers from the 82nd Airborne, National Guardsmen and even tanks. Over 7,000 National Guard and US Army troops had been called into service.

Very similar to the hot, passionate emotional summers in Northern Ireland, Detroit's predominantly African American neighborhood of Virginia Park was a simmering tinderbox of racial tension. About 60,000 low-income residents were crammed into the neighborhood's 460 acres, living in squalid, small, subdivided apartments, similar to the situation in the Derry Bogside at the time.

Just like the RUC, the Detroit Police Department was majority White. There were many accusations of racial profiling and police brutality by the Black residents. The entire city was going through a situation where the Whites

170 GOOD TROUBLE

left the city and moved into the suburbs, leaving widespread unemployment and poverty within the Black community that was in the city of Detroit.

Eamonn McCann said about the RUC, "The RUC was nakedly sectarian and they clearly made no differentiation between students marching for 'one person, one vote' and decent housing and all the rest of it, and people who were out to destroy the state and create a united Ireland."[1]

The worst riots in the United States occurred after the assassination of Dr. King outside of the Lorraine Motel in Memphis, Tennessee, on April 4, 1968. Reverend Burton was at the funeral of Dr. King, which was by invite only. He had a chance to see Dr. King's remains, and it was an experience he still remembers to this day. Even though the riots were awful times for America after the murder, Reverend Burton still had hope for the civil rights cause.

"After King's assassination, there was still a Civil Rights movement, and it was going to be enhanced by the death of Dr. King because he would become a hero after his murder. He died for the cause. White and Black people felt they had to further the cause. I didn't feel that all hope was gone."[2]

The first to panic about what they saw in the United States and what could happen in Northern Ireland were senior figures in British military and intelligence. Seeing soldiers on the streets of American cities, the chiefs-of-staff grew increasingly "uneas[y]" about "the possibility [...] that troops might have [to be] called upon [...] to help cope" with the second Grosvenor Square march on October 27, 1968. The Defense Secretary informed the Home Secretary that "the troops are not trained in riot control." The march passed off without significant trouble. But, much to the frustration of the Home Office, the generals "clearly remain unbelieving that the day will not come when the police will have to turn to the Armed Services for help in coping with a 'Grosvenor Square type' (the Ministry's term) demonstration." On January 8, 1969, Home Office and Security Service representatives told a meeting at the Ministry of Defense that "they could not envisage situations arising in this country which could necessitate the use of troops in [...] aid to the civil power." This assessment proved to be a serious misjudgment.

In August of 1969, Bernadette Devlin headed to the United States on behalf of the Northern Ireland Catholic population to seek relief for their civil rights fight. This was around the same time as an Apprentice Boys march in Derry led to increased violence, prompting the British government to send army troops to intervene on August 14. No doubt, this was again pushed because of what British intelligence had seen in Detroit and other US cities with the Black Civil Rights movement. Devlin was also determined that none of the money raised would be used for any violence. She was shocked that some couldn't see the connection between the Black civil rights movement and the Catholic one in Northern Ireland. Devlin said, "I'd ask them, 'do you support civil rights in Ireland and, if so, are you doing it because you're Catholic or because you support justice? And if so, are you working to see that your Black countrymen are being granted the justice you demand for Ireland? And if not, why not?' Maybe I'm being overly optimistic, but I had the feeling I got through to at least some bigoted Irish Americans. I hope so, anyway."[3] Devlin ended up raising almost $100,000 on her trip, but it was way below her goal of one million.

The riots during the Apprentice Boys parade resulted in heavy clashes between residents of the Bogside and the RUC. Barricades were barricades erected as protestors used stones and petrol bombs to throw at the RUC men to keep them out of the Bogside. That prompted the British Home Secretary, James Callaghan to send in and deploy British soldiers. There were negotiations between the Army and local political leaders, and it was agreed to pull the RUC and B Specials behind the Army outside the Bogside.[4] Unfortunately, the violence led to more deaths across Northern Ireland.

In September 1969, Lord Cameron compiled a report on civil unrest in Northern Ireland in 1968 and 1969. The Commission of Inquiry under Lord Cameron dealt with the religious confrontations, particularly the ones near and around Derry. The Government of Northern Ireland announced in mid-January 1969 that the commission would do the following: "hold an enquiry into and to report upon the course of events leading to, and the immediate causes and nature of the violence and civil disturbance in Northern Ireland on and since 5 October 1968; and to assess the composition, conduct and aims of those bodies involved in the current agitation and in any incidents arising out of it."[5]

Lord Cameron was joined by Sir John Biggert and James Campbell.

The commission found with regret considerable evidence of grave misconduct by the RUC in 1968 and 1969, particularly in the months of January and April in 1969. The report mentioned that RUC officers had been limited in their resources when it came to the marches. It also said that the police should be investigated for charges of assault and malicious damage.

The report was extremely detailed, especially dealing with the Belfast to Derry march in January 1969. It went on to praise John Hume as it mentioned his "outstanding" work in Derry and his "astonishing achievement" in persuading the residents of the Derry Bogside to leave the area for a meeting on April 20, 1969. His actions that day prevented what was an extremely dangerous situation. The report continued, saying that Hume's work had been "honestly exercised towards non-violent protests against wrongs."[6]

172 GOOD TROUBLE

The commission also warned against the possible distortion of the events that happened in those months because of news reports or film with these words: "The aimless and vicious hooligans of the streets and alleys to the extremists of Right or Left, of whatever creed, Catholic or Protestant, all would appear to bear a share of blame for the tragic events which have occurred and in which the vast majority of the population of Northern Ireland have neither hand nor concern and which we have no doubt they most deeply deplore."[7]

Major Bunting refused to give evidence at the inquiry, and Lord Cameron concluded that Bunting was wrong in claiming that the rioters in Derry on January 3 were civil rights protestors. He went on to say about the long march from Belfast to Derry, "For moderates this march had disastrous effects. It polarized the extreme elements in the communities in each place it entered. It lost sympathy for the civil rights movement and led to serious rioting in Maghera and Londonderry."[8] While he criticized the People's Democracy, he also said that the protection that the marchers deserved was not adequate. This was a criticism of the RUC police officers.

The commission continued to speak about Bernadette Devlin. It mentioned Devlin by name and said that they didn't doubt the genuine ideals that she carried about the civil rights movement. However, it did go on to say that they didn't doubt that she would use force to achieve her objectives if other methods such as nonviolence failed. They continued to say that People's Democracy had ties to the far-left movement in England.

The report did show some brute honesty by mentioning that some of the causes of the disorder in the streets were "deep-rooted," such as the Catholic resentment at the failure to remedy injustice in the cities. It also acknowledged the Protestant fears on the other side about the possible economic and political domination by a future Catholic majority.[9]

Overall, the Cameron report found that the civil rights protestors had been right about what they were marching for: housing, discrimination, gerrymandering, and one man, one vote. It also pointed a huge finger at the Unionist government, describing them as being complacent toward the Catholic community as a whole.

Major Bunting broke away from Ian Paisley and his followers in 1970.

Devlin said when she landed in the States, "I am going to America to look for a million dollars. We have 500 people homeless in Belfast. They will have to be rehoused."[10] Devlin planned to stay for a week and visit the cities of New York, Boston and Philadelphia.

Devlin mentioned her plan to also meet with Dr. Coretta Scott King, widow of the Reverend Martin Luther King Jr. She greatly admired King and his widow because of their fight for civil rights in America for the Black population. Devlin saw the clear connection between what the Catholics were fighting for and the Black population. She said, "The Irish Civil Rights struggle and the Black liberation movement in the US were basically the same battle, and Irish Americans should support Black liberation in the US as a primary duty."[11] Devlin had been disappointed in how the Irish Americans had treated the Black Civil Rights movement in the States.

Gerry Duddy said about King, "Martin Luther King Jr. People always brought up his name when we talked about Civil Rights here."[12]

Julieann Campbell said about the US Civil Rights movement's influence in Northern Ireland, "People started to get TVs in the late 60s. They were gathered around them and saw what was happening there. We saw a direct link with us through them."[13]

When questioned in the States about the partition of Ireland, Devlin said, "I will stress the injustice of the Unionist regime all down through the years, and I will stress the injustice of the Stormont government."[14] The Black Panther movement had started to influence the civil rights movement in Ireland. Devlin returned to Northern Ireland disillusioned by the Irish population in America, but her relationship with the Black Panthers remained strong over the years. The key to New York City, which she'd been gifted, was, on her behalf, presented to the Black Panthers. A few years later in 1971, Devlin would visit Black Panther leader Angela Davis in prison, who would, in turn, support Devlin's daughter in the 1990s.

This visit came at a particularly important time for Northern Ireland because of the tensions in the country following the Burntollet march and others.

In a strategic move to help calm the tensions across the country, the commander of the British occupation forces, General Ian Freeland, took the 8,000-man 'B Specials' Protestant volunteer police force off riot control duty. The B Specials were formed and hated by the Catholic minority and had been accused of arson and directed attacks on Catholic areas during the past few weeks of fighting in Northern Ireland cities, something that had been seen across the United States in race riots as well.[15]

Back in Northern Ireland, General Freeland said, "Because the army is now in control it will be possible to relieve the Ulster Special Constabulary of all riot control duties. But, because of the threats of the outlawed Irish Republican Army to intervene in Northern Ireland, the B Specials would remain to guard vital installations."[16]

174 GOOD TROUBLE

In response to the violence at Burntollet Bridge and the summer's violence in Derry's Bogside, the Ulster B Specials were ordered to be disbanded. The British government accepted the recommendations of Home Secretary Jim Callaghan. He ordered a complete reorganization and disarming of the RUC. His recommendations included:

> "An existing reserve force to be renamed the Special Patrol Group to carry out routine police duties, and its members limited to a three year term of service
>
> "A new volunteer reserve police force to aid police at local level, recruited in Belfast, Derry and the six counties"
>
> "A cadet corp

Reverend Paisley attacked the proposal, saying, "[...] an absolute sell-out to the republicans and the so-called civil rights movement which is only a smoke-screen for the republican movement."[17]

The B Specials were disbanded in 1970. In their place, the RUC Reserve was formed as an auxiliary police force. All military-style duties were handed over to the Ulster Defence Regiment, which was under military command.

***

Northern Ireland in the early '70s was looking like the United States in the late '60s. There were riots constantly. Riots preoccupied the minds of citizens throughout the country. Everyone was wondering where the next riot would be. Who was throwing stones and petrol bombs? What building was on fire?

There was also a split within both the IRA and Sinn Fein in 1970. Most people decided the best thing to do would be to take a political approach and fight for civil rights through the government. However, a number of them felt that was giving in and created the Provisional Army Council, which was more anti-government, sectarian and believed in fighting in the streets and not with the ballot box. One faction of Sinn Fein aligned itself with the Provisional IRA and the other, which later became the Worker's Party, aligning with the Official IRA.

The problem was also that not everyone knew exactly what was going on in some of these so-called "no-go areas," especially in the Bogside of Dublin. Because of the neighborhoods being separated and the schooling, this is not a surprising fact.

Conflict with Various Groups 175

Gerry Duddy said, "People in the Waterside (Protestant area in Derry-across the Peace Bridge from the city centre) that I worked with had no idea about what was happening where I lived."[18]

The other issue was that of the media in some places, especially what was going back to England on the television. Some people didn't know what was going on in Northern Ireland because of what was being broadcast on the news. Some media outlets showed what they wanted to show and the British government knew what they were doing in terms of showing the impact of the Troubles.

How much had things changed in that two-year period for the British Army? Wharton was still deployed in Northern Ireland and said the following, "We had dog shit thrown at us. The kids used sticks to throw it at us. And they were kids, what were you going to do with kids?"[19] This was a long way from tea and sandwiches being served to Wharton two years ago.

Wharton admitted that since his first time in Northern Ireland, the entire atmosphere in the country had changed for the worse. He said, "Some Catholic communities hated the British by now."[20]

Even the Catholic citizens remarked on how things had changed with the British Army, such as nighttime raids for searches. The troops were now angry and shouting and being physical with the Catholic communities. There were no more tea and sandwiches with them. And from the troops, there was no apology when the searches and destruction of property didn't turn up anything.

Billy McVeigh talked about the nighttime searches: "Even if you weren't a member of anything you could be picked up. Or if your grandpa was involved in the 50s. The sins of your father."[21]

The number of house searches and invasions brought a number of complaints from the Catholic communities in Northern Ireland. Wharton had been interviewed by the BBC in 1971 and said the following, "So, you go into a Protestant area and they give you tea and cakes. They're friendly. You go into a Catholic area, they throw bottles, stones and they shoot at you. So it's only natural that you're going to be biased. And I'm Catholic. I just don't like the Irish Catholics over here."[22] Wharton said in 2023, "Not everyone was out there to kill you but there are some."[23]

It was a difficult time for everyone in Northern Ireland. Bombs were going off several times each day in shops, pubs and workplaces. There were many victims—men, women and children—and it crossed religious lines with both Catholic and Protestant casualties. The savagery of what was happening was being seen all around the world. Even the tactics of the British Army changed. Wharton said, "Our whole tactics changed. The IRA weren't messing around.

176 GOOD TROUBLE

They were killing people. We had to come up with something and that's all we had-internment."[24]

In late 1971, the disarming of the RUC ended because of the chaos throughout the cities in Northern Ireland. In that same year, sidearms were issued once again to the dismay of the Catholic communities.

Wharton saw the destruction firsthand, and it is amazing that he has kept his humor through all that he dealt with during his tour in Northern Ireland. He explained that over a period of almost five months, his team lost five people and over a hundred were injured. Wharton went home, and he ended up surviving a nail bomb. He went home with shrapnel in his legs and his left hand had almost been completely shattered through the bombing.

Internment was the new way of doing things in Northern Ireland. It impacted people who were sometimes just sitting in their homes, minding their own business. The paranoia that ran through Wharton and other military and police was at the highest level. The British government now said that they had the right to detain anyone without trial whom they deemed to be a suspect for terrorism. That meant houses turned upside down and innocent people being harassed on a daily basis.

Billy McVeigh explained that internment deprived the Catholic citizens of their freedoms since there was no judge or jury. People were locked up and that was it.

Because of internment and the disillusionment of the Civil Rights movement in the late '60s, along with the presence of British troops in the country, the Provisional IRA saw a growth in numbers that they'd never seen before. You could also see that everyday citizens started to see the IRA in a different light as well. People in cities like Derry would see IRA volunteers in the streets, working checkpoints and using everything at their disposal to fortify Catholic neighborhoods. Free Derry was a place that the volunteers tried to keep an eye on and protect the people living there. As one Catholic woman said, "Many provisionals seem to be well respected in the community."[25]

People from the outside, myself included, would often wonder what would make someone join the Provisional IRA at that time. I often think of the saying that one man's freedom fighter is another man's terrorist. Ricky O'Rawe was an IRA volunteer and is now a former member who is very open about his time with the organization, or as open as one can be.

O'Rawe's explanation for joining the IRA at the time could have been the standard answer for other young Catholics, at the time, in Northern Ireland: "As far as I was concerned, I was doing the right thing. The absolute right thing, the patriotic thing. To fight these foreigners who were on Irish soil. I was

Conflict with Various Groups 177

involved with the struggle for Irish freedom. As far as I was concerned, this was war. We saw ourselves like the French Resistance fighting against the Nazis."[26]

At the time in late 1971, both sides had their own paramilitary forces that were getting worked up again. However, the Provisional IRA was relatively new. They had been formed in 1970 after the destruction of Belfast which followed the Battle of the Bogside. There were still some old folks who were part of the IRA from the 1950s, but they had grown quiet over the decades since then.

Another event that created a number of recruits into the IRA was the controversial issue of internment in August 1971.

Internment without trial was officially called Operation Demetrius. This was implemented by Northern Ireland and the Stormont Unionist government to help stem the tide of paramilitary activity at the time. It involved the mass British arrests of close to 350 people from Catholic backgrounds. Rumors were that not everyone on the Unionist side was in favor of internment, but many feared a political backlash if they didn't do something to help fight the IRA. The ironic side was that many of the subjects who were arrested during this time were mostly civil rights protesters and had no ties at all to the IRA. Out of the 350 or so who were arrested, many were released within days because of the intelligence being faulty. The people who were jailed at that time were held in a place called the new Long Kesh near the city of Lisburn. This later became known infamously as the Maze prison. There were also prisoners who were held in a British Army camp in Derry and onboard the Maidstone ship in Belfast Harbour.

The latter part of 1971 had the British security raiding Catholic homes across the country. This included men and sons being dragged out of their beds in the middle of the night and families petrified that their loved ones would never return.

Billy McVeigh was one of these young men who was arrested. He would end up being arrested over nine times during the early '70s.

McVeigh described what he went through during his time under arrest: "The last two times I was arrested I was in a place called Ballyhenny, they called it the Torture chamber. And I got real bad abuse. Teeth made loose, gun to my throat with them pulling the trigger. Pulled my hair out. They tried to pin a bombing on me. They wanted me to sign and confess. Batons and boots on me. They used white lighting—in a room that was totally white, lights flickered all night. Three days and three nights of that. All to get you to sign. They couldn't break me but some signed and you can't blame them. They told me they wouldn't harass me anymore if I signed. Eventually, they released me

178   GOOD TROUBLE

but they said they would take me out sooner or later. Scary for someone 18 and 19 years old."[27]

Internment became another recruitment surge for the IRA at the time. The British had underestimated the reaction of the Catholic population to the controversial issue of internment. Before internment, the IRA had killed 10 soldiers. By the end of 1971, they had killed 40.[28]

Things were getting bad, worse than anyone could have imagined for Northern Ireland. In 1970, twenty-nine people were killed and those numbers were startling. But in 1971, with internment and other issues, the number jumped to 180. It was no surprise that the rise in numbers was attributed to internment. And the stories of those who had been interned were horrible, with interrogation tactics such as hooding suspects and depriving them of both sleep and food and sometimes worse.

                                    ***

In January 1972, things changed for the worse across the country. Bloody Sunday was the reason for that. There have been numerous books written on that subject, one excellent one being *On Bloody Sunday*, by my friend and fellow writer, Julieann Campbell.

On January 30, 1972, a Civil Rights march was held to protest internment. The government had declared that the march was illegal, but the marchers decided that they would go ahead with the protest. The march left the Creggan area of Derry on a cold, crisp day with a clear blue sky. Nobody could have predicted what would happen on that day. There were over 20,000 people in Derry that day. A large number were in front of the Guildhall for the march. But before the majority of the numbers could get there, barricades forced them back into the Bogside. There were a number of young men, about twenty, who started throwing rocks at the army, but there were no guns or petrol bombs, nothing out of the ordinary. Suddenly, the paratroopers charged at the young men and started to fire into the crowd indiscriminately. They shot at anything and anyone for at least twenty minutes.

Gerry Duddy explained why Jackie went to the march that day. "I was only 14 at the time of Bloody Sunday. Our whole family was behind the march. Everyone wanted to hear Bernadette (Devlin). That was Jackie's excuse to go to the march. Jackie had never been to a march before. But I had to sneak out since I was only 14."[29]

In a nutshell, 13 unarmed civil rights demonstrators were shot dead by British Army paratroopers. The protestors were all Catholics and had been

Conflict with Various Groups   179

marching in protest of the internment of suspected Irish nationalists. Most had
been shot in the back. British authorities had ordered the march banned and
sent troops to confront the demonstrators when it went ahead. The soldiers
shot indiscriminately into the crowd of protestors. They ended up killing 13
and wounding 18.

Bernadette Devlin was there as well and said, "The British paratroopers
were gunning down people all around me [...] They murdered 13 unarmed
people. As I saw them fall, I said to myself, Christ! I'm going to die here [...] I
felt no horror, no fear, not even anger. Just a cold realistic assessment that they
had murdered a lot of us."[30]

Devlin flew to London the next day for an emergency parliament emergency meeting. As one speaker tried to blame the Catholics, she explained that
she was there. She couldn't take it anymore and charged him. His name was
Reginald Maudling, who was the home secretary. Devlin punched him over
and over again in the face. It was the first time in history a woman had ever
assaulted a cabinet minister during a session of Parliament.

Delia McDermott still remembers the nightmares from Bloody Sunday. "I
was 18 at the time of the Bloody Sunday march, the year I was getting married. It was horrific. They tried to break the barrier of William Street. I was
there when they were spraying the water. They were spraying us with a blue
dye. I ran towards the platform but I could hear the shooting. Once I heard the
shooting, we all ran into the houses. When my husband (boyfriend at the time)
and I went to get the car beside where the shooting took place, they asked us to
take the bodies to the hospital. It was an awful experience."[31]

Billy McVeigh said about what he had experienced on that day, "I ended up
at a phone box and two people were shot dead right beside me. I'll never forget,
the blood coming towards me."[32]

The murders of the innocent Catholics brought attention from around the
world to the situation in Northern Ireland. Even my parents at the time, both
of whom were barely 30-year-old teachers, remember to this day hearing about
what had occurred in Derry on that day and they were stunned.

One of the iconic pictures of the day was Father Edward Daly as he helped
carry Julieann Campbell's uncle, Jackie Duddy, after being shot. Father Daly
said, "I waved my handkerchief, which, by now, was heavily bloodstained [...]
We then proceeded to the corner of Waterloo Street and Harvey Street. At
this point, Willie Barber took off his coat, spread it on the ground, and we laid
Jackie Duddy on it [...] We waited until the ambulance arrived. I am not sure
how long it took."[33]

180 GOOD TROUBLE

Eamonn McCann described what he saw, "It happened literally on the street that I was born and grew up [...] it was personal. Bloody Sunday was personal to the whole of the Bogside. Bloody Sunday was done in broad daylight, by men in British uniforms using Nato-issue self loading rifles, lethal at 1,000 yards, and they were shooting across the street."[34]

Gerry Duddy believed that Bloody Sunday was also the moment that everyone started to turn against the British Army. Gerry mentioned that his family rarely talked about what happened on Bloody Sunday in the years afterward. He understandably still has not given up hope that some of the soldiers will one day be charged and punished for what they did on that day to the innocent citizens, including his brother.[35]

The British government attempted to cover up the truth about this atrocity with the 1972 Lord Chief Justice Widgery Report. That report falsely blamed the deaths on the march organizers and unconditionally exonerated soldiers.

McCann later became the chair of the Bloody Sunday Trust, which advocated for the second inquiry into the killings.

Decades later, the 2010 Lord Saville report found none of the victims posed a threat, and the soldiers acted without justification. It had taken 38 years, but blame and responsibility for Bloody Sunday was finally given to the Parachute Regiment where it should have been in the first place. Eamonn McCann was there on the steps of the Guildhall in Derry when the victims were found innocent.

When the report came out, many Protestants were shocked because what they were told by the media really did not happen that way. They had been led to believe for years that the unarmed Catholics were the ones who were at fault. The Protestants had been told that and believed it for decades afterward.

Unfortunately, Bloody Sunday became the biggest recruitment drive ever for the Irish Republican Army. In 1972, close to 500 people were killed in Northern Ireland, which to this day remains the worst year of the Troubles in terms of casualties.

After Bloody Sunday, Northern Ireland's parliament in Belfast fell within a few months. This established direct rule of Northern Ireland from London, England.

Julieann Campbell, whose uncle, Jackie Duddy, was killed on that day as a 17-year-old, said the following: "Bloody Sunday killed the Civil Rights Movement. Now, everyone wanted to join the IRA. Even if they didn't lose someone on Bloody Sunday. It was 100% the biggest recruitment for them. There were queues everywhere for the IRA. A huge surge of four thousand active in the weeks after. A lot of people were turned down by the IRA because

Conflict with Various Groups

181

they were relatives of the deceased. They were told they were joining for the wrong reasons. People like me were doing this because of our loved ones, no other reason."[36]

Billy McVeigh explained the impact of Bloody Sunday, "It was a big mistake for people joining the IRA because people were angry. They weren't genuine. The IRA told them, come back in two months' time when you aren't so angry."[37]

The years after Bloody Sunday and the unofficial end of the Civil Rights Movement rocked Northern Ireland with a huge increase in sectarian violence from both sides, including bombings and other atrocities. The new IRA was determined to get its hands on the latest and most dangerous weapons.

Father Daly said, "Countless young people were motivated by the events of that day to become actively involved in armed struggle and, as a direct result, joined the Provisional IRA...I am not at all sure about how I would have reacted, had I been a teenager and witnessed those same events."[38]

Gerry Duddy remarked how the day resonated with him and others, "I was a young, angry boy. Because of Bloody Sunday, people began to take up arms."[39]

Northern Ireland turned into a war zone after Bloody Sunday, with hardended Army posts throughout cities such as Derry. Forty thousand Catholics still lived in the Bogside area, with barricades everywhere, burned-out vehicles, barbed wire, IRA no-go areas and checkpoints. The mood had truly turned.

The frustration of what was ahead was evident in what Bernadette Devlin said later in 1972, "The crime of sectarianism and it is a crime that runs very deep in our society. It has perverted and poisoned even the best people, the truly good people on both sides. If we are to make Northern Ireland a decent place to live, we must stop thinking of ourselves as Catholic or Protestant, Irish or British, and start thinking of ourselves as human beings, with the same social and economic problems and the same social and economic enemies."[40]

Now the people were at a time in Northern Ireland when the government and security had become perilous.

It would remain so for the next 30 years.

CHAPTER 24

CONCLUSION

I took a walk through the stone-walled city of Derry in the summer of 2022 and got to the very top where you can look down into the Bogside. I think about the story that our tour guide told us about a kid being shot by a soldier who was sitting up on this hill, taking out people with a bird's eye view of them. You could feel and taste the history in the air.

We were lucky enough to have a Catholic man from Derry who knew the area well to show us around and give us the stories that peppered the area.

The Civil Rights campaign in Derry was seen around the world and recognized as a formidable movement because it followed the blueprint of the Civil Rights movement in the United States. They borrowed the wording of the Black Civil Rights movement, the commitment to nonviolence and the tactics such as sit-ins and civil disobedience.

There may not have been a Northern Ireland Civil Rights movement were it not for Martin Luther King Jr., John Lewis, the Courageous Eight and others. Today, Bernadette Devlin McAliskey (now her married name) works with the organization she helped found: STEP (South Tyrone Empowerment Program), a community development scheme in Tyrone. She has survived being shot fourteen times in various assassination attempts and continues to seek justice and work toward her goals. She said in her autobiography, "In this movement which is still struggling to free our people from the bonds of economic slavery, I am only one amongst hundreds of my generation. We were born into an unjust system; we are not prepared to grow old in it."[1] She continued when talking about the Unionist government that ruled her country, "For half a century it has misgoverned us, but it is on the way out. And with traditional Irish mercy, when we've got it down we will kick it into the ground."[2]

183

184   GOOD TROUBLE

When people think of Bloody Sunday in Alabama, one tends to think of Governor George Wallace and his proclamations for segregation. On the other side, J. L. Chestnut spoke eloquently about how Wallace treated him with respect and told others to do so as well during his time of practicing law in Selma before Wallace became governor. Chestnut said, "Judge George Wallace was the most liberal judge I ever practiced law in front of. He was the first judge to call me mister in an Alabama courtroom."[3] How do you explain those words about the person who ordered the beating of innocent people at the Pettus Bridge in 1965? I don't know if anyone can.

Other examples are crystal clear. Sheriff Jim Clark, who masterminded the attack on the protestors at Bloody Sunday in Selma, said the following in 2006: "Basically, I'd do the same thing today if I had to do it all over again."[4]

Before John Hume accepted the Nobel Prize in 1998, he said, "Martin Luther King was very much our inspiration," when he and others addressed the problems of discrimination and prejudice throughout the country. He continued, "We believed in the words of Dr. Martin Luther King. We believed in inclusivity, not exclusivity. We believed that true unity among all Irish people was unity of the heart, not unity of the soil."[5]

King's widow, Coretta Scott King, praised Hume when she presented him with the 1999 Martin Luther King Jr. Nonviolent Peace Prize. She said, "Like Dr. King, he has demonstrated the power of one person who provided a spark of leadership that provided a way out of no way."[6]

***

The work of Martin Luther King Jr., John Hume, John Lewis, Eamonn McCann, Bernadette Devlin and the Courageous Eight is not finished. Much progress has been made but the issues of racism and poverty in the United States and Northern Ireland, respectively, continue to challenge both countries today. There is an obligation for us to speak out like King, Hume, Lewis, the Courageous Eight and Devlin did.

The events of Bloody Sunday were never far from John Lewis's mind. Every year until he died, he traveled to Selma to commemorate the anniversary of the march. For many, attitudes did change over the centuries. At the commemoration ceremony in 1988, Joseph T. Smitherman, who had been Selma's segregationist mayor in 1965 at the time of the march and was still mayor, gave Lewis a key to the city. Mayor Smitherman said at that time, "Back then, I called him an outside rabble-rouser. Today, I call him one of the most courageous people I've ever met."[7]

Conclusion 185

I ask all visitors to Northern Ireland to go to the Free Derry Museum in Derry, Northern Ireland. It is a humbling experience. At Free Derry Corner stands the white gable wall where in 1969 Catholics defiantly painted the slogan: "You are now entering Free Derry." It gave me goosebumps seeing that in person. It was a declaration of an area from which police and the British Army were banned until 1972, when the army broke down the barricades.

What makes the Free Derry Museum even more symbolic is that it was officially opened by the Civil Rights activist Reverend Jesse Jackson in 2017. Rev. Jackson marched with Dr. King for many years. This show of support for Derry was another shining example of the strong bond between the Catholic and Black Civil Rights movements.

Probably the most incredible point of the visit to the museum was the outside area. You could still see bullet holes in some of the buildings that surrounded the museum and the alleyways where people hid on Bloody Sunday. Frighteningly historical.

The trauma that the Catholic population dealt with between 1968–1972 is incredible, and television and cameras brought it into the living rooms of people all around the world, just like the March on Washington and the Selma to Montgomery marches did in the United States.

One of the batons that was used on Bloody Sunday in March 1965 is on display at the National Voting Rights Museum in Selma, Alabama.

John Lewis said in 2018: "Do not get lost in a sea of despair. Be hopeful, be optimistic. Our struggle is not the struggle of a day, a week, a month, or a year, it is the struggle of a lifetime."[8]

Devlin said in 1969, "Keep up the pressure; keep down the temperature."[9]

The struggles that the Black population and the Catholic population went through showed their determination to fight for their rights. Dr. King had a great quote for what both populations dealt with: "Freedom is never given to anybody for the oppressor has you in domination because he plans to keep you there and he never voluntarily gives it up. That is where their strong resistance comes. We've got to keep on keeping on in order to gain freedom. It is not done through the pressure that comes about from people who are oppressed. Privileged classes never give up their privileges without strong resistance."[10] We also need to remember that there were many White allies in the civil rights movement in the United States and Protestants who supported the same movement in Northern Ireland.

Julieann Campbell said, "The Civil Rights movement wasn't just a Catholic movement, there were lots of Protestants involved."[11] Many Protestants did not understand why some of their own people sided with the Catholics. They believed that those Protestants in the civil rights movement were being used. Used, as "tokens" in the movement and not realizing that the Catholics had a different agenda in their minds.

Those words resonate for the Black population in the United States and the Catholic population in Northern Ireland, even today after all those years. Both Selma and Derry were the sites of seismic events in the Civil Rights world, which would transform the futures of both countries. The world and history would come to know Selma in 1965 and Burntollet in 1969 forever.

The most incredible thing is that both of these movements were led and created by young people—people like my parents who weren't even twenty when they started marching. Whenever I talk to young people, I remind them of what their parents and grandparents went through to give them the advantages that they have today, myself included.

Eamonn McCann said about the legacy of the Civil Rights movement, "The only thing that ever got us anywhere in this town was not paramilitary manoeuvre. In my view, it certainly wasn't armed struggle. What it was, was the sound of marching feet."[12]

Young people need to know that they can change the world. And don't let anyone tell you that you can't. You have the power to make our world an even better place for future generations.

BREXIT, IRISH UNITY, AND THE TROUBLES IN NORTHERN IRELAND TODAY

July 2001, almost 20 years since I first visited Belfast, Northern Ireland, the beautiful and tragic land I had studied about for three years during my master's in history at Hollins University. The Good Friday peace agreement had so much promise and freshness to it, seeing the Unionist leaders accept the fact that political representatives such as Gerry Adams and others who had links to violence would be a part of a power-sharing government. The Nationalists agreed that Northern Ireland would remain part of the United Kingdom unless the majority of their constituents voted for a united Ireland. Realistically, the peace process involved backroom deals with former terrorists and other unsavory people. Sadly, with recent events, we have to ask ourselves what happened to the reconciliation of the two communities. Don't get me wrong; there has been progress, much progress overall. However, the threats of Protestant Loyalist paramilitaries wanting to review ceasefire agreements and an Irish Times newspaper poll indicating most people don't think the chant glorifying the IRA, "Up the Ra," is a bad thing would make you think it was 1982. Sadly, they were from 2022.

I may be in the minority, but not all the blame can be placed at Brexit's door and the Irish Sea Border controversy. Northern Ireland voted against Brexit, but that is only part of the problem and honestly, Brexit had nothing to do with Northern Ireland. The other part stems from years of fear. Fear has always been a hallmark of Northern Ireland.

More than 3,500 people were killed in Northern Ireland during the thirty years of the Troubles. The ramifications of that violence are still being felt with the prosecutions of British war veterans occurring recently. Also, monetary payments given to victims of the violence. The difficult thing is that the question always comes up about who is truly the victim and who is the bad guy when it comes to past violence. Even someone who was blown up by the same bomb that they planted can be counted as a victim. Strange, but true. Jennifer

188   GOOD TROUBLE

Jordan's father was murdered by the IRA and she can't believe the bomber could be counted as a "victim." "What other country in the world would do that?" Ms. Jordan is now seventy-five years old and she had six relatives die over the 30-year period of the Troubles. The past is never truly the past when it comes to Northern Ireland. The heartbreak of the killings still looms large in the country.

I was so excited to visit the country I had studied. When I told my father about the trip, he said, "You're gonna mess around and get shot over there." I ignored that fatherly advice that he gave me, but I will not lie; I was nervous when I heard that while I was there in July 2001, riots had broken out nearby because of the marching season. The marching season is in full effect in July across Northern Ireland when bands from the Protestant community flow into the streets to mark July 12, a commemoration of a centuries-old military victory of a Protestant king over a Catholic one. There often is sporadic violence that includes bonfires and sometimes riots that break out because of the marches.

What do the Civil Rights marchers and activists think of what they did today? One thing I learned from all of my interviews is how traumatic some of the incidents that happened still affect the people involved today. A great example is that my parents were very hesitant for me to go to Alabama to speak to people who took part in the Selma to Montgomery march. They both still have strong memories of the horrific things that happened to many Black people in the state during the mid-'60s.

Gerry Duddy said, "If we hadn't heard King speak, I don't know if we'd gotten to the stage where we knew what we were doing with the Civil Rights movement. I can still remember the signs of No Dogs, No Blacks, No Irish. Unfortunately, the Troubles still overshadows the Northern Ireland Civil Rights movement and what the people did. It also took time for my parents to be able to talk about the past."[1]

Delia McDermott, who now lives in Ireland, said the following, "I did what I did because I wanted a better life for my kids and my grandkids."[2]

When I interviewed Julieann Campbell, she told her uncle, Gerry Duddy, the following: "Because of what you all did, I didn't need to fight. When I was growing up, I was worried I'd have to take up the fight for the Bloody Sunday campaign because I was the only one interested but I didn't want to do that, but I would have for the family."[3]

In the '70s, Northern Ireland saw violence and sectarian/paramilitary groups becoming highly active on both sides—Catholic Republicans/Nationalists and Protestant Loyalists; chaos was everywhere. Those traumas

Northern Ireland Today

live on today as we witnessed adults in the summer months during the marching season using youths as young as sixteen to set buses ablaze, attack photographers, and throw petrol bombs and rocks at police officers. Over 3,500 lives were lost during what NI citizens call "The Troubles."

The ties that bind the Catholic Civil Rights movement in Northern Ireland and the Black Civil Rights movement were strong even back in 1966 when Dr. King addressed a group in Chicago, "If my Catholic brothers said to me amid bigotry towards Catholics we don't need your support in this because we have enough Catholic power to deal with it. I would still take a stand against bigotry towards Catholics because it is wrong, it is evil and it is unjust."[4]

How much have things changed? I remember after leaving Derry in the summer of 2022, and I went to Belfast and took a black cab tour (very popular to visit both Nationalist and Loyalist communities) into the East Belfast area— Union Jack flags were on every lamppost, so I knew where I was. I visited the peace wall that divided the Shankill Road (Protestant area) and the Falls Road (Catholic area). Interestingly enough, more peace walls have been erected since the Good Friday Agreement. On a positive note, you can still see the beautiful mural of Dr. King and John Hume in Derry's Bogside area. To me, Northern Ireland is still an incredible, beautiful place and it is definitely because of the people. They have a keen sense of humor, probably because they have dealt with a dark history. As people say there, it's a country filled with great craic (fun in Northern Ireland vernacular).

As a young student, I was intrigued by Northern Ireland because of the similarities to what had occurred between Whites and Blacks over the years in the United States. The parallels are striking—segregated neighborhoods (even today in the United States), disillusioned youth, joblessness and hopelessness in some places. Hard to believe? Look at the major areas around the Belfast area—Short Strand Interface (the place of riots), Albert Road (strong Protestant area), Larne (stronghold for Protestants), Glenarm (mixed town). It gets better—Protestants holiday on the north coast, Catholics holiday in Donegal.

Another wrinkle that occurred in September 2023 was the Legacy Act law that shuts down all historical inquests after May 1, 2024, and has already prevented new civil cases from being taken up in the courts. The Conservative government in the United Kingdom backed this law, but most in Northern Ireland are against it. Annette McGavigan was 14 when she was killed by a British soldier in the Bogside and Billy McGreanery was 41; both of these murders took place in 1971. The families of the deceased had been attempting to get charges put on the soldiers, but they were told that both cases had insufficient evidence to provide a chance of any type of conviction. Both families were angered by the decision to not go through with it before the May 1, 2024 cut-off date for prosecution.

The Legacy Act is a delicate matter, where soldiers who were responsible for deaths on Bloody Sunday in January 1972 may now may not be prosecuted for what they did. Gerry Duddy said about this, "The people responsible for the killings, nothing has been done. With the other crimes, hundreds of families out there don't know who to turn to. We had our group for Bloody Sunday."[5] Very similar to the Truth Commission that occurred in South Africa after Apartheid ended. Could it help? Possibly. However, will some people truly admit to some of the heinous crimes that they committed during the era of the Troubles? Only time will tell.

Currently, this is being fought over in several courts. It has been opposed by all Northern Ireland politicians at Stormont and Westminster. It remains to be seen if it will move forward.

Prosecutions which began before May 1, 2024, such as Soldier F in relation to Bloody Sunday in Derry, will continue to reach a conclusion. The biggest impact of the law is that it will stop all Troubles-related inquests. This will apply to inquests which have not been started, or haven't reached the stage where there are substantial findings. The new ICRIR (Independent Commission for Reconciliation and Information Recovery) will look at addressing the legacy of the past. It will be headed by former Lord Chief Justice Sir Declan Morgan. He will have the power to do replacement inquests and investigate any Troubles-related incidents where people were killed or seriously injured. However, the main goal of the group will be to provide new information to relatives and survivors.

The Legacy Act will end 38 inquests from the Troubles era. The Labour Government has said they would repeal the law if they win the election in Summer 2024.

They won. Time will tell.

***

Going back to Brexit—is it the whole problem? No. Has it helped? No. Northern Ireland is a complicated place with a complex history (again very similar to the US). The majority in all the communities want peace and a voice at the table. They want hope, hope that was created from the many people who died over the years (again, similar to the number of Americans who died in the United States fighting for civil rights). Yes, Brexit is partly responsible,

Northern Ireland Today 191

but peace has always been fragile. Now, we are all seeing the stress of politics and newly active sectarian/paramilitary groups taking advantage of a perilous situation. There is still much to do for true peace in the region, but I know from friends that I communicate with in social work, politics and writing that in Northern Ireland it can be achieved. However, make no mistake—this is a dangerous time, just as it was in the '70s. Both sides will need to come together, compromise and agree to disagree on some things. Anger and distrust persist on both sides. Some issues have evolved, but fundamentally, the tension remains the same since the 1830s—home rule vs. outside dominance. Even today, Northern Ireland has had no devolved government for two years because of a dispute over trade borders dealing with Brexit.

In 2000, I wrote this about the peace process in my masters work, "Can peace survive? Yes, it can." The majority of people in Northern Ireland do not want any more unnecessary violence. I loved my time in Derry and Belfast and met some of the most friendly people over there during my visits. They are proud of their country, both sides, for what they've accomplished having moved forward. Are there still issues? Of course, there are. But the same can be said for my own country, the United States. The violence in both countries is long gone. In terms of the United States, my parents lived through segregation, marched for equal rights and have now seen the first-ever Black president. That is progress. Northern Ireland is in the best position that it has been for decades. For leaders like Bernadette Devlin McAliskey, Gerry Adams and John Hume to come from where they began, it is truly amazing. Adams knew he was taking a chance of being killed as he oversaw the destruction of the IRA's arsenal during the beginning of the Good Friday Agreement. And we cannot forget David Trimble, who at the time of the peace agreement, was the leader of the Ulster Unionists, which at the time was the biggest Unionist party. Even though he would barely talk to Adams, they did what they had to do to secure peace in the region. They all made sure that power sharing between the Unionists and Nationalists had to happen. The leading party on one side provided the first ministers, the other side gives the deputy, and the key votes must be passed by majorities representing both. This had to be done to end the carnage since even in the 1990s, over 400 lives were lost to the Troubles.

What these people did to preserve peace should give hope to every Catholic and Protestant in Northern Ireland. It gives hope to the rest of the world, including the United States, where polarizations on both sides are the norm. Northern Ireland has shown in the last decade that the two extremes can learn to rule together.

192 GOOD TROUBLE

Both Selma and Derry were the sites of shocking events that accelerated both countries to look at their marginalized citizens in a different way when it came to Civil Rights. Bloody Sunday in Selma and the Burntollet Bridge incident both caused a huge expression of public sympathy around the world and helped both Civil Rights movements gain momentum. Both moments were watershed events in the lives of Black and Catholic citizens in the United States and Northern Ireland, respectively.

In April 2014, then-Congressman John Lewis visited Derry and walked across the Peace Bridge. It is a bridge that runs parallel to the Craigavon Bridge. It was there that Lewis met with John Hume. At that time, Lewis would still do a ceremonial walk each year to commemorate the Selma march across the Edmund Pettus Bridge. To see Lewis and Hume on that bridge together was showing everything full circle in both the Black and Catholic Civil Rights movements and what they had accomplished.

EPILOGUE

It is hard to believe that it has been well over 25 years since the Good Friday Agreement was signed and peace was secured for the people of Northern Ireland. President Bill Clinton stood near the historic walls of Derry and recited the famous lines of the poet Seamus Heaney, "Once in a lifetime, the longed for tidal wave of justice can rise up and hope and history rhyme."[1] This was symbolic of what was to come for the country in the next few years. The peace agreement was a testament to the more than 3,500 people who had lost their lives during the Troubles and the close to 40,000 people who were maimed during those violent years.

I still remember my first visit to the country fondly, visiting Belfast, looking around and seeing that I was one of the few people of color in the city. I had my first pint across the street from the Europa Hotel (the most bombed hotel in Europe—33 explosions at the property between 1970 and 1994) and received a kiss on the lips from a friendly Northern Irish lass after I'd only been in the country for a couple of hours. You could say that I fell in love with the country instantly after that! And no doubt, the Guinness tastes better in Ireland and Northern Ireland than in any other place in the world!

And the changes it has seen over the years: the new buildings without any fear of bomb attacks, the new and tasty restaurants across the country, now you see people from both religions enjoying themselves in the city center without a care in the world in places like the Cathedral Quarter. When I walked through the area with the new Titanic museum and its hotels and restaurants, you realize that none of this could have been accomplished without the work for peace. The site of the construction of the Titanic had become a barren area by 1998, but now it has not only the museum but worldwide companies like Microsoft and CitiBank. However, yes, people do socialize with each other more than ever across the religious divide, there are 100 peace walls in Belfast that divide the Protestant and Catholic communities in West Belfast, more than there were in 1998 when the Good Friday Agreement was signed.

I joke with my parents that for people their age, they have seen more changes in the world than anyone at any age. The list is impressive in terms of civil rights—Segregation in the 1940s, Rosa Parks and the bus boycott in the 1950s, the landmark *Brown v. Board of Education* that ended school segregation in the 1950s, the rise of Martin Luther King Jr., The March on Washington in 1963, Selma in 1965, the assassination of King in 1968, the rise of Black Power in the '70s, the first Blacks to run for president in the '80s, and the election of President Barack Obama in 2008. I can still remember my parents telling me when Obama was running that there was no way that he would win. To say that they were stunned when he was triumphant would be a huge understatement. They had tears of joy. From both of them drinking out of 'colored' water fountains and marching against the Klan during college to seeing Barack Obama is worth a book on its own. I am humbled by them and love to hear their stories, even to this day. Some people say the country still is not where it should be. I say maybe, but we have come so, so far. The progress is staggering and that in itself is worthy to celebrate, but at the same time still we work to make it even better. Both countries are dysfunctional but overall the good outweighs the bad.

Visiting Northern Ireland again in the spring of 2024 was another amazing experience. The changes that I've seen there have been so good to see. Yes, you still have the peace walls in Belfast, and you still have your "Protestant" and "Catholic" pubs in Derry. Living life in Northern Ireland always has some political slant to it. It has now been over 100 years since the partition of Ireland. But, and this is a big but, the violence has ended. And that is a huge accomplishment compared to the times this book focuses on. The people who have grown up now are lovingly called, "Ceasefire babies" because they don't know about the Troubles. They don't remember the awful bombings in the cities. And that, in my mind, is a good thing.

During my June 2024 interview with Eamonn McCann, a Derry citizen stopped at our table, shook hands with McCann, and said, "I love you as a man and as a person. You speak and we listen and you speak your mind."

Eamonn McCann is still held in high regard in the city of Derry and throughout Northern Ireland for what he did in the Civil Rights movement. That interaction with the gentleman from Derry is a great example. He laughs when he looks back at what he did, "There were great moments and moments where we f....d it up completely. However, it was a relief that what we did had a wider international significance. We weren't some narrow minded

Epilogue

Nationalist group, we spoke up at meetings for civil rights solidarity here and in the States."[2]

A colleague of mine once said to me in the school where I worked that his students can't relate to the pre-Civil Rights years; they don't understand how people could be so cruel. We both agreed that this is good. Like Northern Ireland, many people who were born after the Good Friday Agreement in 1998 have no memory of those days. Yes, my friends in Derry still complain about the lack of opportunity and jobs there compared to Belfast. And yes, many students still attend segregated schools there. Both of those are still issues. However, overall the climate has improved so much regarding how people get along with each other. Again, progress has been made like in the States, but there is still work to be done. Even today, Unionists will call the 67-page peace agreement document, 'The Belfast Agreement,' which is the official title, while others like the Nationalists enjoy the more theatrical 'Good Friday' in front of it. However, some still have a little animosity toward the agreement since it did free well over 480 terrorists who had been jailed long before their sentences had ended, including Patrick Magee, the man who tried to assassinate Prime Minister Margaret Thatcher in 1984 and Loyalist sympathizers who killed pub-goers in 1993 in the Greysteel Pub Attack.

In conclusion, both the United States and Northern Ireland are still grappling with their histories. In the United States, there are mayors and governors of Southern states across the nation. In Northern Ireland, Michelle O'Neill (Sinn Fein's vice president) was just made first minister of the Stormont government, which will end a two-year impasse there. She has made history as the first nationalist first minister of Northern Ireland in 103 years of rule, something that would have been unheard of years ago. This equates with Barack Obama being elected President in the United States. Her comments showed the significance of her new position for the country: "We mark a moment of equality and progress, a new opportunity to work and grow together, confident that wherever we come from, whatever our aspirations, we can and must build our future together. We must make power-sharing work because collectively, we are charged with leading and delivering for all our people, for every community."[3]

But both countries still grapple with legacies. Sinn Fein leadership recently attended a graduation for officers in the PSNI (Police Service of Northern Ireland), formerly known as the RUC. Years ago, this would have never happened because of the distrust between Catholics and the police, but this is more proof that even that relationship is evolving in a positive direction. This was one of the most controversial parts of the peace agreement for Unionists when the RUC, which was only 8 percent Catholic, transformed itself into the PSNI in 2001. Now, the force is close to 35 percent Catholic overall.

The Tulsa, Oklahoma massacre in 1921, where many Blacks were forced out of their homes and killed, leaves a legacy victims still want to be compensated for what their families lost. Victims and families of the Troubles continue to seek some type of closure for the people they lost during those horrific years. As a former history teacher, I believe the worst thing both countries could do would be to try to forget the history, wait until the survivors or family members are dead and pretend that there's nothing that can be done.

I continue to say that education is the key. Schools are so important in teaching our kids the history of the past so we don't repeat it. My brother tells a story of students getting Martin Luther and Martin Luther King mixed up. Another teacher showed a picture of John Lewis. Nobody knew who he was.

A recent poll by the Times UK newspaper showed that almost 25 percent of young people in Ireland admitted to not knowing key events of the Troubles. Worse, they are learning about it on social media instead. Only 7 percent said they received their information about the Troubles from schools. For people ages 18–34, only 2 percent had 'reasonable knowledge' of the Burntollet Bridge incident, 13 percent the Battle of the Bogside, and 62 percent Bloody Sunday in 1972.[4] Those numbers are staggering and sobering.

This falls on the schools. We have to be the ones to educate our young people on the sacrifices that the people before us made to get to where we are today. The past cannot be forgotten or ignored just because it happened "a long time ago." There is no hiding from the fact that horrible atrocities were committed by the Ku Klux Klan, white supremacists, the IRA, the British Army, and Loyalist paramilitaries. It is very important for young people to know about these acts of violence, terrorism or whatever you want to call it, committed against innocent people. The history is important for people who were killed during those horrible years and their relatives who are with us today. I can relate to this, as my great-grandfather disappeared mysteriously in Georgia in 1938 and was never seen again. My grandfather never ever got over that.

Racism and bigotry will never completely end. This was seen clearly in the Far Right race riots that occurred in Belfast in the summer of 2024. Permanently ending racism is a pipe dream and a panacea that will never be fulfilled. But, we can continue to change the mindsets of our young people, especially. Talk about our history in both countries, learn from our history and heal from our history. That won't make racism and bigotry go away, but it will continue to improve relations.

Epilogue 197

Education is the key to giving kids the skills for either university or the job market so they can be functional, well-balanced citizens for each country's economy. We also need our kids to communicate and be social with each other in the classroom and on the fields, providing opportunities for kids to truly get to know each other. Even though schools in both nations are still mostly segregated between Black and White, rich and poor in the United States and in Northern Ireland, more than 90 percent of children attend separate religious schools. Only 9 percent attend integrated schools in Northern Ireland.

Bernadette Devlin said this in 1972 about education, and still rings true for many: "One of the tragedies of Northern Ireland is that children of both groups are educationally segregated; Catholics go to Catholic schools and Protestants go to Protestant schools, so Catholic and Protestant children seldom get to know one another as human beings. [...] And eventually, ignorance gives way to fear, and fear to hate; and hate ultimately to violence."[5]

However, schools are still the key to improving everything. Good teachers are key. Learning your history is key.

Education is the great equalizer, no matter if you're a Black kid in Selma, Alabama, or a Catholic kid from the Bogside in Derry.

You have to acknowledge your past and history, or you will be doomed to repeat it in the future. People have to get over being afraid to talk to each other, especially people from different backgrounds. We continue to be afraid to talk about it. We are a product of our lived experiences. We need to listen to people who have lived in different shoes, not just our own.

We can't be unwilling to listen.

It is hard to hate when people are beside you, and you are learning from each other. Society would be much better if we continued to do that.

The Black and White communities and the Catholic and Protestant communities in the United States and Northern Ireland, respectively, need to continue to work together, listen together, even if it is tough, to make sure both countries continue to improve life for all.

Both countries have come a long way because of their Civil Rights movements, but there is still work to do.

However, we need to think about how far both countries have come. Both the United States and Northern Ireland have persevered, even though the path hasn't always been as smooth as people in both countries would have liked.

Reverend Burton, who has seen many things over his ninety-six years on the earth, said, "This is a country that I'm not ashamed to be a part of. We've had our dark past but we've made progress and I know people say we have a long ways to go. However, having a long ways to go needs to be added to where we have come from."[6]

Billy McVeigh said a young girl had thanked him for helping her get a job. She explained how what he and others did allowed her to get an education. He also added that the best change he has seen is that there is no more hunger in Derry the way it was when he was growing up, when people were begging on the streets. His first cousin had been involved in the controversial hunger strikes in 1981.

McVeigh was also proud of how he and others fought and the inspiration taken from what was happening in America, "We took on the mighty British Empire with sticks and stones, and we kicked their a [...] The American Civil Rights movement definitely influenced what was happening here in Northern Ireland 100% because we saw this clear injustice."[7]

Visiting Derry and Belfast in Spring 2024, I was able to see that they are different places today. The dark, industrial cities with flak-jacketed soldiers everywhere have vanished. Both cities are in their renaissance stages, with movies and shows being filmed in both cities. Even Selma today has an African American mayor, the city council is multiracial and the police chief is African American. I also smiled when I saw that John Hume's former party, the SDLP, just recently elected the first Black mayor in Northern Ireland. Her name is Lilian Barr and I loved her quote when they picked her, "I am proud to be a Maasai woman and a Derry girl."[8] Former MP Colum Eastwood put her appointment perfectly when talking about Derry now, "I think it's fitting that she will make history as the Mayor of Derry [...] a city and region known the world over for standing up against oppression."[9]

Sadly, there were numerous ugly racially motivated attacks on social media after Barr was named Mayor of Derry. The attacks were condemned immediately, but we all know it is very easy to hide behind social media avatars and shoot racist and hurtful language at people. Former SDLP Leader Shauna Cusack said the following about the attacks, "[...] this is not what Derry people are."[10]

All three cities are in a much better place today than they were in years past. Civil Rights progress in both the United States and Northern Ireland resulted from protests, marches and unfortunately violent upheavals such as Bloody Sunday in Selma and Burntollet. Both Northern Ireland and the United States saw political assassinations, murders, bombings and other violence on the path to reconciliation. Segregated and poor Black and Catholic communities in the United States and Northern Ireland, respectively, took part in a number of uprisings and eventually tanks came into the neighborhoods of both countries.

Epilogue 199

All of this has resulted in many changes. Of course, it can always improve, but the key thing is that it has gotten better.

My parents both comment on the amount of change that they have seen over the years. I can still remember both of them being amazed when Barack Obama was elected as President.

That is true change.

However, continued work for equality everywhere is not only the moral thing to do, but it is also important to our democratic ideals.

We can never forget the words of John Lewis, "The right to vote is precious, almost sacred." (Lewis) and John Hume, "If we are to live together, the first lesson that we must learn is that we need each other. We will discover how much we need each other, and how we are to live together, only when we sit down and talk about it."[11]

History judges all of us with wide open eyes. It reveals all of its warts and gives us the chance to remember and not repeat them. This is something the people in the United States and Northern Ireland both need to remember. I remember feeling my heart quicken as I did my extensive research and personal interviews, hearing and reading the firsthand accounts of people who were there and saw this history in the making.

While researching and interviewing for the book, I often felt like I was seeing a movie being shown in front of my eyes—the feel, the smells, the emotions, all of it. It was sometimes overwhelming but exhilarating at the same time.

History is watching us. Our children must know history and learn from it for the good of all people and future generations.

If you want to learn more about Northern Ireland and the United States in terms of their civil rights movements, check out these:

1. *Belfast* (movie)
2. *Derry Girls* (TVshow)
3. *This is the Sea* (movie)
4. *Selma* (movie)
5. *An Irish Goodbye* (short film)
6. *The Exodus* (Jonathan Burgess, playwright)
7. *Malcolm X* (movie)
8. *Give My Head Peace* (TVshow)
9. *Rustin* (movie)
10. *Mississippi Burning* (movie)
11. *Once Upon A Time in Northern Ireland* (documentary)
12. *Selma, Lord, Selma* (movie)

NOTES

Prologue

1. George Wallace's *inaugural address,* January 14, 1963.
2. Major Roger Bunting, *RTE Archives, People's Democracy March Leaves Belfast: War and Conflict,* 1969.
3. Reverend Ian Paisley, *Once Upon a Time in Northern Ireland,* 2023.
4. Reverend Ian Paisley, *Once Upon a Time in Northern Ireland,* 2023.
5. Reverend Ian Paisley, *Belfast City Hall Speech,* 1985.
6. Dr. Martin Luther King, Jr. Speech, *King: A Film Record,* 1970.
7. David Blight, *Frederick Douglass,* 153.

Chapter 1

1. Julieann Campbell, *BBC Sounds,* 2023.

Chapter 2

1. Tim Pat Coogan, *Michael Collins.*
2. Tim Pat Coogan, *Michael Collins,* 9.
3. *Guardian UK Newspaper,* April 29, 1916.
4. Tim Pat Coogan, *Michael Collins,* 40.
5. *Guardian UK Newspaper,* April 29, 1916.
6. *Guardian UK Newspaper,* April 29, 1916.
7. *Guardian UK Newspaper,* April 29, 1916.
8. *Guardian UK Newspaper,* April 29, 1916.
9. *The Memoirs of Desmond Fitzgerald,* 1968, 90.
10. *The Memoirs of Desmond Fitzgerald,* 1968, 95.
11. *The Memoirs of Desmond Fitzgerald,* 1968, 99.
12. *The Memoirs of Desmond Fitzgerald,* 1968, 99.
13. James Connelly, *Quote,* Selected Writings, Pluto Press. 1988.
14. *Irish Independent,* May 26, 1917.
15. Dean McGlinchey, *Letter, Irish Independent,* 1917
16. Tim Pat Coogan, *Michael Collins,* 92.

202 *Notes*

17. Tomas O Deing, *Michael Collins Jail Letter,* National Library of Ireland, 1918.
18. Tim Pat Coogan, *Michael Collins,* 116.
19. *Civil and Military Gazette,* July 28, 1920.
20. *Civil and Military Gazette,* July 28, 1920.

Chapter 3

1. Sean O'Hagan, *Guardian UK,* April 22, 2018.
2. Susan Miller, *Playboy Interview,* September 1972.
4. *Guardian UK Newspaper,* August 24, 2022.
5. *Guardian UK Newspaper,* August 24, 2022.
6. *Guardian UK Newspaper,* August 24, 2022.
7. *Manchester Guardian,* August 24, 1922.
8. Bernadette Devlin, *The Price of My Soul,* 1969.

Chapter 4

1. Betty Coates Jones, *Interview,* January 12, 2024.
2. Forest Grant Jones, *Interview,* January 12, 2024.
3. Forest Grant Jones, *Interview,* January 12, 2024.
4. *SNCC Digital Website,* 2023
5. Cantarow & O'Malley, *Moving Mountains: Women Working for Social Change,* 1980.
6. *SNCC Digital,* 2023.
7. Forest Grant Jones, *Interview,* January 12, 2024.
8. Forest Grant Jones, *Interview,* January 12, 2024.
9. Betty Coates Jones, *Interview,* January 12, 2024.
10. Betty Coates Jones, *Interview,* January 12, 2024.
11. Betty Coates Jones, *Interview,* January 12, 2024.
12. Forest Grant Jones, *Interview,* January 12, 2024.
13. Betty Coates Jones, *Interview,* January 12, 2024.
14. *SNCC Digital,* 2023.
15. *SNCC Meeting Minutes,* July 14, 1961.
16. *SNCC Digital,* 2024.
17. James Chaney, *Funeral,* 1964.

Chapter 5

1. John Lewis, *Walking with the Wind,* 1998.
2. Betty Coates Jones, *Interview,* January 12, 2024.
3. *Washington Post,* August 25, 2023.
4. John Lewis, *Walking with the Wind, 1998.*
5. *Washington Post,* August 23, 2023.
6. Betty Coates Jones, *Interview,* January 12, 2024.
7. Betty Coates Jones, *Interview,* January 12, 2024.
8. Betty Coates Jones, *Interview,* January 12, 2024.
9. *Washington Post, Interview,* August 25, 2023.

Notes 203

10. John Lewis, *Walking in the Wind*, 1998.
11. *Washington Post, Interview*, August 25, 2023.
12. Betty Coates Jones, *Interview*, January 12, 2024.
13. *Washington Post, Interview*, August 25, 2023.

Chapter 6

1. Carolyn Doyle King, *Interview*, April 23, 2024.
2. Carolyn Doyle King, *Interview*, April 23, 2024.
3. Carolyn Doyle King, *Interview*, April 23, 2024.
4. Carolyn Doyle King, *Interview*, April 23, 2024.
5. Carolyn Doyle King, *Interview*, April 23, 2024.
6. Carolyn Doyle King, *Interview*, April 23, 2024.
7. Carolyn Doyle King, *Interview*, April 23, 2024.
8. Dr. Shannah Tharp-Gilliam, *Interview*, April 23, 2024.
9. Linda Gildersleeve-Blackwell, *Interview*, April 26, 2024.
10. Linda Gildersleeve- Blackwell, *Interview*, April 26, 2024.
11. Linda Gildersleeve- Blackwell, *Interview*, April 26, 2024.
12. Linda Gildersleeve- Blackwell, *Interview*, April 26, 2024.
13. Linda Gildersleeve- Blackwell, *Interview*, April 26, 2024.
14. Linda Gildersleeve- Blackwell, *Interview*, April 26, 2024.
15. Alan Reese, Jr. & Marvin Reese, Jr., *Interview*, May 7, 2024.
16. Alan Reese, Jr. & Marvin Reese, Jr., *Interview*, May 7, 2024.
17. Alan Reese, Jr. & Marvin Reese, Jr., *Interview*, May 7, 2024.
18. Dr. Shannah Tharp-Gilliam, *Interview*, April 26, 2024.
19. Carolyn Doyle King, *Interview*, April 23, 2024.

Chapter 7

1. *State of Louisiana Literacy Test*. 1960.
2. *Reverend ET Burton Interview*, April 16, 2024.
3. Linda Gildersleeve- Blackwell, *Interview*, April 26, 2024.
4. Linda Gildersleeve- Blackwell, *Interview*, April 26, 2024.
5. J. L. Chestnut, Jr. & Julia Cass, *Black in Selma, 1980*.
6. Courtland Cox Interview, *Washington Post, 2023*.
7. Aaron Bryant Interview, *Washington Post, 2023*.
8. *NY Times*, March 21, 1965.
9. *NY Times*, March 21, 1965.
10. *NY Times*, March 21, 1965.
11. John Lewis, *Walking with the Wind, Lewis*, 1998.

Chapter 8

1. Paul Arthur, *The People's Democracy 1968–73*, 1974.
2. Paul Arthur, *The People's Democracy 1968–73*, 1974.
3. Paul Arthur, *The People's Democracy PD 68–73, 1974*.

204 *Notes*

4. Paul Arthur, *The People's Democracy 1968–73*, 1974.
5. Eamonn McCann, *Interview*, June 26, 2024.
6. Paul Arthur, *The People's Democracy 1968–73*, 1974.
7. Eamonn McCann, *Interview*, June 26, 2024.
8. Paul Bew, *Ireland: The Politics of Enmity, 1789–2006*, 2007.

Chapter 9

1. David Halberstam, *Nashville Tennessean*, 1960.
2. John Lewis, *Good Trouble Documentary*, 2020.
3. John Lewis, *Good Trouble Documentary*, 2020.
4. David Greenberg, *Washington Post*, August 27, 2023.
5. David Greenberg, *Washington Post*, August 27, 2023.
6. John Lewis, *Walking in the Wind*, 1998.
7. *Washington Post*, August 25, 2023.
8. John Lewis, *Walking with the Wind*, 1998.
9. David Greenberg, *Washington Post*, August 27, 2023.

Chapter 10

1. Bernadette Devlin, *The Price of My Soul*, 1969.
2. John Lee, *NY Times*, April 19, 1969.
3. Susan Miller, *Bernadette Devlin: A Candid Interview with the Fiery Irish Revolutionary, Playboy Interview*, September 1972.
4. Bernadette Devlin, *The Price of My Soul*, 1969.
5. Bernadette Devlin, *The Price of My Soul*, 1969.
6. Susan Miller, *Bernadette Devlin: A Candid Interview with the Fiery Irish Revolutionary, Playboy Interview*, September 1972.
7. Susan Miller, *Bernadette Devlin: A Candid Interview with the Fiery Irish Revolutionary, Playboy Interview*, September 1972.
8. Bernadette Devlin, *The Price of My Soul*, 1969.
9. John Lee, *NY Times*, April 19, 1969.
10. Susan Miller, *Bernadette Devlin: A Candid Interview with the Fiery Irish Revolutionary, Playboy Interview*, September 1972.
11. Susan Miller, *Bernadette Devlin: A Candid Interview with the Fiery Irish Revolutionary, Playboy Interview*, September 1972.
12. John Foley, *Daily World*, January 3, 1970.
13. *Once Upon a Time in Northern Ireland Documentary*, 2023.
14. Bernadette Devlin, *The Price of My Soul*, 1969.
15. *Once Upon a Time in Northern Ireland Documentary*, 2023.
16. *Once Upon a Time in Northern Ireland Documentary*, 2023.
17. *Once Upon a Time in Northern Ireland Documentary*, 2023.
18. *Newsweek*, April 1969.

Chapter 11

1. Gerry Duddy, *Interview*, April 27, 2024.
2. Julieann Campbell, *Interview*, April 27, 2024.
3. Dick Grogan, *Irish Times*, January 22, 2022.
4. Ed Neafsey, *Irish Central*, January 19, 2022.
5. Ed Neafsey, *Irish Central*, January 19, 2022.
6. Julieann Campbell, *Interview*, April 27, 2024.
7. Gerry Duddy, *Interview*, April 27, 2024.
8. Eamonn McCann, *Irish Times*, October 7, 2023.
9. John Hume Interview, *Irish Times*, October 7, 2023.
10. Stephen Walker, *John Hume: The Persuader, 2023.*
11. Aoife Moore, *Irish Examiner*, August 4, 2020.

Chapter 12

1. Eamonn McCann, *Interview*, June 26, 2024.
2. Freya McClements, *Irish Times*, March 10, 2023.
3. Freya McClements, *Irish Times*, March 10, 2023.
4. Freya McClements, *Irish Times*, March 10, 2023.
5. Eamonn McCann, *Interview*, June 26, 2024.
6. Eamonn McCann, *Interview*, June 26, 2024.
7. Eamonn McCann, *Interview*, June 26, 2024.
8. Freya McClements, *Irish Times*, March 10, 2023.
9. Eamonn McCann, *Interview*, June 26, 2024.
11. Eamonn McCann, *Interview*, June 26, 2024.
12. Eamonn McCann, Interview, June 26, 2024.
13. Freya McClements, *Irish Times*, March 10, 2023.
14. Freya McClements, *Irish Times*, March 10, 2023.
15. Julieann Campbell, *Interview*, April 27, 2024.

Chapter 13

1. Richard Smiley, *Interview*, May 1, 2024.
2. Richard Smiley, *Interview*, May 1, 2024.
3. Richard Smiley, *Interview*, May 1, 2024.
4. Sheyann Webb-Christburg, *Interview*, May 9, 2024.
5. Sheyann Webb-Christburg, *Interview*, May 9, 2024.
6. Sheyann Webb-Christburg, *Interview*, May 9, 2024.
7. Sheyann Webb-Christburg, *Interview*, May 9, 2024.
8. Sheyann Webb-Christburg, *Interview*, May 9, 2024.
9. Gillian Brockell, *Washington Post*, February 21, 2021.
10. *King: A Film Record Documentary*, 1970.
11. *King: A Film Record Documentary*, 1970.

206 *Notes*

12. *King: A Film Record Documentary*, 1970.
13. *King: A Film Record Documentary*, 1970.
14. *King: A Film Record Documentary*, 1970.
15. *NY Times*, 1965.
16. J. L. Chestnut, Jr. & Julia Cass, *Black in Selma*, 1990.
17. Richard Smiley, Interview, May 1, 2024.
18. John Lewis, *Walking with the Wind*, 1998.
19. *NY Times*, September 30, 2008.
20. *King: A Film Record Documentary*. 1970.
21. Dr. Shannah Gilliam, Interview, April 26, 2024.
22. Alan Reese, Sr. & Marvin Reese Jr., *Interview*, May 7, 2024.
23. Carolyn Doyle King, Interview, April 23, 2024.
24. Linda Gildersleeve Blackwell, Interview, April 26, 2024.
25. Richard Smiley, *Interview*, May 1, 2024.
26. *NY Times*, March 8, 1965.
27. *NY Times*, March 8, 1965.
28. *NY Times*, March 8, 1965.
29. Richard Smiley, Interview, May 1, 2024.
30. *NY Times*, March 8, 1965.
31. Sheyann Webb-Christburg, Interview, May 9, 2024.
32. John Lewis, *Walking with the Wind*, 1998.
33. Richard Smiley, Interview, May 1, 2024.
34. John Lewis, *Walking in the Wind*, 1998.
35. John Lewis, *Walking in the Wind*, 1998.

Chapter 14

1. J. L. Chestnut, Jr. & Julia Cass, *Black in Selma, 1990.*
2. John Lewis, *Walking with the Wind*, 1998.
3. Roy Reed, *NY Times*, March 8, 1965.
4. *NY Times*, March 8, 1965.
5. John Lewis, *Walking in the Wind*, 1998.
6. *NY Times*, March 8, 1965.
7. *NY Times*, March 8, 1965.
8. *NY Times*, March 8, 1965.
9. Sheyann Webb-Christburg, *Interview*, May 9, 2024.
10. Richard Smiley, *Interview*, May 1, 2024.
11. *UPI*, March 1965.
12. *NY Times*, March 8, 1965.
13. *NY Times*, March 8, 1965.
14. *NY Times*, March 8, 1965.
15. Alan Reese Sr & Marvin Reese Jr., *Interview*, May 7, 2024.
16. Sheyann Webb-Christburg, *Interview*, May 9, 2024.
17. *NY Times*, March 8, 1965.
18. John Lewis, *Walking in the Wind*, 1998.
19. Linda Gilldersleeve- Blackwell, *Interview*, April 6, 2024.

Chapter 15

1. *King: A Film Record,* 1970.
2. *King: A Film Record,* 1970.
3. Richard Smiley, Interview, May 1, 2024.
4. *King: A Film Record,* 1970.
5. Richard Smiley, Interview, May 1, 2024.
6. John Lewis, *Walking in the Wind,* 1998.
7. *King: A Film Record,* 1970.
8. John Lewis, *Walking in the Wind,* 1998.
9. Linda Gildersleeve- Blackwell, Interview, April 6, 2024.
10. *King: A Film Record.* 1970.
11. *King: A Film Record.* 1970.
12. Sheyann Webb- Christburg, Interview. May 9, 2024.
13. Richard Smiley, Interview. May 1, 2024.
14. Alan Reese, Sr. & Marvin Reese, Jr., Interview, May 7, 2024.
15. John Lewis, *Walking with the Wind,* 1998.
16. *King: A Film Record,* 1970.
17. *King: A Film Record,* 1970.
18. *King: A Film Record,* 1970.
19. *King: A Film Record,* 1970.
20. Sheyann Webb-Christburg, Interview. May 9, 2024.
21. Richard Smiley, Interview. May 1, 2024.
22. Alan Reese, Sr. & Marvin Reese, Jr., Interview, May 7, 2024.
23. Sheyann Webb- Christburg, Interview. May 9, 2024.
24. John Lewis, *Walking in the Wind,* 1998.
25. *King: A Film Record.* 1970.
26. *CBS News,* March 15, 1965.
27. Carolyn Doyle King, April 23, 2024.
28. Richard Smiley, Interview, May 1, 2024.
29. Richard Smiley, Interview, May 1, 2024.
30. *King: A Flim Record,* 1970.
31. *King: A Film Record,* 1970.
32. *King: A Film Record,* 1970.
33. Linda Gildersleeve- Blackwell, Interview, April 6, 2024.
34. Sheyann Webb Christburg, Interview, May 9, 2024.

Chapter 16

1. Freya McClements, *Irish Times,* August 24, 2018.
2. Freya McClements, *Irish Times,* August 24, 2018.
3. Bernadette Devlin, *The Price of My Soul,* 1969.
4. Bernadette Devlin, *The Price of My Soul,* 1969.
5. Freya McClements, *Irish Times,* August 24, 2018.
6. Bernadette Devlin, *The Price of My Soul,* 1969.
7. Bernadette Devlin, *The Price of My Soul,* 1969.
8. Bernadette Devlin, *The Price of My Soul,* 1969.

208 *Notes*

9. Freya McClements, *Irish Times*, August 24, 2018.
10. Freya McClements, *Irish Times*, August 24, 2018.
11. Freya McClements, *Irish Times*, August 24, 2018.
12. *Daily World*, January 3, 1970.
13. *NY Times*, March 3, 1970.
14. Eamonn McCann, Interview, June 26, 2024.
15. Eamonn McCann, Interview, June 26, 2024.
16. Eamonn McCann, Interview, June 26, 2024.
17. *Derry Journal*, September 18, 2021.
18. Fionbarra O'Dochartaigh, *Ulster's White Negroes*, 1994.
19. Sean O'Hagan, *Guardian UK Newspaper*, April 22, 2018.
20. Bernadette Devlin, *The Price of My Soul, 1969.*
21. Billy McVeigh, Interview, March 27, 2024.
22. Billy McVeigh, Interview, March 27, 2024.
23. Delia McDermott, Interview, December 28, 2023.
24. Bernadette Devlin, *The Price of My Soul*, 1969.
25. Susan Miller, *Bernadette Devlin: A Candid Interview with the Fiery Irish Revolutionary, Playboy Interview*, September 1972.
26. Tim Pat Coogan, *The Troubles*, 1996.
27. Sean O'Hagan, *Guardian UK Newspaper*, April 22, 2018.
28. Fionnbarra O'Dochartaigh, *Ulster's White Negroes*, 1994.
29. Delia McDermott, Interview, December 28, 2023.
30. Susan Miller, *Bernadette Devlin: A Candid Interview with the fiery Irish Revolutionary, Playboy Interview*, September 1972.
31. Tim Pat Coogan, *The Troubles*, 1996.
32. Tim Pat Coogan, *The Troubles*, 1996.
33. *Daily World*, January 3, 1970.
34. *Irish Times*, September 5, 2021.
35. Freya McClements, *Irish Times*, August 24, 2018.
36. Bernadette Devlin, *The Price of My Soul*, 1969.
37. Bernadette Devlin, *The Price of My Soul*, 1969.
38. Bernadette Devlin, *The Price of My Soul*, 1969.

Chapter 17

1. Paul Arthur, *People's Democracy 1968–73*, 1974.
2. Susan Miller, *Bernadette Devlin: A Candid Interview with the Fiery Irish Revolutionary, Playboy Interview*, September 1972.
3. Tim Pat Coogan, *The Troubles*, Page 33, 1996.
4. Bernadette Devlin, *The Price of My Soul*, 1969.
5. Paul Arthur, *People's Democracy 1968–73*, 1974.
6. Paul Arthur, *People's Democracy 1968–73*, 1974.
7. Susan Miller, *Bernadette Devlin: A Candid Interview with the Fiery Irish Revolutionary, Playboy Interview*, September 1972.
8. Paul Arthur, *People's Democracy 1968–73*, 1974.
9. Paul Arthur, *People's Democracy 1968–73*, 1974.
10. Paul Arthur, *People's Democracy 1968–73*, 1974.

Notes

11. Paul Arthur, *People's Democracy 1968–73*, 1974.
12. Paul Arthur, *People's Democracy 1968–73*, 1974.
13. Paul Arthur, *People's Democracy 1968–73*, 1974.
14. Captain Terence O'Neill, *National Archives UK*, December 23, 1968.

Chapter 18

1. Eamonn McCann, Interview, June 26, 2024.
2. Michael Farrell, *Northern Ireland and the Orange State*, 1976.
3. Tim Pat Coogan, *The Troubles*, page 34, 1996.
4. *RTE Archives*, 2024.
5. *Irish News*, October 15, 2010.
6. Eamonn McCann, *Interview.* June 26, 2024.
7. Eamonn McCann, *Interview.* June 26, 2024.
8. Bernadette Devlin, *The Price of My Soul*, 1969.
9. Eamonn McCann, *Interview.* June 26, 2024.
10. Eamonn McCann, *Interview.* June 26, 2024.

Chapter 19

1. Bernadette Devlin, *The Price of My Soul*, 1969.
2. Bernadette Devlin, *The Price of My Soul*, 1969.
3. Bernadette Devlin, *The Price of My Soul*, 1969.
4. Eamonn McCann, Interview, June 26, 2024.

Chapter 20

1. Bernadette Devlin, *The Price of My Soul*, 1969.
2. Bernadette Devlin, *The Price of My Soul*, 1969.
3. Bernadette Devlin, *The Price of My Soul*, 1969.
4. Eamonn McCann, Interview, June 26, 2024.
5. Eamonn McCann, Interview, June 26, 2024.
6. *Irish News*, October 15, 2010.

Chapter 21

1. Bernadette Devlin, *The Price of My Soul*, 1969.
2. Eamonn McCann, Interview, June 26, 2024.
3. Adrian Kerr, *Free Derry Protest and Resistance*, 2013.
4. Tim Pat Coogan, *The Troubles*, page 80. 1996.
5. Bernadette Devlin, *The Price of My Soul*, 1969.
6. Bernadette Devlin, *The Price of My Soul*, 1969.
7. Freya McClements, *Irish Times*, January 4, 2019.
8. Eamonn McCann, Interview, June 26, 2024.
9. Bernadette Devlin, *The Price of My Soul*, 1969.

210 *Notes*

10. Freya McClements, *Irish Times,* January 4, 2019.
11. Sidney Buchanan, *Boston Globe.* January 5, 1969.
12. Freya McClements, *Irish Times,* January 4, 2019.
13. Tim Pat Coogan, *The Troubles,* page 81, 1996.
14. Freya McClements, *Irish Times,* January 4, 2019.
15. Tim Pat Coogan, *The Troubles,* Page 81. 1996.
16. Tim Pat Coogan, *The Troubles,* page 81. 1996.
17. *The Irish Journal,* August 11, 2019.
18. Bernadette Devlin, *The Price of My Soul,* 1969.
19. Freya McClements, *Irish Times,* January 4, 2019.
20. Freya McClements, *Irish Times,* January 4, 2019.
21. Eamonn McCann, *Interview,* June 26, 2024.
22. Eamonn McCann, *Interview,* June 26, 2024.
23. Billy McVeigh, *Interview,* March 27, 2024.
24. Gerry Duddy, *Interview,* March 27, 2024.
25. Freya McClements, *Irish Times,* January 4, 2019.
26. Eamonn McCann, *Interview,* June 26, 2024.
27. Tim Pat Coogan, *The Troubles,* page 80, 1996.
28. Freya McClements, *Irish Times,* January 4, 2019.
29. Eamonn McCann, Interview, June 26, 2024.
30. *The Sunday Press,* January 5, 1969.
31. Terence O'Neill. *Belfast Telegraph,* January 6, 1969.
32. Billy McVeigh, Interview, March 27, 2024.
33. Michael Farrell, *Northern Ireland and the Orange State,* 1976.
34. Bernadette Devlin, *The Price of My Soul,* 1969.

Chapter 22

1. Bernadette Devlin, *National Archives UK,* April 22, 1969.
2. *National Archives UK, Home Office,* July 14, 1969.
3. *Scarman Tribunal,* 1969.
4. Russell Stetler, *Battle of the Bogside: The Politics of Violence in Northern Ireland, CAIN,* 1970.
5. Russell Stetler, *Battle of the Bogside: The Politics of Violence in Northern Ireland, CAIN,* 1970.
6. *Eamonn McCann, Interview,* June 26, 2024.
7. *Billy McVeigh, Interview,* March 27, 2024.
8. Bernadette Devlin, *The Price of My Soul,* 1969.
9. Russell Stetler, *Battle of the Bogside: The Politics of Violence in Northern Ireland, CAIN,* 1970.
10. Tim Pat Coogan, *The Troubles,* 1996.
12. Russell Stetler, *Battle of the Bogside: The Politics of Violence in Northern Ireland, CAIN,* 1970.
13. Bernadette Devlin, *The Price of My Soul,* 1969.
14. Eamonn McCann, *Interview,* June 26, 2024.
15. Billy McVeigh, *Interview,* March 27, 2024.
16. Billy McVeigh, *Interview,* March 27, 2024.

Notes 211

17. *Irish Journal,* August 11, 2019.
18. *Irish Journal,* August 11, 2019.
19. Tim Pat Coogan, *The Troubles,* 1996.
20. Delia McDermott, *Interview,* December 28, 2023.
21. Adrian Kerr, *Perceptions: Cultures in Conflict,* 1996.
22. Delia McDermott, *Interview,* December 28, 2023.
23. Billy McVeigh, *Interview,* March 27, 2024.
24. Billy McVeigh, *Interview,* March 27, 2024.
25. Julieann Campbell, *Interview,* March 27, 2024.
26. Edward Daly, *Mister, Are You a Priest?,* 2000.
27. Gerry Duddy, *Interview,* March 27, 2024.
28. Julieann Campbell, *Interview,* March 27, 2024.
29. Eamonn McCann, *Interview,* June 26, 2024.

Chapter 23

1. Adrian Kerr, *Perceptions: Culture in Conflict,* 1996.
2. ET Burton, *Interview,* April 16, 2024.
3. Susan Miller, *Bernadette Devlin: A Candid Interview with the Fiery Irish Revolutionary, Playboy Interview,* September 1972.
4. *RTE Archives,* August 7, 1969.
5. *RTE,* 2024.
6. Alan Smith, *Guardian UK Newspaper,* September 12, 1969.
7. Alan Smith, *Guardian UK Newspaper,* September 12, 1969.
8. *Irish News,* October 15, 2010.
9. Alan Smith, *Guardian UK Newspaper,* September 12, 1969.
10. *Daily World,* August 22, 1969.
11. *Daily World,* August 22, 1969.
12. Gerry Duddy, *Interview,* March 27, 2024.
13. Julieann Campbell, *Interview,* March 27, 2024.
14. *Daily World,* August 22, 1969.
15. *Daily World,* August 22, 1969.
16. *Daily World,* August 22, 1969.
17. BBC, 1969.
18. *Gerry Duddy, Interview,* March 27, 2024.
19. *Once Upon a Time in Northern Ireland Documentary,* 2023.
20. *Once Upon a Time in Northern Ireland Documentary,* 2023.
21. Billy McVeigh, *Interview,* March 27, 2024.
22. *Once Upon a Time in Northern Ireland Documentary,* 2023.
23. *Once Upon a Time in Northern Ireland Documentary,* 2023.
24. *Once Upon a Time in Northern Ireland Documentary,* 2023.
25. *Once Upon a Time in Northern Ireland Documentary,* 2023.
26. *Once Upon a Time in Northern Ireland documentary,* 2023.
27. Billy McVeigh, *Interview,* March 27, 2024.
28. *Once Upon a Time in Northern Ireland,* 2023.
29. Gerry Duddy, *Interview,* March 27, 2024.

30. Susan Miller, *Bernadette Devlin: A Candid Interview with the Fiery Irish Revolutionary*, *Playboy Interview*, September 1972.
31. Delia McDermott, Interview, December 28, 2023.
32. Billy McVeigh, Interview, March 27, 2024.
33. *Edward Daly, *Mister, Are You a Priest?*, 2000.
34. Freya McClements, *Irish Times*, March 10, 2023.
35. Gerry Duddy, Interview, March 27, 2024.
36. Julieann Campbell, Interview, March 27, 2024.
37. Billy McVeigh, Interview, March 27, 2024.
38. Edward Daly, *Mister, Are You a Priest?*, 2000.
39. Gerry Duddy, *Interview*, March 27, 2024.
40. Susan Miller, *Bernadette Devlin: A Candid Interview with the Fiery Irish Revolutionary*, *Playboy Interview*, September 1972.

Chapter 24

1. Bernadette Devlin, *The Price of My Soul*, 1969.
2. Bernadette Devlin, *The Price of My Soul*, 1969.
3. *NY Times*, September 30, 2008.
4. *Montgomery Advertiser*, 2006.
5. John Hume, *Nobel Peace Prize Speech*, 1998.
6. Coretta Scott King, *MLK Non-Violent Peace Prize*, 1999.
7. Joseph T. Smitherman, *Bloody Sunday Commemoration*, 1988.
8. John Lewis, 2018.
9. *Boston Globe*, April 27, 1969.
10. *King: A Film Record Documentary*, 1970.
11. Julieann Campbell, Interview, March 27, 2024.
12. BBC, *Eamonn McCann: A Long March*, October 7, 2018.

Brexit, Irish Unity, and the Troubles in Northern Ireland Today

1. Gerry Duddy, *Interview*, March 27, 2024.
2. Delia McDermott, *Interview*, December 28, 2023.
3. Julieann Campbell, *Interview*, March 27, 2024.
4. Gerry Duddy, *Interview*, March 27, 2024.

Epilogue

1. *Seamus Heaney Poem*, 1990.
2. Eamonn McCann, *Interview*, June 26, 2024.
3. Patrick O'Donoghue & Kieran McDaid, *London Times*, February 4, 2024.
4. Claire Scott & Rachel Lavin, *The London Times*, April 2, 2023.
5. Susan Miller, *Bernadette Devlin: A Candid Interview with the Fiery Irish Revolutionary*, *Playboy Interview*, September 1972.

6. ET Burton, *Interview*, April 16, 2024.
7. Billy McVeigh, *Interview*, March 27, 2024.
8. Brendan McDaid, *Derry Journal*, April 29, 2024.
9. *Derry Journal*, April 29, 2024.
10. Kevin Mullan, *Derry Journal*, May 1, 2024.
11. John Hume, *In His Own Words*, 2018.

BIBLIOGRAPHY

Arthur, Paul. *The People's Democracy 1968–73*. Blackstaff Press, 1974.

BBC. October 10, 1969 BBC News.

BBC. *Eamonn McCann: A Long March*. October 7, 2018.

Bew, Paul. *Ireland: The Politics of Enmity*. Oxford University Press, 2007.

Blackwell-Gildersleeve, Linda. *Interview*. April 26, 2024.

Blight, David. *Frederick Douglass: Prophet of Freedom*. Simon & Schuster, 2018.

Boston Globe. January 6, 1969.

Boston Globe. April 27, 1969.

Brockell, Gillian. *Washington Post*. February 21, 2021.

Bunting, Roger Major. *RTE Archives, People's Democracy March Leaves Belfast: War and Conflict*. 1969.

Campbell, Julianne. *BBC Sounds*. 2023.

Campbell, Julieanne. *Interview*. April 27, 2024.

Cantarow, Ellen & O'Malley Susan. *Moving Mountains: Women Working for Social Change*. The Feminist Press at CUNY, 1980.

CBS News. March 15, 1965.

Chaney, James. *Funeral*, 1964.

Chestnut, J. L & Julia Cass. *Black in Selma: The Uncommon Life of J. L. Chestnut, Jr.*, Fire Ant Books, 1990.

Christburg, Sheyann-Webb. *Interview*. May 9, 2024.

Civil and Military Gazette. July 28, 1920.

Connelly, James. *Quote*. 1921.

Coogan, Tim Pat. *The IRA*. St. Martins, 2002.

Coogan, Tim Pat. *Michael Collins*. Random House UK, 2016.

Coogan, Tim Pat. *The Troubles*. St. Martin's Press, 1996.

Daily World. August 22, 1969.

Daily World. January 3, 1970.

Daly, Edward. *Mister, Are you a Priest?* Four Courts Press, 2000.

Derry Journal. September 9, 2021.

Derry Journal. April 29, 2024.

Devlin, Bernadette. *National Archives UK*. April 22, 1969.

Devlin, Bernadette. *The Price of My Soul: The 22 year-old Member of Parliament from Northern Ireland Tells Her Story*. Knopf, 1969.

216 *Bibliography*

Duddy, Gerry. *Interview,* April 27, 2023.

Farrell, Michael. *Northern Ireland and the Orange State.* Pluto Press, 1976.

Fitzgerald, Desmond. *The Memoirs of Desmond Fitzgerald.* Routledge and K Paul, 1968.

Foley. *Daily World.* January 3, 1970.

Greenburg, David. *Washington Post.* August 27, 2023.

Gilliam-Tharp, Dr. Shannah. *Interview.* April 23, 2024.

Grogan, Dick. *Irish Times.* January 1, 2022.

Guardian Newspaper. September 29, 1916.

Guardian Newspaper. August 24, 1922.

Guardian Newspaper. August 30, 1924.

Halbestam, David. *Nashville Tennessean,* 1960.

Heaney, Seamus. *Poem,* 1990.

Hume, John. *In His Own Words.* Four Courts Press, 2018.

Hume, John. *Nobel Peace Prize Speech.* 1998.

Irish Journal. August 11, 2019.

Irish News. October 10, 2010.

Jones, Betty Coates. *Interview.* January 12, 2024.

Jones, Forest Grant. *Interview.* January 12, 2024.

Kerr, Adrian. *Free Derry Protest and Resistance.* Guildhall Press, 2013.

Kerr, Adrian. *Perceptions: Cultures in Conflict.* Guildhall Press, 1996.

King, Carolyn Doyle. *Interview.* April 23, 2024.

King, Coretta Scott. *MLK Non Violent Peace Prize.* 1999.

King, Jr., Martin Luther. *King: A Film Record.* 1970.

Lee, John. *NY Times.* April 19, 1969.

Lewis, John. *Twitter.* June 27, 2018.

Lewis, John. *Good Trouble Documentary.* 2020.

Lewis, John. *Walking with the Wind: A Memoir of the Movement.* Simon & Schuster, 1998.

McCann, Eamonn. *Interview.* June 26, 2024.

McGlinchey, Dean. *Letter, Irish Independent.* 1917.

McClements, Freya. *Irish Times.* August 24, 2018.

McClements, Freya. *Irish Times.* March 10, 2023.

McDermott, Delia. *Interview.* December 28, 2023.

McVeigh, Billy. *Interview.* March 27, 2024.

Miller, Susan. *Bernadette Devlin: A Candid Interview with the Fiery Irish Revolutionary.* Playboy Magazine. September 1972.

Moore, Aiofe. *Irish Examiner.* August 8, 2020.

Montgomery Advertiser. 2006.

Mullan, Kevin. *Derry Journal.* May 1, 2024.

Neafsey, Ed. *Irish Central.* January 19, 2022.

Newsweek. April 1969

New York Times. March 8, 1965.

New York Times. March 3, 1970.

New York Times. September 30, 2008.

O'Deing, Tomas. *Copy of Michael Collins Jail Letter.* National Library of Ireland, 1918.

O'Dochartaigh, Fionbarra. *Ulster's White Negroes.* AK Press, 1994.

O'Donoghue, Patrick & Kieran McDaid. *London Times.* February 4, 2024.

Bibliography 217

O'Hagan Sean. *Guardian UK Newspaper.* April 22, 1918.
O'Neill, Terence. *Belfast Telegraph.* January 6, 1969.
O'Neill, Terence. *National Archives UK.* December 23, 1968.
Paisley, Ian Reverend. *Belfast City Hall Speech.* 1985.
Paisley, Ian Reverend. *Once Upon a Time In Northern Ireland.* 2023.
Reese, Jr. Marvin & Alan Reese, Jr.. *Interview.* May 7, 2024.
RTE Archives. August 7, 1969.
RTE Archives. 2024.
Scott, Claire & Rachel Lavin. *The London Times.* April 2, 2023.
Smiley, Richard. *Interview.* May 1, 2024.
Smith, Alan. *Guardian Newspaper.* September 12, 1969.
Smitherman, Joseph T. *Bloody Sunday Commemoration.* 1988.
Stetler, Russell. *Battle of the Bogside: The Politics of Violence in Northern Ireland.* CAIN
    (Conflict Archive on the Internet). 1970.
SNCC Digital Website. 2023.
SNCC Digital Website. 2024.
SNCC Meeting Minutes. July 14, 1961.
Sunday Press. January 5, 1969.
United Press International. March 1965.
Wallace, George. *Inaugural Address.* January 14, 1969.
Walker, Stephen. *John Hume: The Persuader.* Gill Books, 2023.
Washington Post. August 23, 2023.

INDEX

Abernathy, Ralph 96–97
Alabama: Alabama Freedom March to Montgomery 48–49; Alabama National Guard 49–50; blacklisted families 104; Bloody Sunday in 184; Bombingham 31; Clark 80; federalized Alabama National Guardsmen 49; Jim Crow Alabama 57; landscape 45; National Voting Rights Museum 185; Pettus Bridge 82; Selma-Montgomery march (*see* Selma to Montgomery march); sharecropping 45; state troopers 84, 92–93; violence after Reeb's death 84, 92–93
American Civil War 2, 18, 36, 45
Anglo-Irish Treaty 17–20
Anglo-Irish War 15
Apprentice Boys parade 171

B Specials 20, 107, 143, 146, 150, 155, 162, 164–65, 167, 171, 173–74
Baez, Joan 34, 101
Baker, Ella 24–25, 27; Mother of the Civil Rights Movement 24–25; organizer for NAACP 25; SNCC 25, 27
Battle of the Bogside 64, 76, 115, 148, 165–67, 177, 196; Apprentice Boys, march through Derry 158; B Specials 164–65; DCDA 164; devastation 166; evolution of Civil Rights movement 167; first day 162; loss of homes 166; Protestant marchers 159; RUC barriers

159–60; second and third day 164; siege 158; use of CS 161–63; violence 166–67
Battle of the Boyne 2, 7
Belafonte, Harry 101
Belfast Agreement 195
Belfast to Derry long march: anti-Catholic group 130; B Specials 143; beatings and violence 144; Bunting and Paisley 133–34; Bunting's supporters 129; Burntollet 147; counter-riots 148; day one-January 1, 1969 127–30; day three 139; day two, Toome 133–36; Dolorus and Marian Price 139; Free Derry wall 148; last day 141–46; Loyal Citizens of Ulster (LCU) 128; nonstudents, control of 141; nonviolent protest 144; People's Democracy, march 127; police entry 130–31; police games 134; radio reports 137; rioting in Derry 139; riots in Derry 149; risks 130; RUC's action 142, 146; strong group of marchers 135–36; students from the People's Democracy 135; UVF 128; walk from Belfast to Antrim 128
Bennett, Tony 101
Bernstein, Leonard 101
Berry, Marion 24
bigotry 98, 189, 196
Black Civil Rights Movement 6, 67, 80, 94, 110–11, 123–24, 131, 170, 173, 183, 185, 189

220 *Index*

Black Panthers 21, 24, 111–12, 121, 123, 173
Blackmon, Ulysses 37
Blackwell, Linda Gildersleeve 40–42, 84, 94, 98, 105
Blake, Eugene Carson 60
Bloody Sunday: -1972 (Derry) 3–5, 61, 69–70, 76, 178–81, 190, 196; -1965(Selma) 6, 37–38, 43, 77–88, 95–96, 99, 105, 115, 144, 146, 151, 184–85, 192, 198; Free Derry Museum 5
Bloody Sunday Museum 115
Boer War 11
Boynton-Robinson, Amelia 37–38
Bray, Robert 111
Brexit 187, 190–91
British Army 4, 11, 21, 65, 69, 115, 175, 177–78, 180, 185, 196
Brown vs. Board of Education 31, 194
Browns Chapel Church 92
Bryant, Aaron 35, 49
Bunting, Ronald 11, 127–31, 134, 139, 149, 172
Burntollet Bridge 51, 76, 120, 139, 142–43, 146–51, 158, 167, 173–74, 186, 198; incident 150, 192, 196; march 173; violence at 174
Burton, Reverend E. T. 47–48, 170, 197

Campbell, Julieann 3–5, 70, 73, 76, 148, 154, 166–67, 171, 173, 178–80, 185, 188
Carmichael, Stokely 24, 112
Catholic Church 7, 133, 157
Catholic Civil Rights movement 53–54, 66–67, 107–23, 125–26, 133, 150, 189, 192; and Black Civil Rights movement 189; Black Panthers 111; Derry Citizens Action Committee 117; Duke Street march 117–19; first Civil Rights march 108; Homeless Citizen League 109; kettling 114; middle-class Catholics 120; People's Democracy, The 124; posters and signs 113; poverty 119; Protestant Orangemen 111;

self-defense 113; SNCC's slogan "One Man, One Vote" 119; water cannons against Black marchers 117
Ceasefire babies 194
Chaney, James 28–29
Che Guevara 21
Chestnut, J. L. 83, 184
Chestnut, J. L., Jr. 82, 89
Churchill, Winston 3
Civil Rights Act 29, 60
Civil Rights Association 4, 108, 110, 113–14, 121, 127, 129, 132, 157, 162
civil rights bill 32, 36, 58–59
civil rights marchers 48, 51, 109–10, 128, 148, 188
Civil Rights Movement: Black (*see* Black Civil Rights Movement); Catholic (*see* Catholic Civil Rights movement)
Civil War: American 2; Irish 18–19; Reconstruction period after 36
Clark, Sheriff Jim 80–82, 86, 91, 95–96, 99, 184
Clinton, Bill 193
Cloud, John 85–86, 88
Collins, Michael 7–10, 13–15, 18–19; boyhood 8; death of 19; and Easter Rising (*see* Easter Rising of 1916); reorganization 13; Royal Irish Constabulary (RIC) 14–15; Twelve Apostles 14; worked with the provisional government 18
Commission of Inquiry under Lord Cameron 171–72
Congress of Racial Equality 51
Connelly, James 9, 11–12
Coretta Scott King 102, 172, 184
Courageous Eight 37–43, 84, 98–99, 105, 183–84; bravery 43; voting rights for 40
Craigavon, Lord 17
Crazy Eight, The: *see* courageous eight
Crimean War 3
Cromwell, Oliver 7
Currie, Austin 109–10, 119

Index

Dallas County Voters League (DCVL) 38–39, 42
Daly, Edward 4, 179
Davis, Angela 112, 173
Davis, Ossie 101
Davis, Sammy, Jr. 101–2
de Valera, Eamon 12, 18, 20
Dennis, Dave 29
Derry: 1963 March 6; Bloody Sunday 5, 6; Catholics 3–4; Church of Ireland Chapel of St. Augustine 1; Civil Rights campaign in 183; Daire Calgaich 1; Duke Street confrontation 153; electoral system 4; Free Derry Museum 5; Londonderry 1; Peace Bridge 1, 3; Protestant majority in Northern Ireland 4; UK City of Culture 3
Derry Citizens Defence Association (DCDA) 164
Detroit Police Department 169
Devenny, Sam 153–54
Devlin, Bernadette 17, 20, 55, 61, 108, 111, 113; Catholic oppression 64–65; character description 61–62; early life and family 62; goal of nonpolitical social justice 63; leaders of the Catholic civil rights movement 65; Member of Parliament 61–65; Republican anti-Free State songs 63
Disappeared, The 139
discrimination 25, 35, 45, 54–55, 57, 59–60, 74, 76, 108–9, 123, 127, 151, 153–54, 172, 184
Doyle, Ernest 38–40, 43, 104
Du Bois, W. E. B. 34, 112
Dublin 9–14, 18–19, 65, 121, 174; Bloody Sunday 4; destruction 13; IRA 18
Duddy, Gerry 69–70, 147, 167, 173, 175, 178, 180–81, 188, 190
Duke Street 76, 113–16, 118–20, 153, 158, 167
Dylan, Bob 34

Easter Rising of 1916 7–14, 20, 62; case of rebellion prisoners 12; casualties 13;

Easter Monday 10; flag of truce 12; rebels, fight against the British 10–11
education 5, 24, 197–98
extremism 53–54

Farrell, Michael 121–22, 125, 127–28, 130, 141–46, 148, 150–51; Civil Rights movement 122; family 122; leaflets and slogans 122
Free Derry 2, 4–5, 148, 164, 169, 176, 185; corner 2, 4–5, 164, 185; Museum 4–5, 185
Free Presbyterian Church of Ulster 133
Freedom Summer 28–29

George, Lloyd 13, 15, 17
Gerrymandering 54–55, 127, 153–54, 172
Gildersleeve, James 38–41, 48
Gildersleeve-Blackwell, Linda 40–41, 84
Gilliam, Shannah, Dr. 39–40, 43, 83, 84, 106
Good Friday peace agreement 67–68, 166, 187
Good Samaritan Hospital 92
Graham, Henry V. 50

Henry II 7
Henry VIII 7
Hieronimo Marino 2
Hitler, Adolf 23
home rule bill, third 9
Hoover, J. Edgar 36
Hume, John 3, 55, 64, 67–71, 76, 116–17, 123, 159–60, 162, 164, 171, 184, 189, 191–92, 198–99; Bloody Sunday march 70; Civil Rights movement campaign 68–69; Derry Credit Union 68; early life and family 67; Good Friday Peace Agreement 67; Magilligan 69; retribution bombing by the UDA 71; Sinn Fein 71
Hunter, Reverend J. D. 38

Independent Commission for Reconciliation and Information Recovery (ICRIR) 190

222 *Index*

Internment without trial 4, 12, 177–78
Irish Citizen Army 9
Irish Civil War 18–19
Irish Republic 10
Irish Republican Army (IRA) 15,
17–21, 27, 54, 61, 69–70, 104–5, 110,
120, 139, 153, 168, 174–78, 180–81,
184, 187–88, 191, 195–96, 198;
bombing campaign 20; deployment
of British Army into Northern
Ireland 21; destructive tactics 21;
Provisional Irish Republican Army
21
Irish Republican Brotherhood 9, 13
Irish Sea Border controversy 187
Irish Volunteers 9, 11

Jackson, George 112
James I 1–2, 7
James II 2, 7
Jim Crow rules 36, 57, 107
Johnson, Lyndon B. 29, 36, 50, 92, 94,
98, 103, 105

Kennedy, Bobby 60
Kennedy, John F. 28, 31–32, 59
kettling 114
King, Carolyn Doyle 8, 37–40, 84, 92,
104–6
King, Coretta Scott 102, 172, 184
King, Martin Luther 35, 57–58, 99,
125, 127, 184, 196
King III, Martin Luther 36
King, Martin Luther, Jr. 25–26, 31,
33–34, 37, 51, 67, 78
King William 2, 7
Ku Klux Klan (KKK) 25–26, 32, 43,
107, 133, 196

Labour Party 54, 68
Legacy Act law 189–90
Lewis, John 3, 24, 32–33, 35, 49, 51,
57–60, 62, 67, 80, 83, 93, 95–97,
99–100, 103, 106, 111, 123, 127,
183–85, 192, 196, 199; evolution of
SNCC 58; meeting with President
Kennedy 59; segregation and racial
discrimination 57; speeches 58

Lincoln Memorial 33–35
Literacy Test, Louisiana 46–47
Livingstone College 23, 26, 33
Londonderry (Belfast Derry) 1, 20,
113, 123, 150, 155–57, 172
Londonderry Citizens' Action
Committee 123
Loyal Citizens of Ulster (LCU) 128, 149
Loyal Orange Institution (Orange
Order, The) 124
loyalism 133
Loyalists 4, 20, 61, 68, 70, 109–10,
113–14, 124, 128–31, 133–35, 139,
142–44, 147–48, 150–51, 153,
159–60, 165, 167, 187–89, 195–96

Magilligan Beach 69–70
Malcolm X 32, 58
Malloy, Francie 109
March On Washington 1963 6, 31–36,
49, 58–60, 185, 194; Independence
Avenue and Constitution Avenue
33; program for 32–33; signs 34
Mathis, Johnny 101
Maxwell, John 11, 50
McCann, Eamonn 55–56, 70, 73–76,
112, 114, 118, 127, 129, 131–32, 136,
139, 141, 144, 146–50, 160, 163–65,
167, 170, 180, 184, 186, 194; belief
in socialism 73; central to the Civil
Rights movement 75–76; family
73; Fight For Gaza 76; People's
Democracy group in Belfast 74
McCormack, Vinny 144–45
McDermott, Delia 116–17, 164–65,
179, 188
McGavigan, Annette 189
McGreanery, Billy 189
McLoughlin, Michael 108
McVeigh, Billy 115, 147–48, 150, 160,
163–65, 175–77, 179, 181, 198
media 175

Naegle, Walter 36
National Association for the
Advancement of Colored People
(NAACP) 24–25, 27, 33, 38–39, 60,
98, 117, 123

Index

National Council of Churches 60
National Voting Rights Museum 185
no-go areas 174
nonviolence 113, 172, 183
Northern Ireland 4, 6, 17, 20–21, 23,
  25–29, 32, 45, 52–58, 61–71, 73–74,
  76, 106–11, 113–15, 117–24, 126–30,
  132, 137, 147–48, 150, 153–58,
  163–81, 183–95, 197–99
Northern Ireland Civil Rights
  Association (NICRA) 4, 108, 110,
  113–14, 116, 119, 121, 127, 129
Northern Ireland Civil Rights
  movement 183, 188

Obama, Barack 104, 194–95, 199
O'Connor, Paul 146, 148
O'Connor, T. P. 12
October 1968 march 20, 53, 55–56,
  63, 65, 75–76, 111, 113, 116, 118–23,
  153, 167, 170–71
O'Dochartaigh, Fionnbarra 113,
  118
Oklahoma massacre 196
On Bloody Sunday (Campbell) 3, 178
O'Neill, Michelle 195
O'Neill, Terence 119, 124, 126, 150
Operation Demetrius 177
Orange Day 158
O'Rawe, Ricky 176

Paisley, Ian 53, 109, 129, 133–35, 139,
  142, 149, 172, 174
paramilitaries 70, 169, 187, 196
Parks, Rosa 99, 194
Peace marches 4
peaceful march 4, 110, 116, 150
Peadar O'Donnell (pub) 3
Pearse, Patrick 9
People's Democracy (PD) 23, 25, 27,
  53–56, 58, 68–69, 74, 111, 118–19,
  121–25, 127–31, 133–35, 141–42,
  148, 151, 157, 172; CSJ (Campaign
  for Social Justice) 54; police
  brutality 56; Protestant extremism
  54; riots between Paisley's followers
  and UVF 53–54; unemployment 55;
  unequal housing 54

Police brutality 34, 56, 96, 98, 113,
  119, 169
Police Service of Northern Ireland
  (PSNI) 195–96
Ponderosa, The (pub) 137
Pope Adrian IV 7
poverty 2, 35, 53, 62, 67–68, 113, 120,
  126, 128, 170, 184
power-sharing work 195
Protestant 2, 4, 7–9, 17, 21, 54, 62, 65,
  67, 69, 71, 74, 107, 109, 111, 116,
  119–22, 124, 128–29, 146, 156–58,
  160, 165, 167, 172–73, 175, 181,
  187–89, 191, 194, 197
Protestantism 7
Provisional Army Council 174
Provisional IRA 168, 174, 176–77, 181

Queens University- Belfast 23, 55, 61,
  63, 119, 122

racism 103, 184, 196
Randolph, Philip A. 32, 59
reconstruction 36, 45, 107
Reed, Roy 90
Reese, Marvin, Jr. 42–43, 84, 100, 102
Reese, Rev. Frederick Douglas 37,
  42–43
remedy measures 1969 154–55
Republic of Ireland 8, 10, 55, 74, 163,
  167
Republican (Northern Ireland) 11, 13,
  18–21, 41, 62–63, 70–71, 113, 139,
  157, 173–74, 180, 188
riots/rioting 25, 34, 50, 53, 55, 65, 69,
  74–76, 91, 97, 111, 118, 139, 142,
  144, 146, 148–49, 155, 158–60,
  165–67, 169–74, 176, 188–89, 196;
  casualties and arrests 156; Dungiven
  155–56; Londonderry 156; use of
  troops 156–57
Rose, Richard 53
Royal Irish Constabulary (RIC) 14–15
Royal Ulster Constabulary (RUC) 13,
  55, 107–8, 113–14, 116, 118, 121,
  128–30, 134, 142–43, 146, 148–50,
  153, 157, 159–66, 169–74, 176, 191,
  195–96

224   *Index*

Rustin, Bayard 36

Salisbury (North Carolina) 23–27, 134; attempt to integrate local movie theater 26; Grand Dragon of the KKK 24

Say Nothing (Keefe) 139

segregation 24–25, 28, 32, 35–36, 48, 54, 57, 80, 82, 94, 184, 191, 194

Selma to Montgomery march: aftermath 96–105; agents for the FBI in Selma 93; Alabama state troopers 84; attack on Pettus Bridge 91; Bloody Sunday (*see* Bloody Sunday); confrontation on the Edmund Pettus Bridge 96; equality and voting rights 48; events surrounding the Selma march 105–6; federalized Alabama National Guardsmen 49; feelings for voting rights legislation 96; hospitalized marchers 92; march process 82–85; negative impacts 104; nonviolent protest in Selma 98, 103; planning for the march 50; procession 51; schedule 50; tear-gas bombs 88, 90; Turnaround Tuesday 97; video of Bloody Sunday 94; violence after Reeb's death 97–98; voter disenfranchisement 100; Voting Rights Act 105

Shannon, Reverend Henry 38

sheriff's posse, the 80

Simone, Nina 101

Sinn Fein 8–9, 13, 15, 71, 109, 174, 195

Sinn Feiners 9

Smiley, Richard 77–78, 92, 96, 99, 102, 104; early days 77–78; march, preparation 82–87; Selma to Montgomery march 77–78; tear-gas 88, 90; use of force by marchers 87

Smitherman, Joseph T. 184

Social Democratic and Labour Party (SDLP) 68, 71, 198

South Tyrone Empowerment Program (STEP) 183

Southern Christian Leadership Conference (SCLC) 25, 49, 51, 80–81, 83, 98, 104

Special Powers Act 107, 125

student nonviolent coordinating committee (SNCC) 23–25, 27–29, 32, 34, 38, 42, 49, 53, 55, 58–59, 76, 83, 98, 111, 119–20, 123; impact on World War II 25; sit-ins and freedom rides 28; threats and violence 28–29; voter registration campaign in US South 27

summer's violence in Derry's Bogside 174

tear gas 80, 87–93, 161

terrorist campaign 20

Titanic museum 193

Torture chamber 177

Trimble, David 191

Troubles, The 3, 20, 29, 76, 117–18, 128, 139, 151, 166, 175, 180, 187–91, 193–94, 196

Truth Commission 190

Turnaround Tuesday 97

Twelve Apostles 14

Ulster 1, 14, 18–19, 64, 130; Free Presbyterian Church of Ulster 133; Loyal Citizens of Ulster (LCU) 128, 149; Protestants 124, 128, 158; RUC (*see* Royal Ulster Constabulary (RUC))

Ulster B Specials 174

Ulster Defence Regiment 174

Ulster flags 129

Ulster Special Constabulary 173

Ulster Unionists 191

Ulster Volunteer Force (UVF) 54, 128

Unionists 4, 20–21, 53–54, 64, 68, 70, 121, 157, 191, 195

United Kingdom (UK) 8, 17, 71, 126, 155, 161, 166, 187, 189

University of Ulster's Conflict Archive 129

US Civil Rights campaign 109

US Voting Rights Act 96, 105

Index

Valera, Eamon De 12, 18, 20
Vitry-le-Francois 2
Vivian, C. T. 80–82
Voter registration 27–28, 38–39, 42, 80, 105
Voting Rights Act 96, 105

Wallace, George 48, 51, 87, 92, 96, 98, 102, 128, 184
walled city 2, 118, 183
Washington DC 24, 29, 31, 93
"*We Shall Overcome*" 26, 33, 69, 98, 105, 109–10, 119, 146

Webb-Christburg, Sheyann 78–79, 85, 86, 91, 93, 99, 101–2, 106
Wharton, Tom 65, 175–76
Wilkins, Roy 33, 60
William of Orange 7
Williams, Hosea 51, 85, 91–93, 127
Wilson, Harold 56, 125–26, 134
Winters, Shelley 101
World War I 9, 12, 15

Year of Terror in Ireland 15
Young, Andrew 51, 83
Young Liberals, The 108
Young Socialists, The 108

www.ingramcontent.com/pod-product-compliance
Lightning Source LLC
Jackson TN
JSHW022303110425
82437JS00002B/2